TEMPLE OF LIBERTY

TEMPLE
OF LIBERTY

Building the Capitol for a New Nation

PAMELA SCOTT

Published in cooperation with

the Library of Congress

Washington, D.C.

New York   Oxford
OXFORD UNIVERSITY PRESS
1995

OXFORD UNIVERSITY PRESS

Oxford   New York
Athens   Auckland   Bangkok   Bombay
Calcutta   Cape Town   Dar es Salaam   Delhi
Florence   Hong Kong   Istanbul   Karachi
Kuala Lumpur   Madras   Madrid   Melbourne
Mexico City   Nairobi   Paris   Singapore
Taipei   Tokyo   Toronto

and associated companies in
Berlin   Ibadan

Development and publication of this book was made possible by a generous gift from Philip Morris
Companies Inc. The book accompanies an exhibition at the Library of Congress, February 24–June 24, 1995.
Support for the exhibition came from Philip Morris and the James Madison Council of the Library
of Congress. This exhibition is part of the project to establish a Center for American
Architecture, Design, and Engineering at the Library of Congress.

Library of Congress Cataloging-in-Publication Data
Scott, Pamela, 1944–
Temple of Liberty: building the capitol for a new nation / Pamela Scott
p.   cm.
"Published in cooperation with the Library of Congress, Washington, D.C."
"Accompanies an exhibition at the Library of Congress, Feb. 24-June 24, 1995"—T.p. verso.
ISBN 0-19-509857-9 (cloth)
ISBN 0-19-509858-7 (paper)
1. United States Capitol (Washington, D.C.)—Exhibitions.
2. Neoclassicism (Architecture)--Washington (D.C.)—Exhibitions.
3. Signs and symbols in architecture--Washington (D.C.),—Exhibitions.
4. Architecture and state--Washington (D.C.)—Exhibitions.
5. Washington (D.C.)--Buildings, structures, etc.—Exhibitions.
I. Library of Congress. II. Title
NA4412.W18S37   1995
725'.11'09753—dc20   95-8122

1 3 5 7 9 8 6 4 2
Printed in the United States of America
on acid-free paper

Foreword

On September 18, 1993, Congress and the nation observed the bicentennial of the United States Capitol, the two-hundredth anniversary of the day George Washington laid the building's cornerstone. Planning for this celebration began a few years earlier and resulted in a series of exhibitions, symposia, publications, ceremonies, and restoration projects that commemorate the early history of the Capitol. The seven-year celebration will end in 2000, the bicentennial of the relocation of the federal government to its permanent home in Washington, D.C.

The Office of the Architect of the Capitol has been pleased to participate in numerous bicentennial observances that will have a lasting impact. Restoration of the statue *Freedom Triumphant in War and Peace* was perhaps the most visible project in this series. The statue's removal from atop the dome on May 9, 1993, and the subsequent conservation work were watched by thousands; its return on October 23, 1993, was a thrilling sight enjoyed by an even larger crowd that included President Clinton.

An idea for another bicentennial project consisted of a major exhibition that we proposed to be held at the Library of Congress; it seemed a natural partnership of resources and purpose. Like the restoration of *Freedom,* thousands could enjoy the event and learn more about the Capitol and its history. From this initial idea has grown a major exhibition that explores the early history of this great building: *Temple of Liberty: Building a Capitol for a New Nation.* We are grateful to Dr. James Billington, Librarian of Congress, and his talented staff for transforming an idea into a handsome and fascinating exhibit. Guest curator Pamela Scott, assisted by our staff and by designers and curators at the Library, has drawn together an impressive and instructive collection of objects that tell an important story. The story is about creation, for the Capitol was a new type of building designed for a new type of government. It is also a story of signs and symbols, because the Capitol has never been mere shelter; it is also an expression of national pride and perception. And it is the story of famous and forgotten people, wise and foolish, gifted and greedy, but all very human and joined by the compelling idea of building a Capitol suited to a great republic. *Temple of Liberty: Building a Capitol for a New Nation* celebrates the taste, talents, and plain hard work of many uncommon persons united in pursuit of a common goal.

George M. White, FAIA
Architect of the Capitol

Preface

The Library of Congress is the proud keeper of some of the most important documents of the early Republic. The exhibition *Temple of Liberty: Building a Capitol for a New Nation,* one of the events marking the bicentennial of the United States Capitol, gives us the opportunity to present to the public many of the rare drawings and prints assembled by the Library during the past two centuries, together with related documents and artifacts from many other institutions that illuminate the history and significance of the design and construction of the Capitol. Almost a century has passed since the last such exhibition, and much new and interesting material has come to light to expand our understanding and appreciation of this great structure. Guest curator Pamela Scott has done a fine job of bringing clarity and new insight to this complicated story.

American architecture can be said to have begun with the United States Capitol, conceived as early as 1791 and largely completed by 1865. Designed to serve a revolutionary new form of government, it was the first example of an entirely new building type. Like the Declaration of Independence, the Constitution, and the Bill of Rights, the Capitol was a tangible expression of the ideas of the Founding Fathers. The chambers necessary to the functions of the executive, judicial, and legislative branches of the new government determined the plan of the Capitol, and the two houses of the legislature established its symmetry and symbolized the balance of powers. Thomas Jefferson described it as the "first temple dedicated to the sovereignty of the People," and its central and uniting feature was a great domed rotunda originally styled "the Hall of the People."

George Washington and Thomas Jefferson played important roles in the design and construction of the Capitol. Early in the process, both indicated their preference for a domed building, and in 1793 Washington chose William Thornton as the winner of one of the first public architectural competitions in America. Jefferson worked closely with Washington, pressing his own architectural ideas and securing the talents of Benjamin Henry Latrobe to guide the Capitol toward its first phase of completion, accomplished by Charles Bulfinch in 1826.

Both before and after its enlargement through the addition of wings and a new dome by Thomas U. Walter and Montgomery C. Meigs in the 1850s and 1860s, the United States Capitol served as a model for countless state capitols, county courthouses, and city halls in this country, as well as for capitol buildings in other parts of the world. It remains the functioning home of our federal legislature, and one of the most recognizable symbols of the United States.

To the nation's early leaders, including Washington, Jefferson, Madison, Monroe, and Lincoln, there was no question about the importance of architecture. They recognized clearly architecture's symbolic and expressive role as well as its functional possibilities. Abraham Lincoln strove to complete the Capitol's great cast-iron dome in the midst of a war to preserve the Union of which it was the primary symbol. He and his predecessors sought to provide more than just the walls and roof within which the government could carry out its business. Their Capitol was intended to serve as the principal and most visible manifestation of the identity of a new nation, of its components and their structure, of its permanence and aspirations, and of its seriousness of purpose.

The documents in this exhibition provide clear evidence of the talent, imagination, and skill of those who participated in the creation of the Capitol and represent the origins of the professions of architecture, design, and engineering in this country. Throughout the early history of the Capitol, shortages of funds, materials, and skilled craftsmen together with intrigues of every sort plagued the efforts of those who struggled to complete it. While the influence of contemporary French and British architectural developments is clearly evident, the remarkable plan of the Capitol and its details, such as elegant columns based on native plant forms, mark the beginnings of the search for a distinctively American architecture. The building's many technical innovations reflect the young Republic's appetite for experimentation in engineering, mechanics, and new building materials and techniques.

It is especially appropriate that this exhibition serve as the inaugural event of the Library of Congress's Project for a Center for American Architecture, Design, and Engineering, intended to focus attention on and encourage support for its preeminent holdings in these areas.

We thank our partners from the beginning of this enterprise, George White, the Architect of the Capitol, and his able staff, for their generous contributions to the planning and realization of this exhibition.

James H. Billington
The Librarian of Congress

Contents

Color plates follow page 80

Acknowledgments

This publication and the exhibition on which it is based were prepared by the Library of Congress in collaboration with the Architect of the Capitol and coordinated by the Library's Interpretive Programs Office, under the direction of Irene Burnham. The many details connected with the preparation of this catalog as well as the exhibit were overseen by Martha Hopkins, Coordinator of Exhibitions. Debbie Durbeck, Production Officer, also played an invaluable role in the development of the exhibition. Others in the Interpretive Programs Office who contributed to the project are Tambra Johnson and Sally Livingston, Registrars, and Juliet Acker, Denise Agee, Jennifer Bride, Tina Carr, Kimberly Curry, Jennifer Chisholm, Kendall Christian, Christopher O'Connor, Gene Roberts, and Gwynn Wilhelm. Yusef El-Amin, Marita Clance, and Jim Higgins, Photoduplication Service, assisted in providing the many necessary photographs. John Cole and Margaret Wagner, Publishing Office, also were instrumental in the development of the catalog. Norma Baker and Jan Lauridsen of the Library's Development Office assisted in raising funds for the exhibition.

Ford Peatross, Curator of Architecture, Engineering, and Design in the Prints and Photographs Division, first suggested an exhibition on the Capitol's early development as the inaugural event of the Library's Center for American Architecture, Design, and Engineering Project. He has guided both the exhibit and the project from their inception. Harry Katz, Curator of Popular and Applied Graphic Arts, led us to many treasures. Mary Ison and her reference staff in the Prints and Photographs Division—Sam Daniel, Jan Grenci, Marilyn Ibach, Maja Keech, Pamela Posz, and Jane Van Nimmen—were unfailingly helpful in locating drawings, photographs, and curatorial data.

The reference staff of the Rare Books Division—Anthony Edwards, Clark Evans, Joan Higbee, Charles Kelly, and Robert Shields—patiently helped us in our searches among the division's collections. Declan Murphy of Rare Books translated Latin mottos. Frank Carroll,

Georgia Higley, and Mark Sweeny of the Serials and Government Publications Division were particularly helpful at the last minute. Marvin Kranz of the Manuscript Division assembled materials under his care. Special thanks are also due to the following members of the Library of Congress Conservation Office: Thomas Albro, Riki Condon, Ken Grant, Doris Hamburg, Renata Mesmer, Margo McFarland, Marilee Oliver, Ann Sibert, Linda Steiber, Heather Wanser, and Mary Wooten. Tim Blount, Fred Harrison, Kimberly Lord, James Redd, John Richardson, and Onnetta Benoit of Office Systems Services expedited publication of the exhibit brochure, poster, and related graphics. The Friends of the Law Library also rendered invaluable assistance.

William C. Allen, Architectural Historian of the United States Capitol, faithfully commented on several versions of the text, always offering valuable suggestions. Barbara Wolanin, Curator of the Capitol, was instrumental in guiding the exhibit's direction. Members of her staff Linnea Dix, Ann Kenny, Eric Paff, Kim Soucy, Dana Strickland, and Sarah Turner were cheerfully helpful many times in many ways. Pamela Violente McConnell deserves special thanks for answering innumerable questions, measuring drawings, and coordinating their reproduction.

In order to present the rich history of the Capitol, it was necessary to reach outside the substantial holdings of the Library of Congress and the Architect of the Capitol. With gratitude, we acknowledge the participation of the many institutions and private collectors who have so kindly shared their holdings. Special thanks are owed to the following individuals: Michael Plunkett and George Riser, Alderman Library, University of Virginia; Beth Carroll-Horrocks and Rita Dockery, American Philosophical Society; Bruce Laverty, Athenaeum of Philadelphia; Andrée Pouderoux, Bibliothèque Nationale de France; Ruth O'Brien, Carpenter's Company of the City and County of Philadelphia; Dan Kany and Janet Parks, Avery Fine Arts Library, Columbia University; Ann Baker Horsey, Delaware State Museum; Lee Langston-Harrison, James Monroe Museum and Memorial Library; Elizabeth Gombosi, Harvard University; Bonnie Hedges, Historical Society of Washington; James Greene, Library Company of Philadelphia; Elizabeth Gordon and Jeff Goldman, Maryland Historical Society; Peter Drummie and Chris Steele, Massachusetts Historical Society; Kevin Avery, American Wing, Catherine Bindman and Raphael Pita, Department of Drawings and Prints, and Patricia Farrar and Mary Doherty, Photograph Library, Metropolitan Museum of Art; Elizabeth Kirwan, National Library of Ireland; Silvie Péharpré, Musée National de la Coopération Franco-Américaine; James Zender, National Archives; Sarah Sibbald, National Gallery of Art; Mary Beth Betts, Annette Blaugren, Jim Francis, and Jack Rutland, The New-York Historical Society; Roberta Waddell, Print Division, New York Public Library; Sherry Birk and Charlotte Krull, Octagon Museum, American Institute of Architects Foundation; Judy Gardner-Flint, The Johns Hopkins University; Courtney D'Angelis, National Museum of American Art, John Fleckner and Ann Kuebler, Archives Center, Richard Doty, Department of Numismatics, and Sheila Alexander, Bonnie Lillianfeldt, and Susan Meyers, Department of Ceramics and Glass, National Museum of American History, Smithsonian Institution; Katheleen Betts, the Society of the Cincinnati; Franz Jantzen, Supreme Court; James Danke, State Historical Society of Wisconsin; Mindy Black, Ann Lucas, and Susan Stein, Thomas Jefferson Memorial Foundation/Monticello; James Ketcham and Melinda Smith,

United States Senate; Eleanor Preston and Ann Webb, Tudor Place Foundation, Inc.; and Betty Monkman, The White House. Private collectors who were of great assistance include Arthur D. Arendt, Clarence and Joyce Brown, John Long, Jack and Diane Louv, Mr. and Mrs. Set Charles Momjian, Arthur J. Phelan, and Murray B. Woldman and Joel M. Woldman.

Additional scholars who generously shared their time and knowledge include Kevin Avery, Douglas Ball, Neil Bingham, Charles E. Brownell, Jeffrey A. Cohen, Olive Graffam, Diana Hale, Don Alexander Hawkins, Alvin Holm, Richard Janson, Anne Poulet, Catherine Rubincam, and Thomas P. Somma.

The exhibition and associated graphics were designed by George Sexton Associates, Washington, D.C. Those staff members involved were George Sexton III, Terry Ammons, Thomas Biggar, Simon Blakey, Rebecca Davies, Joseph Geitner, Steve Heidlauf, Nelson Jenkins, Elizabeth Jones, Peter Kozloski, Jeanne Krohn, Diana Pabon, Doug Pierson, Roy Robinson, Karin Salch, Mary Sarant, Jean Sundin, David Tozer, and Tom Uzzell.

Development and publication of this book was made possible by a generous gift from the Philip Morris Companies Inc. Support for the exhibition came from the Philip Morris Companies and the James Madison Council of the Library of Congress. This exhibition is part of the project to establish the Center for American Architecture, Design, and Engineering at the Library of Congress.

Chronology of the United States Capitol

1790 July 16   "An act for establishing the temporary and permanent Seat of the Government of the United States."

1791 April 10   Secretary of State Thomas Jefferson writes to Pierre Charles L'Enfant that he hopes the Capitol will be based on "some one of the models of antiquity which have had the approbation of thousands of years."

1792 March   L'Enfant's "Plan of the City of Washington," depicting the ground plan of his Capitol with a vast circular room facing west, is published in the *Universal Asylum and Columbian Magazine* (Philadelphia).

1792 March 24   Advertisement for Capitol designs are first published in *Dunlap's American Daily Advertiser,* (Philadelphia).

1792 July 15   Competition entries are due; none is found acceptable.

1792 July–December   French-born and -trained architect Stephen Hallet is retained to produce revised designs.

1792 October 8   Hallet's third Capitol design is exhibited at the second sale of Washington city lots.

1793 January   Hallet's fourth plan and a design by physician and amateur architect William Thornton are shown to President George Washington in Philadelphia.

1793 February 1   Jefferson reports to the Commissioners of the District of Columbia that he and Washington prefer Thornton's design, as it is "simple, noble, beautiful, excellently distributed, and moderate in size."

1793 March 11   Commissioners formally award Thornton the first prize; Hallet, the second.

1793 April   Thornton writes a lengthy description of his Capitol design: "the house of the people . . . which is meant to serve them for many Centuries, and which the richest people in the world cannot surely hesitate to erect in a manner worthy of their dignity."

1793 July 15   Meeting is called by Washington and Jefferson in Philadelphia to review criticism of Thornton's plan; outcome is the "conference plan," which marries Thornton's exterior to Hallet's plan. Hallet is hired as the superintending architect.

1793 August–September   Foundations are dug under Hallet's direction.

1793 September 18   Cornerstone is laid with Masonic rites; Washington participates.

1794 June 26   Hallet is reprimanded for altering Thornton's design.

1794 September 12   Thornton is appointed one of three commissioners with oversight of the Capitol.

1794 November 15   Hallet is dismissed as the Capitol's superintending architect. His semi-elliptical Senate chamber is a two-story room entered at ground level (Jefferson's suggestion); its shape is defined by an arcade below and a colonnade above the public gallery.

1795 January 2   Commissioners authorize American painter John Trumbull (in London) to hire English architect George Hadfield to replace Hallet.

1795 October 15   Hadfield is appointed Architect of the Capitol.

1795 November 18   Hadfield's suggestion of eliminating Thornton's rusticated basement and adding a second attic story is rejected by Thornton and James Hoban, architect of the White House. His idea of an octagonal drum for the dome and a substantial east front staircase entrance to the rotunda is eventually executed by succeeding architects.

1797–1798   Thornton revises his original design to have on the west front a tall, colonnaded "Temple of Fame," or "Temple of Virtue," to commemorate the Revolution's civic and military heroes.

1798 May 28   Hadfield is dismissed. Hoban is appointed architect of the Capitol.

1799 December 14   Washington dies.

1800 January 2   Thornton writes to John Marshall recommending that Washington's tomb be placed "in the Center of that National Temple which he approved of for a Capitol."

1800 May 15   Commissioners report 109 brick and 263 wood houses in Washington; population is about 3,000.

1800 November 22   Sixth Congress meets in the completed north wing: the Senate in a two-story, east-facing room designed as its permanent chamber; the House temporarily in a large room across the hall.

1801 March 4   Jefferson is inaugurated president.

1801 May–December   Chamber for the House of Representatives ("the oven"), designed by Hoban as a free-standing oval room in the center of the south wing's rectangle, is built; exterior walls are to be carried up later.

1802 May 1   Board of Commissioners of the District of Columbia is abolished by Congress.

1802 October 24   Committee of architects and builders appointed by Jefferson reports that Hoban's House chamber is unstable.

1803 March 6   Jefferson appoints Benjamin Henry Latrobe as Surveyor of Public Buildings.

1803 April 4   Latrobe first suggests to Jefferson a hemispherical room for the House of Representatives.

1804 February 28   Latrobe reports proposed changes due to poor design and faulty workmanship of both the north and south wings. He receives from Thornton plans for a new oval House chamber, but revives Hallet's hippodrome shape in order to accommodate skylit roof proposed by Jefferson.

1804 March 29   Latrobe shows Jefferson section drawings of the new House chamber: one with Roman Doric from the Theater of Marcellus, and the other with Greek Doric from the Tower of the Winds. By the end of April, they settle on the elaborate Greek Corinthian from the Choragic Monument of Lysicrates in Athens.

1804 Spring   Hoban's House chamber is dismantled.

1805 March 6   Latrobe writes to Philip Mazzei asking for his help in securing Italian sculptors. By September, Mazzei has contracted with brothers-in-law Giuseppe Franzoni and Giovanni Andrei.

1805 August 31   Latrobe suggests to Jefferson that the Senate wing be "compleatly *gutted,* and solidly constructed in the interior."

1805 September 8   Jefferson writes to Latrobe that the House chamber's skylights will make it the "handsomest room in the world, without a single exception."

1806   Latrobe presents Jefferson with a perspective watercolor of the Capitol's new east facade: a single, low Roman Pantheon-inspired rotunda and dome to be entered via a combined portico-colonnade that spans the center and approached by a deep, wide staircase. Rotunda is labeled "Hall of the People" on matching plan of the main floor; House of Representatives is hippodrome-shaped; Senate is semicircular. Washington's mausoleum is proposed for a crypt below the rotunda.

1806 December 6	Latrobe credits Jefferson with an idea of east front portico, modeled on a source "said to be of *Dioclesian*['s]" reign.
1807 September 1	Franzoni's plaster model of figure representing American Liberty is set in place behind the Speaker's chair in the House of Representatives. Allegorical relief figures of Agriculture, Art, Science, and Commerce are carved in the frieze.
1807 November 22	Latrobe's detailed description of his changes to the Capitol is published in the *National Intelligencer.*
1808 April 26	Jefferson orders Latrobe to divide the two-story Senate chamber in half horizontally, arranging the ground floor for the Supreme Court and the second floor for the Senate.
1808 September 19	Section of Latrobe's wide single arch in Supreme Court falls, killing Clerk of the Works John Lenthall.
1808–1809	Latrobe designs a two-and-a-half-story room for the Library of Congress in the Egyptian Revival style; the Library is located on the west side of the north, or Senate, wing.
1809	Latrobe designs the corn order—corncobs for the capitals and cornstalks for the convex ribbed shafts—for the Supreme Court vestibule; the columns are carved by Franzoni.
1809 September 8	Latrobe reports to President James Madison on completion of the rebuilt Senate chamber, boasting that its brick vaulted half-dome, with a span of 110 feet, is "one of the most extraordinary ever attempted."
1810–1811	Latrobe proposes Doric Greek Revival propylaea (gateway in the form of a temple) as the entrance on the Capitol's west front and a statue of *Athena as American Liberty* atop the portico overlooking the Mall. Dome's octagonal drum to have relief sculpture based on Panathenaic Procession from the Parthenon in Athens.
1812 July 21	Franzoni proposes to carve six emblematic figures of Bellona, Agriculture, Commerce, Science, Minerva, and Art for the Senate chamber.
1814 August 24	Capitol is burned by British troops during the War of 1812.
1815	Latrobe adds a west wing to the Capitol to gain more offices and a new Library of Congress.
1815 March 14	Latrobe is reappointed architect of the Capitol by President James Madison; Board of Commissioners is to act as intermediary.
1815 July 12	Latrobe writes to Jefferson (at Monticello) describing the extent of damage caused by the fire.
1815 August	Latrobe sends Giovanni Andrei back to Italy to oversee the execution of Corinthian capitals for the House of Representatives in white Carrara marble.
1816	Latrobe designs the double-story tobacco-leaf rotunda for the north wing to replace Thornton's flying staircase, destroyed in the fire; it is sculpted by Antonio Iardella. For enlarged Senate, he designs thirteen caryatid figures representing the original states for the railing of the public gallery.
1816 February 6	For the Rotunda, Congress commissions from American painter John Trumbull four large history paintings depicting major civic and military events of the Revolution.
1817 May	Carlo Franzoni's plaster relief of Justice is placed on the west wall of the Supreme Court chamber.
1817 November 20	Latrobe resigns as architect of the Capitol.
1818 January 8	President James Monroe officially appoints Boston architect Charles Bulfinch as Architect of the Capitol.
1818 April 17	Bulfinch sends Trumbull a sketch of his west wing design in which he has inserted a subbasement level. Portico above is to have Bulfinch's signature motif of two sets of double columns framing two single columns.
1819	Franzoni carves the *Car of History* clock for the House of Representatives.
1819 February 2	View of one of Hadfield's proposed Capitol alterations is published in the *Washington Gazette.*
1821 January 11	House Committee on Public Buildings reports favorably on Enrico Causici's proposal to carve in marble his figure representing the *Genius of the Constitution* for the House chamber.
1822 February	Bulfinch presents estimates for a dome in wood, brick, or stone.

1822 Summer	Bulfinch plans the Rotunda's decoration: relief-sculpted panels by Italian and French artists depicting pre-Revolutionary War events. Beginning of the idea of the Capitol as a repository of the socio-political theory of Manifest Destiny, the settling of the continent by Euro-Americans seen as inevitable and justified.
1822 December 9	In his annual report Bulfinch describes his double dome's construction: two-thirds of the inner dome is built of stone and brick, the remainder is wood, and the outer dome is of wood sheathed in copper.
1823	Now-lost Bulfinch drawings copied by English architect Charles A. Busby in 1819 are published in London. East elevation shows a return to Thornton's arcaded portico (not executed); plan shows a massive central stair leading from the Rotunda to the crypt and Washington's proposed mausoleum.
1825 May 6	Bulfinch shows President John Quincy Adams about thirty-six designs submitted in competition for east pediment sculpture.
1825 May	Jury consisting of Thornton, painter Charles Bird King, and Colonel George Bomford votes for a composite design that combines elements from several entrants.
1825 May 31	Adams meets with sculptor Luigi Persico and changes his figure of Hercules to one of Hope and replaces his classical fasces with an altar of Liberty. The entire composition is entitled the *Genius of America,* with the central figure accompanied by "Hope" and "Justice."
1832 Summer	New York architect Alexander Jackson Davis spends the summer doing sketches and measured drawings of the Capitol; he returns in the summers of 1833 and 1834.
1834	Persico executes figures *War* and *Peace* for niches flanking the east door.
1843 March 1	Congress requests the secretary of war to prepare a new design for the House of Representatives; it eventually leads to proposals for the Capitol's extension.
1850 Autumn	Senate Committee on Public Buildings announces competition for the Capitol Extension.
1851 June 10	President Millard Fillmore appoints Thomas U. Walter as Architect of the Capitol Extension.
1851 July 4	Daniel Webster gives the oration at the cornerstone-laying ceremony.
1853 March 4	Authority over the Capitol Extension is transferred from the Department of the Interior to the Department of War. Captain Montgomery C. Meigs of the Army Corps of Engineers is put in charge.
1853 August 18	Meigs solicits designs for marble pedimental sculpture and bronze doors from two American sculptors residing in Rome: Hiram Powers and Thomas Crawford.
1853 October 31	Crawford sends designs for the Senate Wing pediment, *The Progress of Civilization,* and for a door depicting major events in Washington's public career.
1855 March 3	Congress passes appropriation for a new cast-iron dome designed by Walter.
1855 May 11	Meigs solicits design from Crawford for a figure of Liberty for the summit of the new dome.
1859	Italian-born and -trained fresco painter Constantino Brumidi makes sketches for a Rotunda frieze, the theme of which is *America and History.* He also does his first sketches for the canopy painting to be suspended between Walter's double dome: *The Apotheosis of Washington.*
1908–1916	Sculptor Paul Bartlett designs and executes a sculptural group, *The Apotheosis of Democracy,* for the House of Representatives pediment.

TEMPLE OF LIBERTY

~ PROLOGUE ~

"Temple of Liberty"

The Capitol in Overview

When Congressman James Wilson of Pennsylvania prophesied in 1787 that America's new federal government would "lay a foundation for erecting temples of Liberty in every part of the earth," he based his expectation on widespread Enlightenment ideas and ideals (Plate 1, Cat. 225). Wilson's analogy was not an isolated metaphor, but a genuine expression of the excitement and sense of purpose among Euro-Americans. The Marquis de Lafayette, in his farewell address to the Continental Congress in Trenton, New Jersey, on December 11, 1784, had proclaimed that the entire United States was a moral allegory: "May this Immense temple of freedom Ever Stand a lesson to oppressors, an Example to the oppressed, a Sanctuary for the Rights of Mankind." By the mid-1780s, George Washington and Thomas Jefferson were already planning a new capital city under the exclusive jurisdiction of Congress where the Revolution's great civic achievement, government of and by the people, would be permanently located.[1]

Ratification of the Constitution in 1788 created the imminent need for housing the new federal government. Accommodations for the president and executive department officers could be readily met by existing buildings. But large, medium, and small auditorium rooms in which the House of Representatives, Senate, and Supreme Court could hold their debates and deliberations were not easily available. Each of the thirteen states had a statehouse, but residual political tensions among the states, as well as conflicting legislative calendars, precluded their simultaneous use by the federal government. The immediate problem was solved by the renovation of New York's old city hall into Federal Hall, an overt bid to locate the national capital in this northern commercial city. Carpenters' Hall and Congress Hall in Philadelphia were subsequently renovated to house Congress temporarily.

After prolonged debate, Congress passed the Residence Act on July 16, 1790. It called for a federal city near Georgetown, Maryland, within a 10-mile square federal district carved out of Maryland and Virginia. In January 1791, Washington hired Pierre Charles L'Enfant (1755–1825) to design the city as well as an impressive array of public buildings for civic, religious, military, utilitarian, and commemorative purposes. The priorities were a residence-cum-office for the president and a "Congress House," both to be ready by the first Monday in December 1800, the date Congress had mandated to move the government to the federal city. L'Enfant was dismissed within a year; his successors were to be chosen by open competitions to obtain designs for the public buildings announced in March 1792. These competitions resulted in a fine design for the President's House, but none of the original entries for the Capitol was considered a suitable expression of its important national purposes.

The process of imagining, designing, constructing, and decorating the Capitol occupied statesmen, architects, and artists from 1791 to 1916. Washington and Jefferson's idea that the Capitol should convey America's new political, social, and cultural order was so strong that it survived continual revisions and major additions to the design they had sanctioned in 1793. Revolutionary-era events provided symbols and allegorical personifications that expressed such concepts as liberty, justice, prosperity, and national union.

Washington's own ideas about how the Capitol might convey political and social concepts must be inferred from changes that architects made after meeting with him. His rare suggestions known from surviving correspondence affirm his own claim to being an amateur in the arts. For instance, he commented on one of the competition entries that the "Dome, which is suggested as an addition to the center of the edifice, would, in my opinion, give beauty & grandeur to the pile, and might be useful for the reception of a Clock—Bell—&c." Jefferson advised him on aesthetic, political, and practical aspects of the Capitol's design and early construction.

Jefferson's active involvement with the Capitol's lengthy gestation and halting growth was more than twice as long as that of Washington. As secretary of state, he suggested an open competition, guided its direction, made a design himself, advised Washington and the commissioners on the selection of a design, and arbitrated the compromise that resulted in a composite design. As president, he oversaw the erection and dismantling of the first hall for the House of Representatives, hired Benjamin Henry Latrobe (the architect whose genius made the Capitol a great building), and collaborated with him to create many of the Capitol's unique and meaningful public spaces: a new Senate chamber, a second (but not final) House of Representatives hall, and a Supreme Court room. Jefferson made several oblique and direct statements about the Capitol's transcendent purposes both in the designs he proposed and fostered and in his correspondence and discussions with the principals. He believed that America's political system was unparalleled in the history of humankind and that the Capitol, which embodied it, should be a worthy container.

Over almost forty years, five excellent professional architects were hired to erect the design that Washington and Jefferson selected. Outwardly, the final building was an approximation of that design; inwardly, it bore little resemblance to what Washington thought the Capitol would look like when he died in 1799. Working in collaboration with the competition judges, French émigré Stephen Hallet (1755–1825), the only professional architect to enter the competition, produced five designs for the Capitol from July 1792 to March 1793. Their architectural forms and sculptural decoration drew on American as well as European traditions to express various concepts of America's history, national character, and destiny. Hallet eventually lost the competition to an amateur architect, physician William Thornton (1759–1828), whose compact and elegant design was universally admired. In August and September 1793, the Capitol's foundations were dug following a composite design of Thornton's elevations and Hallet's plans. The compromise had been negotiated during a conference in Philadelphia called by Washington and moderated by Jefferson on July 15. At that time, Hallet was hired to supervise the construction of the Capitol. In November 1795, President Washington noted that the Capitol's design was "no body's, but a compound of every body's," referring to the varied contributions to the building's design history of himself, Jefferson, Hallet, Thornton, and the federal city's commissioners.[2]

The pragmatic and symbolic functions of the Capitol were inextricably interwoven from the outset. Both Washington and Jefferson believed that the Capitol's outward appearance should reflect important ideas of the new government: national union, the bicameral legislative bodies it housed, and easy accessibility to all Americans. Through their suggestions to some of the competitors—principally Hallet and Thornton—they influenced the Capitol's overall form: the separate wings to accommodate the Senate and the House of Representatives were joined together by a domed rotunda. The building's details, however, were not firmly established by the competition results. Rather, they slowly evolved as each succeeding architect altered the designs of his predecessors.

The Capitol's construction history was even more complex than the competition for its design. Numerous pragmatic and political difficulties—including material shortages, labor problems, inadequate funding, faulty construction, a serious accident, and a major fire—combined with multiple design changes to delay the Capitol's completion. In 1795, the Italian-born, English-trained architect George Hadfield (1763–1826) was hired to replace Hallet. Hallet had been fired in November 1794, Thornton claimed, for having deviated from Thornton's design for the central section of the building. Hadfield had won the Gold Medal in architectural design from the Royal Academy in London in 1784 and, in 1790, as the first holder of the Travelling Scholarship in Architecture awarded by the academy, began several years of study in Italy. The hopes that Washington officials placed in Hadfield's completing the Capitol were dashed as he, too, was dismissed in 1798 as a result of conflicts with Thornton. Echoes of Hadfield's proposed alterations to the Capitol did surface in later designs by his successors.

The commissioners then turned to James Hoban (ca. 1762–1831), the Irish-born and -trained architect who since 1792 had been successfully supervising the construction of his winning design for the President's House. Hoban had supervised both Hallet and Hadfield in their construction of the Capitol, had participated in the conference in July 1793 that settled the Capitol's design, and had acted generally as a mediator among all the factions. His most significant contribution to the Capitol's development was his design in 1801 for the first hall for the House of Representatives; it was dismantled in 1804 because of faulty construction.

Jefferson's decision in 1803 to hire the English-born and pan-European-trained architect Benjamin Henry Latrobe (1764–1820) to complete the Capitol changed the building's aesthetic direction from Thornton's British distillation of Italian Renaissance traditions to Latrobe's radically modern Neoclassical vision, in which space and light were palpable architectural realities, as powerful as his stone colonnades, walls, and vaults. During most of Latrobe's first building campaign, which ended in July 1811, the president and his architect—informed amateur and consummate professional—worked closely together to realize a Capitol whose architectural expression was intended to be unique among the world's public buildings. In 1806, Latrobe proposed a new design for the Capitol's central porticoes, Rotunda, and dome that focused attention on the "Hall of the People," rather than on the legislative chambers. He rebuilt Hallet's and Hadfield's interiors for the Senate wing and erected a hippodrome-shaped House chamber that revived Hallet's plan, but with details, including a skylit ceiling, that reflected his close collaboration with Jefferson.

On August 24, 1814, toward the end of the War of 1812 and in retaliation for the American destruction of York (now Toronto), British troops burned the Capitol (as well as all the other public buildings in Washington except the Patent Office). The fire destroyed most of the Capitol's interiors, leaving a stone shell that was not entirely stable. Latrobe's rebuilding of the gutted Capitol began in April 1815; the job was unfinished when he resigned in November 1817, leaving behind drawings necessary for its completion according to his revised, post-fire design. He had enlarged the Senate chamber, entirely redesigned the hall for the House of Representatives, and extended the west wing to gain space for additional offices and committee rooms as well as a new Library of Congress.

Latrobe devised for the Capitol a comprehensive iconographic scheme intended to be comprehensible to the common man that fused both European and American symbols and personifications. He refuted criticism of his sculptural decoration by remarking, somewhat

Fig. 1. Charles Bulfinch. "Site Plan of the Capitol," ca. 1826–1829. Library of Congress.

Fig. 2. Peder Anderson and Fitz Hugh Lane. "View of the City of Washington," 1838. Library of Congress.

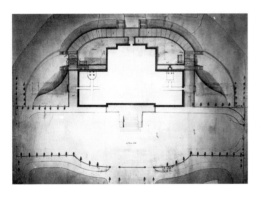

sarcastically, that "it may indeed be said that as good Laws may be made in a Wigwam, as in the Capitol, and that all decoration is useless, and all history mere idle amusement." With his American architectural orders; his Americanized figures of Liberty, Justice, History, and the Genius of the Constitution; and his figures representing the thirteen original states, which are now lost, Latrobe sought to unite the Capitol's architecture and decoration. Together they were to make manifest to the Capitol's users and visitors its actual and symbolic functions as the nation's most important public building.[3]

During the 1820s, an expanded range of historical events, beginning with Columbus's exploration of the New World, introduced to the Capitol's nationalistic iconography the concept of Manifest Destiny. This belief held by Euro-Americans that the spread of European civilization across North America was both inevitable and desirable justified their displacement of Native Americans. Charles Bulfinch

(1763–1844), the only American-born and -trained architect yet consulted (other than Jefferson), was hired in November 1817 to finish the building (Plate 2, Cat. 108). Bulfinch combined considerable experience and skills as an architect and a politician, having designed dozens of public and private buildings in New England, including the Massachusetts State House (1795–1797). He had served as a Boston selectman for a quarter-century before assuming the position of Architect of the Capitol. In general, Bulfinch finished Latrobe's post-fire designs for the interiors of the north and south wings and the east portico, but substituted his own scheme for the west wing and portico and the Rotunda and dome. His final work was to landscape the grounds, which included erecting gatehouses and a terrace (Figs. 1 and 2; Cats. 107 and 223).

Each architect had offered his own solutions to the Capitol's practical and symbolic design questions; their combined efforts resulted in a building that received mixed reviews when it was finally complete almost four decades after Washington had appointed L'Enfant as its designer in 1791. Anne Royall, in her encomium published in *Sketches of History, Life and Manners in the United States*, expressed the opinion of most Americans—an emotive, but not particularly well-informed, evaluation: "The capitol, however, which may aptly be called the eighth wonder of the world eclipses the whole [of Washington's buildings]. This stupendous fabric, when seen at a distance, is remarkable for its magnitude, its vast dome rising out of the centre, and its exquisite whiteness."[4]

In 1830, when Charles Bulfinch retired to Boston, the Capitol was complete but already inadequate to meet the needs of the growing country. By 1836, designs to extend the Capitol were being proposed; the winner of the competition of 1850 and 1851, Philadelphia architect Thomas U. Walter (1804–1887), produced a thoroughly modern Renaissance Revival design that irrevocably changed the nature of the Capitol because of its overwhelming scale and robust design character. Walter worked with a larger professional staff than had any of his predecessors. Montgomery C. Meigs (1816–1892) of the Army Corps of Engineers contributed architectural and aesthetic ideas (he located the new chambers in the center of each wing and supervised the painters and sculptors) as well as engineering and administrative expertise to the Capitol Extension. The Italian-born fresco painter Constantino Brumidi (1805–1880) spent the twenty-five years from 1855 to 1880 at the Capitol, formulating and largely executing an extensive cycle of history and decorative paintings. His work culminated in the great canopy painting suspended between the double-shelled dome. Entitled *The Apotheosis of Washington*, it brought the Capitol's iconographic themes full circle by placing Washington at the center of the maturing nation's many cultural, political, and technological achievements.

In 1858, Walter's new cast-iron dome, hailed as one of the greatest engineering feats of the century, began rising above the original building. The Capitol's first dome had been derived from that of the ancient Roman Pantheon; the second was a descendant of the dome of St. Peter's Basilica in Rome, one of the greatest architectural achievements of the Italian Renaissance. Walter's most immediate source was the cast-iron dome that crowned St. Isaac's Cathedral (1818–1858) in St. Petersburg, but it, as well as the Capitol's wings, underwent an Americanization process. American sculptor Thomas Crawford (1813–1857), working in Rome, collaborated with Meigs and Senator Jefferson Davis to create the Capitol's crowning glory, the bronze statue of *Freedom Triumphant in War and Peace*.

At the same time, Crawford modeled fourteen figures for the pediment of the Senate wing, the whole composition titled *The Progress of Civilization*. The House wing's pediment was not put in place until 1916. Paul Bartlett (1865–1925) was the sculptor; his theme, *The*

Apotheosis of Democracy. Both Crawford and Bartlett created central Athena-like figures that represent some important aspects of the American experience.

Henry James, writing in *The American Scene,* perceptively described the Capitol as the "ark of the American covenant, . . . as a compendium of all the national terms and standards, weights and measures and emblems of greatness and glory, and indeed as a builded record of half the collective vibrations of a people; their conscious spirit, their public faith, their bewildered taste, their ceaseless curiosity, their arduous and interrupted education."[5]

– I –

"A More Perfect Union"

Symbolizing the National Union
of States

In 1754, Benjamin Franklin devised the first symbolic emblem for America whose political content—national union—expressed Euro-American concerns (Cat. 1). European allegorical figures of the New World originating during the Renaissance were Native Americans wearing feather clothing and accompanied by indigenous animals and plants. About the time of the Revolution, the "Indian Princess" was fused with the European figure of Liberty or Minerva (emblematic of strength and civic virtue) to create a new composite personification given various titles but expressive of the new American liberty through representative government.

For those immediately involved in the Revolution and the arduous process of formulating the government under the Constitution, the most important fact about America was the effective union of the states. Most of the Revolutionary-era emblems were primarily symbols of union intended to be understood by the multilingual American population and the illiterate as representing the new political order. The country's very name—United States of America—was devised by Thomas Jefferson to reinforce among all Americans their "common cause," a phrase that originated during the Revolution. Union was the fundamental meaning of the American flag as well as the Great Seal of the United States, both emblems voted by Congress to officially represent the country.

Symbols with thirteen elements were so prevalent during the Revolution that they were satirized by a British officer, Mr. Smythe, who recorded in his diary on January 1, 1780:

A party of naval prisoners lately returned from Jersey say, that the rations among the rebels are thirteen dried clams per day; that the titular Lord Stirling takes thirteen glasses of grog every morning, has thirteen enormous rumbunches on his nose, and that (when duly impregnated) he always makes thirteen attempts before he can walk; that Mr. Washington has thirteen toes on his feet, (the extra ones having grown since the Declaration of Independence,) and the same number of teeth in each jaw; that the Sachem Schuyler has a top-knot of thirteen stiff hairs,

9

which erect themselves on the crown of his head when he grows mad; that Old Putnam had thirteen pounds of his posteriors bit off in an encounter with a Connecticut bear, (It was then he lost the *balance* of his mind); . . . that Polly Wayne was just thirteen hours in subduing Stony Point, and as many seconds in leaving it.[1]

The Capitol's proposed and actual sculpture consisted of emblems and allegorical figures either invented or adapted for America during the latter half of the eighteenth century. All sought to express a commonality of purpose among the politically and culturally diverse populations in the thirteen colonies. Although divided by language, social customs, religious beliefs, and political systems, Euro-Americans did share the visual and written heritage of Greco-Roman antiquity. As political ties with Europe were strained and then severed, symbols and personifications drawn from this rich lode expressed the underlying national political goals sought by the Founding Fathers. The politics of diverse cultural identity was addressed by the range of sources for the new national emblems, which were drawn from British, French, Dutch, Italian, and German traditions. Sometimes their use was further sanctioned by direct classical or Native American precedent. The sources, choices, and, ultimately, synthesis of some of these images help us understand how peoples from different European cultural backgrounds were subtly urged to consolidate into a new nation of Americans.

Fig. 3. Benjamin Franklin. "Join or Die." *Pennsylvania Gazette* (Philadelphia), May 9, 1754. Library of Congress.

Fig. 4. After Pierre Eugene du Simitière. "Design for the Great Seal of the United States," 1776. Library of Congress.

SYMBOLS OF AMERICAN UNION
Severed Snake

Benjamin Franklin was the seminal figure who conceptualized symbols of American union. His snake device was first published in the May 9, 1754, edition of his newspaper, the *Pennsylvania Gazette*. The image and its accompanying motto, "Join, or Die," were Franklin's advice to the Albany Convention, a loose federation of seven colonies seeking a resolution to the French and Indian Wars (Fig. 3; Cat. 1). Franklin labeled the sections of a severed American rattlesnake with the initials of the colonies, arranged geographically from the serpent's head, which represented New England, to its tail, labeled South Carolina. Georgia chose not to be included in the plan of union under consideration in 1754. Franklin's cut snake was redesigned by Paul Revere in 1765 and published widely in newspapers to denote opposition to the Stamp Act, and again in 1774 on the eve of the Revolution; in both cases, the tail terminated with Georgia (Cat. 2). In 1765, Revere changed the logo to "Unite or Die," but in 1774 both "Join or Die" and "Unite or Die" were used.[2]

Great Seal of the United States

The design of the Great Seal of the United States was entrusted first to a congressional committee appointed on July 4, 1776, and composed of Jefferson, Franklin, and John Adams. Designs proffered by five committees were reviewed before Congress finally accepted on June 20, 1782, a composite design made up of elements suggested by all of them. Pierre Eugene du Simitière, a French-born artist and learned antiquarian living in Philadelphia, designed the first committee's seal to express national unity but individual cultural identity (Fig. 4; Cat. 11). The central motif was a large shield divided into six parts, each decorated with the national symbol of one of the six European countries whose immigrants had settled America: England, Scotland, France, Germany, Ireland, and Holland. Around its perimeter, smaller shields were emblazoned with the initials of the thirteen new states arranged geographically. The two supporting heraldic figures were Liberty and America. Du Simitière's central concept, expressed by his proposed motto, "E pluribus unum" (One out of many), and a Masonic device denoting the all-seeing eye of God, were retained in the final design.

The second committee, which reported on March 25, 1780, contributed a shield of thirteen stripes, an olive branch, and a "radiant constellation of 13 stars." William Barton, a Philadelphia lawyer, suggested the heraldic or spread eagle to the third committee, which was appointed in May 1782 (Cat. 7). The eagle, a symbol of royal authority since Roman times, was chosen specifically by Barton, he said, to signify the "supreme power and authority of Congress" (Cat. 4.1).

In June 1782, Secretary of Congress Charles Thomson brought together du Simitière's motto, the stars and striped shield, and Barton's eagle, which Thomson depicted clutching an olive branch with thirteen leaves in one claw and thirteen arrows in the other (Cat. 8). A stepped pyramid of thirteen levels was chosen for the seal's obverse. Adopting traditional European symbols but giving them a new American meaning—transferring the symbol of power from kings to Congress, for instance—was the most common way that American symbols were created.[3]

The Great Seal eagle became the most popular symbol of the federal government and was soon adopted for numerous unofficial purposes to simply denote America (Fig. 5; Cats. 9 and 10). Its widespread acceptance, despite European royalist associations, may have been due to the eagle's dual citizenship. Around 1734, John Faber executed a mezzotint of William Verelst's double portrait of Tomo Chachi Mico and his nephew Tooanahowi, who is shown holding an eagle (Fig. 6; Cat. 5). The portrait was painted when the Creek Indians visited England as members of a delegation from the newly founded colony of Georgia. In September 1734, the *Gentleman's Magazine* reported on the chief's audience with King George II, including his presentation of a gift to the British monarch: "These are the Feathers of the Eagle, which is the Swiftest of Birds and who flieth all round our Nation. These feathers are a Sign of Power in our Land, and have been carried from Town to Town there; and we have brought them over to leave with you, O Great King, as a sign of everlasting peace."[4]

The Indian Peace Medal designed by Robert Scott and struck

Fig. 5. James Trenchard. "Arms of the United States." *The Columbian Magazine* (Philadelphia), September 1786. Library of Congress.

Fig. 6. John Faber, "Tomo Chachi Mico." Frontispiece in Samuel Urlsperger, *Ausfürliche nachricht von den saltzburgischen emigranten*, 1744. Library of Congress.

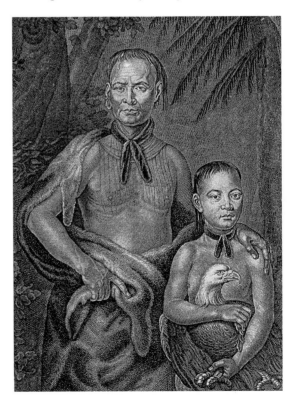

in 1801 also allied the eagle with Native Americans (Cat. 6). The obverse shows the handclasp of an American military officer, identified by the cuff of his uniform, and an Indian wearing a bracelet decorated with an eagle with its wings asymmetrically splayed.

American Flag

The American flag, composed of thirteen red and white stripes and thirteen white stars set on a blue field "representing a new constellation," was adopted by Congress on June 14, 1777. The identity of its designer is not certain, but the weight of evidence suggests the poet Francis Hopkinson, signer of the Declaration of Independence from Pennsylvania. No records concerning the reasons for the choice of the stars, stripes, or colors survive. However, the wording of the congressional resolution suggests the replacement of an "old constellation," perhaps one of the many political unions studied by the Founding Fathers. It has been postulated that the red and white stripes were adapted from the British Union flag. The union of the English and Scottish crowns under James VI (James I of England) in 1603 (the United Kingdom), and the union of their parliaments in 1707 (the Union of Great Britain), may also have provided the idea of the stars to represent the states. In 1603, Francis Bacon introduced a discourse on the union of crowns using cosmological and astrological metaphors to express a "congruity between the principles of Nature and [political] Policy."[5]

Fasces

The insignia of Roman senators, the fasces, or bundles of rods bound together by thongs, symbolized union as well as civil authority. Although fasces were not formally adopted as an official American emblem, they were commonly used as a symbol of national union because they cannot be broken. Jefferson added a later notation to his 1774 account book that indicates he may have originated their official use as an American symbol: "A proper device (instead of arms) for the American states united would be the Father presenting the bundle of rods to his sons. The motto 'Insuperabiles si inseperabiles' [Unconquerable if inseparable] an answer given in parl[iament] to the H[ouse] of Lds, & comm[ons]."[6] The French sculptor Jean-Antoine Houdon's famous statue of George Washington commissioned in 1785 for the new Virginia State Capitol in Richmond depicted Washington with his left hand resting on fasces, over which he has hung his sword, probably intended to symbolize the laying aside of arms and assumption of civic responsibilities.

ALLEGORICAL FIGURES OF AMERICA

Many allegorical figures borrowed from traditional European iconography were suggested as appropriate representations for some fundamental facets of American life. Minerva's association with figures of Britannia seems to have had a long history. In 1769 and 1770, the English astronomer Benjamin West paired Hercules (Strength) with Minerva (Wisdom) as metaphorical supports for the English liberal parliamentarian John Wilkes and the American patriot James Otis (Cat. 12). In 1782, the anonymous designer of the allegorical print "America Triumphant and Britannia in Distress" transferred Minerva's attributes from Britannia to America, adding a pike with a liberty cap and an olive branch (Cat. 13). The shield of this new composite figure of America-Minerva-Liberty was decorated with a snake. Two years later, Pierre Charles L'Enfant modeled his certificate for the Society of the Cincinnati on this print, but depicted America as an armor-clad male warrior holding a flag and aided by a fierce eagle (Cat. 14).[7]

In 1782, Franklin suggested Hercules to represent the young country on his design for the medal to celebrate American independence, the "Allegory of the American Revolution," popularly known as the Libertas Americana Medal. Recent research has established the French sculptor Claude-Michel Clodion (1738–1814) as the artist who made the terra-cotta relief from which the medalist Augustin Dupré worked (Fig. 7; Cat. 15). Franklin used three figures drawn from classical mythology to personify the successful Franco-American alliance. Minerva, carrying a shield decorated with the fleur-de-lys, represents France. She fends off an attacking lion, symbolic of Britain. The infant Hercules, whose strength was likened to that of the young American nation, stands between them and strangles two snakes, one representing the defeat of British troops at Saratoga in 1777 and the other at Yorktown in 1781.[8]

Fig. 7. Benjamin Franklin, designer, and Claude-Michel Clodion, sculptor. "Allegory of the American Revolution," 1783. Musée National de la Coopération Franco-Américaine.

Minerva had an existence in early American allegory apart from her association with Hercules in Franklin's Libertas Americana Medal. She was the Roman version of the Greek warrior goddess Athena, and thus derived her civic associations from Athena's role as the founder of Athens. (Both the Erectheum and the Parthenon on the Acropolis were temples dedicated to Athena.) The helmeted figure of America, used in conjunction with portraits of Franklin and Washington, displays attributes of Abundance, Liberty, and Athena-Minerva on the frontispiece of W. D. Cooper's *The History of North America* (1789) (Cat. 18).

Minerva had long been associated with figures of Britannia and was successfully allied with new figures of America. Traditional attributes of ancient personifications of Liberty merged with the Indian Princess, the primary allegorical figure who expressed the New World in Renaissance and later iconography, to create a new American figure sometimes called America, sometimes Columbia, sometimes American Liberty. The British Britannia-Minerva was easily assimilated with this versatile new American figure, who borrowed attributes from her and took on several related meanings to become a composite representing multiple civic virtues in the Capitol.[9]

As early as the beginning of the eighteenth century, a French designer of stove tiles depicted America as a Hercules figure carrying his traditional club, but wearing a cape of feathers (in emulation of the feather clothing of Native Americans), rather than a lion skin. Franklin's revival of Hercules to represent the fledgling America led to the adoption of the hero in the role of adult victor against tyrants and monsters, recounted in ancient tales of the Twelve Labors of Hercules. One of the federal government's first ships, the *Hercules,* commanded by Moses Browne, sailed for Canton, China, on February 1, 1788. On July 1, 1789, Congressman John Vining of Delaware, in a speech before the House of Representatives, noted that "this government, like HERCULES, rose brawny from the cradle." In 1792, the French minister to America, Barbé-Marbois, presented Secretary of Congress Charles Thomson with a drawing of Hercules astride an arch whose thirteen voussoirs are inscribed with the names of the American states in their geographic order from north to south (Fig. 8; Cat. 16).[10]

Probably the most influential image of the American Hercules is Robert Edge Pine's painting *Allegory of America* (1778), engraved by Joseph Strutt in 1781 (Fig. 9; Cat. 17). Pine's allegory was explained in 1784:

America [kneeling before the altar of peace], after having suffered the several evils of war, bewailed its unhappy cause, and lamented over the victims of its fury—her ruined towns—destroy'd commerce. etc. etc. On the appearance of Peace, is represented in an extacy of gratitude to the Almighty—Heroic Virtue [Hercules]. presents Liberty attended by Concord—Industry followed by Plenty and her train form a group expressive of Population: and ships denote Commerce.

On August 23, 1784, Pine's patron George William Fairfax wrote to his relative George Washington from England: "The figure of 'Heroic virtue' was intended to represent your Excellency, and if your likeness could have been procured, it had been a fine portrait of your person."[11]

Hercules as Heroic Virtue, for Americans at least as meaningful an aspect of the ancient hero's legend as his feats of strength, was based on the "Judgment of Hercules," as retold by the Earl of Shaftesbury in his *Characteristics of Men, Manners, Opinions, and Times* (1711). Hercules had been the arbiter in a contest between Venus, the goddess of beauty, and Minerva, the goddess of wisdom. Hercules chose Minerva, or, as it was interpreted by Shaftesbury and others, he chose a life of virtue and public service over one of frivolity. In 1776, John Adams had suggested Hercules as Heroic Virtue to symbolize America on the Great Seal:

I proposed the Choice of Hercules, as engraved by Gribeline in some Editions of Lord Shaftsburys Works. . . . The Hero resting on his Clubb. Virtue pointing to her rugged Mountain, on one Hand, and persuading him to ascend. Sloth, glancing at her flowery Paths of Pleasure, wantonly reclining on the Ground, displaying the Charms both of her Eloquence and Person, to seduce him into Vice. But this is too complicated a Group for a Seal or Medal, and it is not original.[12]

After the 1790s, Hercules declined as an American symbol, perhaps because his attributes of lion skin and club denoted savagery and the reasoning for his association with America was too abstruse for many Americans to understand.

Fig. 8. François, Marquis de Barbé-Marbois, designer. "Allegory of the American Union," 1784. American Philosophical Society.

Fig. 9. Joseph Strutt, after Robert Edge Pine. "Allegory of America," 1781. Library of Congress.

HOUSING THE CONTINENTAL CONGRESS IN PHILADELPHIA:
CARPENTERS' HALL

On the morning of September 5, 1774, forty-four delegates from eleven of the states that composed the first Continental Congress met at Carpenters' Hall in Philadelphia and voted to hold their sessions in its main meeting room.[13] This choice of a hall offered them by the Carpenters' Company in preference to the more commodious Assembly Room in the nearby Pennsylvania State House, "Independence Hall," bespoke an awareness of the delicate balance that existed between the colonies as well as a sensitivity to the delegates' function. The Continental Congress was meeting in Philadelphia because of its centrality, not as an affirmation of any regional or ideological political position. The Carpenters' Company guild hall had no prior political associations with British sovereignty in America (as the statehouse did), and its selection by the delegates could not be construed as unlawful usurpation of power by the delegates. Their choice silently affirmed their purpose: to decide what joint action the colonies should take in response to the Coercive Acts passed by Parliament during the spring of 1774, not to vote on rebellion.

When Congress reconvened on May 10, 1775, the political situation had altered considerably. George III had refused to receive the "Petition of the Grand American Continental Congress," prepared during the fall 1774 session and addressed to him in an effort to seek peaceful redress of grievances. In addition, on April 19, while some delegates were already en route to Philadelphia, shots had been fired at Lexington and Concord. When the delegates took their seats on May 10, they did so as members of a legislative body preparing to take control of the government rather than as a convention drafting a set of resolutions. This change in function is reflected in their meeting place. The Pennsylvania State House was now deemed appropriate because Congress saw itself, and was seen by other Americans, as representing a new national government. Part of the process of transferring political legitimacy from the old order to the new was occupation of a former seat of government. This consciousness of the symbolic and political significance of the meeting places of the country's national representatives was present throughout the protracted process of building a permanent Capitol for the United States.[14]

HOUSING THE FIRST FEDERAL CONGRESS IN NEW YORK:
FEDERAL HALL

Due to the vicissitudes of war and regional interests, the Continental (1774–1778) and Confederation (1779–1788) congresses met in eight cities, moving ten times between the first session in Philadelphia on September 5, 1774, and the final one in New York on October 11, 1788. Philadelphia and New York were the primary meeting places and the major contenders for the permanent location of the government. Both were centrally located, offered a wide range of urban amenities, and had powerful local interests lobbying to keep "Congress," the embodiment of the government before the Constitution was adopted in 1788. Congress had first debated establishing a separate federal town in 1779; its location was the subject of heated discussion in and out of Congress for the next decade and was unresolved when it disbanded in 1788. More than fifty American cities and towns vied for the honor and the benefits of becoming, or being adjacent to, the proposed permanent seat of government.[15]

In the absence of any consensus about the permanent location of the national capital, Congress voted on September 13, 1788, to remain in New York when it reconvened on

Fig. 10. Amos Doolittle. "View of the Federal Edifice in New York," *The Columbian Magazine* (Philadelphia), August 1789. Library of Congress.

March 4, 1789, under the new Constitution as the First Federal Congress. Congress had been meeting in New York's city hall since January 11, 1785, in the same building where the Stamp Act Congress had been held for seventeen days in October 1765. Immediately after Congress's decision to remain temporarily in New York, a local citizens' committee formed to convert the city hall into Federal Hall in hopes that the government would make the city its permanent home if provided with an impressive meeting place. Within two weeks, the committee chose a design by one of its members, Pierre Charles L'Enfant, a French military engineer and architect who had designed many projects with specifically American emblematic content (Fig. 10; Cat. 25). On October 20, 1788, Hector St. John de Crève-coeur, the French-born author of *Letters from an American Farmer* (1781), reported in a letter to Jefferson that £4,000 had been subscribed by private citizens for the extensive renovations. Five weeks later, the French minister, the Comte de Moustier, who apparently had seen sketches or drawings by L'Enfant, wrote to Jefferson that the renovated and expanded building would be the best work of architecture in America, with its interiors beautiful and perfectly suited to the purpose of accommodating Congress.

Federal Hall was incomplete when the House of Representatives held its first meeting there on April 1, 1789, and the Senate its first meeting five days later, yet the building quickly became the most famous and admired "modern" structure in America. The first account of its major exterior and interior features appeared in the *New-York Journal* on March 26, 1789, and was reprinted in other newspapers within the next two months. A more complete description, accompanied by an engraving by Samuel Hill of the Wall Street elevation, was published in the June 1789 issue of the *Massachusetts Magazine.* Similar engravings and descriptions appeared in Philadelphia's *Columbian Magazine* in August and in the *New York Magazine or Literary Repository* in March 1790. Amos Doolittle's famous frontal view depicting Washington's inauguration at Federal Hall on April 30, 1789, was printed as a broadside to commemorate the occasion.

Thus when the design competition for the Capitol in the new federal city of Washington was announced in March 1792, entrants in major cities had both a visual image and a detailed description of the first building to consciously fulfill the functional needs and express the symbolic importance of the new federal government. The engraved views indicate how imposing and majestic Federal Hall's white classical facade appeared in the context of red brick, stepped-gabled houses and shops, the common remnants of New York's Dutch past.

The architectural significance of Federal Hall is twofold: it was a harbinger of more flexible and cosmopolitan public buildings for America, and it initiated a national emblematic language in both its architectural forms and its decorative details. The main facade, which faced Wall Street, was dominated by a double-story Roman Doric portico set above an arcaded ground story. The portico provided the framework for a recessed balcony specifically designed by L'Enfant for inaugurations and other public events. The balcony's large scale suggests that L'Enfant intended Federal Hall's facade to be a metaphorical statement about America's open and accessible government. Its fusion with a Roman portico signified that America's political system was deeply rooted in Roman republicanism. The only earlier American building to use Roman architectural elements was the Virginia State Capitol, designed in 1784 by Jefferson in conjunction with the French architect Charles-Louis Cleris-seau. Their model, the intact rectangular temple set among Roman ruins in the city of Nîmes, France, known then and now as the Maison Carrée, was chosen by Jefferson because of its supposed associations with the Roman Republic.

An American model did exist, albeit on paper. In 1788, James Trenchard had published his design for a thirteen-column classical temple inscribed "Sacred to Liberty Justice and Peace," with statues of these personifications standing on its pediment (Cat. 24). Columbia, the figure in front of the temple who represents America, carries a cornucopia to signify abundance or prosperity; her companions are Concord and Clio, or History, who records for posterity "We are One."[16]

L'Enfant's most lasting contribution at Federal Hall was the incorporation of numerous American symbols in its decorative sculpture both on the facade and within the two legislative chambers. The four stately Doric columns of the portico supported an entablature whose thirteen metopes were decorated with stars, the symbols of the states on the American flag. L'Enfant also designed a red and white fabric festoon to decorate the balcony for Washington's inauguration on April 30, 1789. The only sculpture in Federal Hall's pediment was an eagle rising amid billowing clouds and set against a backdrop of the rays of the rising sun. Four relief panels on the top story were decorated with clusters of thirteen arrows tied together by olive branches. L'Enfant's adaptation of features from the two emblems specifically designed by congressional order—the Great Seal and the flag—immediately identified Federal Hall's national purpose and imparted to it a distinctive and dignified appearance.[17]

American symbols in Federal Hall's interiors were so novel and so admired that they were described in detail by the building's chroniclers. These descriptions are the only contemporary record of them, as no verified drawings or engravings of Federal Hall's interiors are known. The Senate chamber, a renovated room located on the second floor at the front behind the balcony, was 40 feet long, 30 feet wide, and 20 feet high with an arched ceiling. Its walls were decorated with pilasters whose capitals were of a

> fanciful kind, the invention of Major L'Enfant, the architect & he has appropriated them to this building, for amidst their foliage appears a star and rays, and a piece of drapery below suspends a small medallion with U.S. in a cypher. The idea is new and the effect pleasing; and although they cannot be said to be of any antient order, we must allow that they have an appearance of magnificence. The ceiling is plain with only a sun and thirteen stars in the center.[18]

L'Enfant's invention of an American order—columns with their accompanying capitals and entablature—of architecture for Federal Hall continued an eighteenth-century European practice of national orders at the same time that it initiated a new American tradition. In Europe, capitals of columns decorated with national symbols often replaced traditional classical orders on important public buildings. The French order, decorated with the sun—the emblem adopted by Louis XIV, the Sun King—was initiated at Versailles. L'Enfant's use of sun rays on the exterior of Federal Hall and a full sun on the Senate ceiling may have been intended to recall France's participation in the American Revolution.

The sun also had a specifically American meaning. The rising sun as the insignia of the

Carpenters' Company of Philadelphia was probably drawn from Masonic symbolism. As part of the company's seal, it decorated the room in Carpenters' Hall where the Continental Congress first met in 1774. Perhaps more significantly, new chairs commissioned from John Fowell by the state of Pennsylvania in 1778 for the Assembly Room in the State House were decorated with the rising-sun motif. In 1787, these chairs were used by the delegates to the Constitutional Convention. On the closing day of the convention, James Madison recorded in his journal:

> Whilst the last members were signing [the Constitution] Doctr. Franklin looking towards the Presidents Chair, at the back of which a rising sun happened to be painted, observed to a few members near him, that Painters had found it difficult to distinguish in their art a rising from a setting sun. I have, said he, often and often in the course of the Session, and the vicissitudes of my hopes and fears as to its issue, looked at that behind the President without being able to tell whether it was rising or setting: But now at length I have the happiness to know that it is a rising and not a setting Sun.[19]

L'Enfant may well have incorporated suns into Federal Hall's iconography to commemorate both the first meeting places of the Continental Congresses and the role of France in securing American independence.

L'Enfant designed the hall for the House of Representatives at Federal Hall as a new room attached to the rear of the old city hall. Its internal height was extraordinary for America: 46 feet tall with windows that began 16 feet above the floor. Its richly decorated interior was decidedly French in character, an octagon with curved corners and a cove (curved) ceiling 10 feet deep. Ionic columns and pilasters decorated the upper walls, along with "trophies carved with the letters U.S. in a cypher, surrounded with laurel." L'Enfant planned that a statue of Liberty be placed above the Speaker's chair.[20]

HOUSING THE FEDERAL CONGRESS IN PHILADELPHIA: CONGRESS HALL

Congress occupied Federal Hall for only two sessions, yet seventy-seven pieces of legislation were enacted and the Bill of Rights was adopted there. The Residence Act, passed at Federal Hall on July 16, 1790, stipulated that the government would reconvene in Philadelphia until it moved to its new home in 1800 in a city to be built on the Maryland shore of the Potomac River. The national legislators first met temporarily in Philadelphia's new county courthouse (1787–1789) located to the west of the Pennsylvania State House. A square, hipped-roof building, the courthouse underwent minor structural alterations and was elegantly furnished by the state of Pennsylvania to serve the national government as Congress Hall. For the federal Congress's third session, which opened on December 6, 1790, a public gallery to hold about 300 people was added to the large ground-floor chamber chosen for the House of Representatives. Between 1793 and 1795, Congress Hall was enlarged to accommodate additional representatives, whose number had increased from 68 to 105.

In 1795, when Senate debates were first opened to the public, a public gallery was added on the south wall of the Senate chamber in Congress Hall. The Great Seal rendered in painted plaster was placed on the ceiling above the president's chair. (The vice president of the United States serves as the president of the Senate.) An elaborate carpet made by William P. Sprague included the thirteen state seals, each set within a link of a chain that formed a circle; the eagle of the Great Seal was in the center. The "union chain," composed of thirteen interconnected links, had been designed by Franklin for the first currency issued by the Continental Congress on February 17, 1776. The links inscribed with the names of the states were arranged geographically, with Massachusetts at the top. The union chain rivaled the eagle and stars as a popular symbol of America, appearing in portrait prints of Washington and Adams as well as on Chinese export porcelain and Liverpool creamware, but was never part of the Capitol's iconography.

In 1792, the Italian sculptor Giuseppe Ceracchi's terra-cotta bust *Minerva as the Patroness of American Liberty* was placed behind the Speaker's chair in Congress Hall (Fig. 11; Cat. 19). It may have been the same statue of Liberty that L'Enfant had commissioned for Federal Hall. Ceracchi's helmeted Minerva wears armor, her traditional garb, but her breastplate is decorated with the liberty pike and cap, thus adding Liberty as an additional dimension to her meaning. The 66-inch-tall bust was given to the Library Company of Philadelphia when Congress moved to Washington in 1800.

GEORGE WASHINGTON AND
THOMAS JEFFERSON PLAN A CAPITOL

When George Washington (Fig. 12; Cat. 26) and Thomas Jefferson (Fig. 13; Cat. 27) were sworn in as the first president and first secretary of state, they were veterans of the civic and military events that had brought the United States into being. Both had served in early Continental Congresses; Washington was unanimously chosen as commander-in-chief of the Continental Army on June 15, 1775, and Jefferson was named chairman of the committee that drafted the Declaration of Independence, which was presented to Congress on July 2, 1776. For most Americans, the struggle had ended with ratification of the Constitution in 1788. For Washington and Jefferson, the Constitution was the pivot between the past and the future. The location of the national capital had yet to be determined, and the ability of all three parts of the new government to work together was yet to be tested.

Fig. 11. Giuseppe Ceracchi. *Minerva as the Patroness of American Liberty,* 1792. Library Company of Philadelphia.

The joint efforts of Washington and Jefferson to establish a centrally located federal district separate from the jurisdiction of any single state began in 1783 when Jefferson and James Madison wrote to Governor Benjamin Harrison of Virginia suggesting that Virginia and Maryland "offer a Small tract of Territory . . . in the Neighborhood of George Town on Potowmack" for a future national capital. The Residence Act, passed by Congress on July 16, 1790, established such a territory and stipulated that the federal government would move there on the first Monday in December 1800. A decade was considered ample time to create a city from sparsely settled farmland and to erect its necessary public buildings, initially those for the use of the legislative branch, Congress, and the executive, the president and his cabinet. Washington was given the responsibility of creating the federal city under the Residence Act, and he delegated its oversight to Jefferson as his adviser on national affairs (Cat. 28).

Until the end of their lives, both Virginians dedicated their considerable talents to ensure that the union of states under the Constitution would be a success. The most visible expression of this union was to be the Capitol, the place where America's political ideas and ideals would be permanently enshrined. Washington and Jefferson wanted the Capitol to symbolically perpetuate the goals of the Revolution and the Constitution: political union of people whose history, livelihood, and attitudes varied greatly; equal justice under the law; peace or domestic tranquillity; economic and national independence (the common defense and general welfare of the Constitution's Preamble); and protection of individual liberties.

Fig. 12. Jean-Antoine Houdon. Bust of George Washington, ca. 1786–1793. Gift of Robert L. McNeil, Jr., in Honor of the Fiftieth Anniversary of the National Gallery of Art, © 1994 Board of Trustees, National Gallery of Art, Washington.

Fig. 13. After Jean-Antoine Houdon. Bust of Thomas Jefferson, ca. 1784–1789. Copy, ca. 1948. Library of Congress.

Washington and Jefferson could not have anticipated the difficulties that they and their successors would face in choosing and implementing a design for the Capitol, which was not completed until 1826, thirty-four years after it was first planned. During these decades, the Capitol's architectural form and symbolic language slowly evolved as numerous architects took over its execution, the availability of financial and other resources waxed and waned, and ideas of its meaning changed. The Capitol's most distinguishing architectural form—its dome—was derived from both ancient and modern prototypes, a contemporary Neoclassical structure that synthesized European sacred and civic traditions. In addition, architectural ideas from earlier American buildings, and emblems and personifications adopted during the Revolutionary era, played significant roles in expressing the Capitol's actual and abstract functions. The wish to affirm the uniqueness of the New World experience, yet acknowledge the common classical heritage of Euro-Americans, was part of the Capitol's political and cultural equation.

− II −

"The Most Approved Plan"

The Competition for the Capitol's Design

COMPETITION GUIDELINES

Thomas Jefferson and George Washington's decision to institute a competitive process to obtain a design for the Capitol had far-reaching implications. It set in motion a democratic tradition for American public architecture, but one that had mixed results. Professional architects found open competitions threatening. In 1806, architect of the Capitol Benjamin Henry Latrobe noted:

> The designs of the public buildings at Washington were chosen from a collection obtained by public advertisement offering a reward for the plan most approved by the then President of the United States. This mode of obtaining designs for public buildings, though exceedingly common, is certain of defeating its own end. It brings into competition all the personal vanity of those who think they have knowledge and taste in an art which they have never had an opportunity to learn or practice—of all those who enticed by the reward think that personal influence and interest will procure it for them—and of those who know of design nothing but its execution: and it keeps out of the competition all who have too much self-respect to run the race of preference with such motley companions, and especially of all regularly educated professional men,—who understand their business too well not to know that a picture is not a design, and that to form and elaborate the design of a public work so that it shall be capable of being executed from the papers they present, requires so much expense of time, labor and clerkship, that no reward such as is usually offered can compensate.[1]

Latrobe was not in the United States in 1792 when the Capitol competition was held, but the entries were among the papers of the Office of the Architect of the Capitol. Latrobe's fellow English-trained professional architect, George Hadfield, also judged the Capitol competition entries a "pile of trash." Close examination of them, however, reveals that they were

21

representative of a wide range of architectural practitioners who worked in late-eighteenth-century America.[2]

Only three open competitions to obtain designs for public buildings in America before 1792 are presently documented: those for the Maryland State House in 1769, Bridewell (the almshouse) in New York in 1775, and the Library Company of Philadelphia in 1789. Colonial Americans seem to have followed the common English practice of appointing three or more commissioners to a building committee. One member might be an experienced architect or builder, or designs might be solicited by either invitation or competition. The intermittent duties of such temporary commissions included selecting a design, executing contracts for labor and materials, overseeing general operations, and paying the bills. The purpose of this system was to have intermediaries adjudicate disputes among designers, builders, and suppliers and to ensure that public money was prudently and properly spent.

The building-commission tradition was formally adopted by Congress. Article I, Section 8, paragraph 18 of the Constitution grants Congress "exclusive legislation" over the "seat of government of the United States," while the Residence Act of July 16, 1790, gave Washington the authority to appoint three commissioners and direct their survey of the federal district. Jefferson, probably in consultation with the president, interpreted Washington's authority under the Residence Act to extend to design control over the government's public buildings. At least one and possibly two of the first three commissioners Washington appointed—Thomas Johnson of Annapolis, Maryland, and David Stuart of Alexandria, Virginia—had experience erecting public buildings. In 1769, Johnson had served as a commissioner for the Maryland State House, and Stuart, a physician by profession, but grand master of Alexandria's Masonic lodge, officiated at the ceremony to lay the federal city's first milestone on April 15, 1791.

Before Washington hired Pierre Charles L'Enfant in January 1791 to design the federal city and all its public buildings, Jefferson was planning that designs be acquired through a democratic process, the first in America for which competitors were nationally sought, by advertisement in newspapers in several localities. Within six weeks of the passage of the Residence Act, Jefferson, in his official capacity as secretary of state, outlined his thoughts about implementing its provisions. On August 29, 1790, he noted that the "Commissioners should have some taste in architecture, because they may have to decide between different plans. They will however be subject to the President's direction in every point." Two weeks later, on September 14, he expanded on his earlier thoughts: "The plan for the public buildings is to be approved by the President. The Commissioners will no doubt submit different ones formed by themselves, or obtained from ingenious architects. Should it be thought proper to excite emulation by a premium for the best, the expence is authorized, as an incident to that of the Buildings."[3]

After L'Enfant's dismissal in February 1792, one of Jefferson's major concerns was to move forward quickly to obtain designs for both the Capitol and the President's House. On March 6, he returned to the commissioners an outline, "with some alterations," of the advertisement initially prepared by Johnson and sent to Washington for his approval. Johnson's outline has not survived; Jefferson's amended draft reads:

Washington in the territory of Columbia

A Premium of a lot in this city to be designated by impartial judges and 500. dollars, or a Medal of that value, at the option of the party, will be given by the Commissioners of the federal buildings to the person, who before the 20th day of July 1792 shall produce to them the most approved plan if adopted by them for a Capitol, to be erected in this city, and 500 dollars or a medal for a plan deemed next in merit to the one they shall adopt. The building to be of brick and to contain the following apartments, to wit.

a Conference room [and] a room for the Representatives sufficient to accommodate 300 persons each. a Lobby or Antichamber to the latter. a Senate room of 1200 square feet area. an Antichamber or Lobby to the last. these rooms to be full elevation. 12. rooms of 600. square feet area each for Committee rooms and clerk's offices, to be of half the elevation of the former.

Drawings will be expected of the ground plats, elevations of each front, and sections thro the building in such directions as may be necessary to explain the internal structure; and an Estimate of the Cubic feet of brickwork composing the whole mass of the walls.

THE COMMISSIONERS.[4]

The date was changed to July 15 and the amount of the second prize reduced to $250 when the announcement appeared in newspapers. *Dunlap's American Daily Advertiser,* a Philadelphia paper, first carried it beginning on March 24, 1792 (Cat. 30).

Jefferson probably introduced the term "Capitol" into Johnson's text to refer to the national legislative building, significant because of the political implications of the word's meaning. Most of the structures that had housed America's colonial legislatures had been referred to as statehouses. However, the act of the Virginia House of Burgesses that had moved the seat of government from Jamestown to Williamsburg in 1699 decreed that "for ever hereafter [the building will] be caled and knowne by the name of the *Capitoll."* This act is found among Jefferson's papers in the Library of Congress. The original Capitol was Rome's national temple, dedicated to Jupiter Optimus Maximus and located on the Tarpeian (Capitoline) Hill. Of all the ancient and modern republics studied by Jefferson, Madison, and other Founding Fathers while the Constitution was being written and debated during the ratification process, the Roman Republic was frequently cited as the best model for America's government.

Jefferson had always referred to Congress's building as the Capitol and conceived of it with its full historical meaning. As early as April 10, 1791, he wrote to L'Enfant: "[W]henever it is proposed to prepare plans for the Capitol, I should prefer the adoption of some one of the models of antiquity which have had the approbation of thousands of years." Others who referred to the legislative building as the Capitol about this time may have been influenced by Jefferson's use of the word, for the most frequent references in print and in private correspondence are to "Congress House." On the earliest manuscript map of Washington, preserved in the Geography and Map Division of the Library of Congress, Jefferson replaced L'Enfant's designation "Congress House" with "Capitol." Subsequently, all the engraved maps of the city identified the legislative building as the Capitol (Fig. 14; Cat. 29).[5]

Thus Jefferson subtly shaped the public's conception of the nature of America's national legislative building by having its official name resonate with historical associations of Roman republicanism and hence Roman civic virtues. His intention was to forge a chain among America's political system, the ancient traditions in which it was rooted, and the building where American laws would be enacted. The notion that architecture could be the palpable, visual expression of abstract concepts was an Enlightenment idea that Jefferson wholeheartedly embraced and attempted to transmit to the American populace in general. The history of the design competition for the Capitol is the attempt to secure an architectural design expressive of the new government's unique form and the new nation's republican ideals.

The Capitol and President's House competitions were apparently the first in America to offer substantial premiums solely for architectural designs. These incentives were consciously

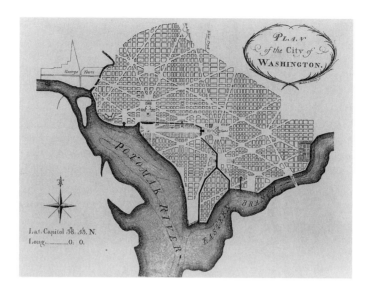

Fig. 14. Pierre Charles L'Enfant. "Plan of the City of Washington," March 1792. Library of Congress.

offered to encourage professional architects to compete, yet few apparently did. Samuel Blodget, Jr., a Boston businessman and amateur architect, wrote to Jefferson on June 25, 1792, that Boston's leading architect, Charles Bulfinch, "through modesty, has declined presenting his Plan & this has fright[e]ned me out of my Intention." Blodget did submit a design, which is now lost, but no Capitol competition plan by Bulfinch is known. Given the slowness of communications in 1792, four months was not adequate time for Europeans or even Americans to respond. A survey of American newspapers from March through July reveals that competition announcements known to have been sent to New England and southern newspapers never appeared in them.[6]

Only four of the known fourteen original competitors can be identified using city directories and newspaper advertisements, yet the same sources list numerous architects and builders actively practicing their professions in America. Although the competition announcement first appeared in Philadelphia newspapers, none of the many well-trained English architects who had recently settled there seem to have submitted designs. With the exception of Blodget and Samuel McIntire of Salem, Massachusetts, who was alerted about the competition by his senator, all the competitors resided in Pennsylvania, Maryland, or Virginia, states where the competition announcement appeared in newspapers.[7]

While the guidelines drafted by Johnson and Jefferson gave much salient information that architects would need to know—including the key spaces and their general size, the range and type of drawing required, and the material of which the building would be constructed—much was left unsaid. The Capitol's intended site was not mentioned, nor was any comment made about the design of the new federal city in which the Capitol was to be the most important element. The absence of any indication in the guidelines of the Capitol's expected cost may account for why three, and possibly four, of the known original competitors submitted multiple designs ranging from simple to complex, from economical to expensive. No mention was made in the competition guidelines of including symbols associated specifically with America.

The desired architectural nature of the building could be inferred from only its name and the requirement that its three assembly rooms, the House and Senate chambers and a conference room (for joint sessions of Congress), be "full elevation"—that is, the height of the entire building, interpreted generally as two stories. The direct architectural result of this stipulation was that most competitors placed the principal rooms on the ground floor, in contrast to the common Renaissance and Neoclassical practice of treating the second floor as the main story. The House chamber at Federal Hall had been a two-story room appended to the back of the old city hall. The "floor" of the House had been accessible either through the building's central entry or via French doors that opened onto a galleried arcade along its east side.

Additional information available to competitors about the nature of the Capitol's site was limited to anonymous newspaper accounts of L'Enfant's design for the city and publication of L'Enfant's "Observations explanatory of the plan." In December 1791 and January 1792, three Philadelphia newspapers copied L'Enfant's lengthy description from the manuscript map on display at Congress Hall. It was general in nature, merely noting that all the major buildings were located "on the most advantageous ground, commanding the most extensive prospects." The first engraving of L'Enfant's plan for Washington was published in Philadelphia's *Universal Asylum and Columbian Magazine* in March 1792. A seemingly immense Capitol almost fills the largest public square in the city; its most salient feature is a large circular room overlooking a long and broad public park: Washington's Mall. The accompanying text notes that the "Capitol will be situated on a most beautiful eminence, commanding a complete view of every part of the city, and of a considerable part of the country around."[8]

Thus competing architects might have known that the Capitol would be a highly visible object on the city's skyline rather than an integral part of a dense urban environment. Those who saw the engraved plan knew that the square planned for the Capitol was shaped like the letter *T* and that L'Enfant's Capitol design was dominated by a domed rotunda facing west. As no list of entrants, only one written description, and very little correspondence from them or concerning their designs survive, competitor's drawings, the cultural traditions of which they were a part, and sparse biographical information must form the basis of our understanding of individual competition entries.

EIGHTEENTH-CENTURY AMERICAN ARCHITECTURAL PRACTICE

The Capitol competition coincided with, and perhaps to some degree influenced, some major changes in American architecture. The majority of entrants were architect-builders who erected the structures they designed rather than professional architects who supervised artisans who constructed their designs. Prior to the late eighteenth century, American society was unable to support architects who were not also craftsmen.

The main stream of architecture in the colonies was a provincial version of late Renaissance design filtered through its English version known as the Georgian, or Anglo-Palladian, style. This tradition was transmitted to America through a wide range of illustrated architectural treatises, pattern books, and carpenter's handbooks. The treatises, usually folio size and emphasizing theory and history, were often English translations of Renaissance works, while the more common pattern books and handbooks were frequently written and illustrated by English architects. One hundred forty-seven such books are known to have been available in American libraries and through booksellers by 1800. Jefferson's collection was one of the finest in the country. When in 1769 he began designing his home, Monticello, he followed principles outlined in the most influential of the Renaissance treatises, Andrea Palladio's *Four Books of Architecture.* First published in Latin in 1570, it was reprinted in numerous Italian, French, and English editions, four of which Jefferson owned. Washington's addition to Mount Vernon of 1773 to 1779 was done with one of Batty Langley's pattern books in hand, *The City and Country Builder's, and Workman's Treasury of Designs,* published in London in

1740. The artisans who built Monticello and Mount Vernon undoubtedly referred to carpenter's handbooks, which contained arithmetic and geometric formulas to calculate correct proportions and carve classical details as well as rules to calculate materials and erect framing.[9]

Treatises provided eighteenth-century American property owners like Jefferson and Washington, often referred to as gentlemen-amateur architects, with design concepts fundamental to Renaissance architecture. Regularity of all parts was essential, with windows of the same width placed above one another and lined up in rows according to level floor divisions. The symmetrical arrangement of windows around a central door or a classical portico gave a single, dominant focus. The use of one module to determine the dimensions of each part resulted in harmonious, well-proportioned buildings. Pattern books were a common ground between designer and workmen because they contained plans, elevations, interior sections, and exterior and interior details from which entire buildings could be assembled. Very frequently, more than one pattern book was employed, and details were often altered. The first American carpenter's handbook, Asher Benjamin's *The Country Builder's Assistant,* not published until 1797, continued the familiar British prototype.

By the 1780s, the American Georgian tradition began to be influenced by a new wave of European Neoclassicism as architects and their clients bypassed the Renaissance and turned directly to antiquity for their architectural sources. Roman architecture was revived before Greek because many artists and patrons sojourned in Rome; until Greece was freed from Turkish rule in 1820, Christian travelers were not welcome there. While ancient Roman monuments had been the inspiration for Renaissance architecture, many eighteenth-century Neoclassicists felt that fundamental ancient principles had been debased through repeated variations and refinements. By the mid-eighteenth century, English and French architects were excited by new discoveries of Roman architecture both in Italy and in the former Roman provinces, as well as Greek architecture on the Dorian mainland, the Ionian islands, in Italy, and in Asia Minor.

Part of the rediscovery of ancient architecture was the realization that mere architectural structure, properly proportioned and simply ornamented, has immense power to affect the human mind and emotions. A second insight was that ancient ruins can evocatively recall the entire social and political structure of a once-great civilization, a powerful stimulus to those with a historical sense who were in the process of creating a new social and political order. Fundamental to Washington and Jefferson's decision to promote Neoclassical rather than Georgian architecture for the Capitol was their belief that America should erect public buildings that would transmit its political and social ideals both to the present generation and to all posterity. Georgian architecture had been a direct by-product of British colonialism; its associations were ephemeral rather than eternal.

After the Revolution, French architectural traditions began to challenge predominantly English ones as French engineers who remained in America, such as L'Enfant, worked as architects, if only intermittently. In addition, beginning in 1789 many French architects were driven to the United States by the revolution in their own country. They brought with them a theoretical approach to architectural problems, the result of a sophisticated national educational system in the arts established in France during the seventeenth century. Formal, spatial, and symbolic solutions that clearly distinguished among building types, particularly those of a public or religious nature, were a priority. Stephen Hallet was the only architect to compete for the Capitol's design who is known to have been trained to the profession in France. Jefferson knew Hallet's work in Paris and Philadelphia, and he actively encouraged his participation in the Capitol competition.

The impact of contemporary French architecture on Jefferson during his tenure as American minister to France from 1784 to 1789 was profound. After his return to the United States, Jefferson immediately began altering his home, Monticello, into a building that partakes of three traditions: Anglo-Palladianism, English Neoclassicism, and French Neoclassicism. The final product is quintessentially American, pragmatic yet grounded in a range of ideas and practices concerning man's habitation in nature. In the public realm, Jefferson was able to direct the character of the Virginia State Capitol, the re-creation of a Roman temple, from its inception by collaborating with the French architect Charles-Louis Clerisseau. For the Capitol in Washington, Jefferson promoted a more famous ancient Roman temple, the Pantheon, as the model to convey American civic purposes. The Pantheon was to be filtered through the rigorous process of rational abstraction that characterized French Neoclassicism. A fundamental difference between English and French Neoclassicism was the French emphasis on the mass and volumes of buildings rather than on a proliferation of decorative surface details. Thus French eighteenth-century public buildings, erected in stone for permanence, had a sense of solidity and a seriousness of purpose that few of their contemporary English counterparts could match.

For Jefferson, many of the Capitol competition entries may have seemed fanciful variations on outmoded domestic themes incapable of expressing the gravity of the Capitol's purpose. After his first-hand experience of monumental French public architecture, Jefferson possibly viewed American pattern-book architecture as an unsuitable design process for public buildings. He recognized the fundamental difference between buildings conceived as spatial and emblematic totalities and those pieced together from preexisting engraved models.

The differences between designs done by professional architects and by architect-builders were due to level of education and experience, not degree of talent. Both groups relied on the history of architecture known to them and manipulated customary forms and details to create new versions of basic types. In this process of transformation, some architects were more academic than others, closely adhering to their models, while others were more creative in their recombinations of prototypes. A few exceptionally talented people of both traditions transcended their models to create modern classics.

The sources used by an architect, as well as his ability to make sophisticated architectural drawings, can be guides to the level of his education, but neither can be used to judge the quality of his architectural ideas or his professional or aesthetic success. Jefferson's architectural drawings were crude in their execution, but rich in their implications; the details of his buildings were executed by workmen following instructions and engravings in pattern books chosen by him and altered to suit his specific needs and his sense of architectural propriety. In his role as arbiter of the Capitol competition, and his later involvement with the Capitol's construction, Jefferson sought to promote professionalism in American architecture. He wished to ensure that it develop from correct principles grounded in antiquity but respond to contemporary circumstances, an attitude analogous to his political thinking as he helped formulate America's governing system.

CAPITOL COMPETITORS

Drawings by ten of the fourteen original and one late entrant in the Capitol competition demonstrate the changes taking place in American architecture after the Revolution. In addition to the new influence of French architects, many trained designers and architect-builders from England, Scotland, Ireland, and Germany had emigrated during the 1780s or remained in the United States after having served in the British army. The entries can be grouped generally according to the background of the designers: builders with little design training who aspired to being architects, talented architect-builders who probably served an apprenticeship that included some academic education, gentlemen-amateurs for whom architecture was a learned avocation, and one man who had been educated to practice architecture as a profession.

Builders

Charles Wintersmith, a German-born and -trained engineer who had served with General John Burgoyne's British regiment during the Revolution, excused the plainness of his Capitol competition entry on the sparse outline in the published advertisement. He wrote to Jefferson (whom he had met at Albemarle, Virginia, in 1778) that he understood from the newspaper notice that a "plain Building Strong, Symetrical and of an Oeconomical [sic] plan" was required. His letter, written on July 17, 1792, just two days after the close of the competition, sheds valuable light on the judging process. He noted that his "plan was not noticed, nor called for full Explanation like the others was done, if it could be build or lined outside with Stones of which I understand [the commissioners] had a Notion." This is the only indication that some of the competitors brought their designs to Georgetown and met directly with the commissioners.[10]

Wintersmith assured Jefferson that his entry was merely a preliminary outline to indicate a general idea, customary when designing a building in his native country before the full panoply of architectural decoration was added. His design does include the eagle of the Great Seal in a curved pediment, the only ornament or symbol on a highly unusual structure (Cat. 34). He planned two great hemicycles back to back for the House of Representatives and the conference room, placing the Senate and offices in four wings that project from each side of the central mass. Twelve entrances lead into each part of his Capitol, but none is on the building's main axes, unprecedented in formal, symmetrical architectural designs.

Jacob Small, Sr. (1746–1794), probably of German descent, founded a dynasty of Baltimore architect-builders. He entered three designs in the competition for the Capitol and two in that for the President's House. For the Capitol, he adapted the same basic idea to three different shapes: a square, a rectangle, and an oblong. Wide, double-story porticoes mark the center of each facade of his square plan, and giant pilasters finish its edges (Cat. 35). Small recognized the need for an important architectural and symbolic focus for the Capitol and accordingly planned an octagonal dome (presumably of wood) to cover the conference room, which is located in the center of his nine-part square (Fig. 15; Cat. 36). Sculptural decoration is minimal, with what seem to be pineapples (a symbol of hospitality) above the portico and rotunda pilasters. As Small's drafting abilities were rudimentary, his drawings convey neither a sense of three-dimensionality nor actual proportional relationships, making it difficult to judge his architectural abilities. He is believed to have been a self-taught architect; his surviving brick Otterbein Church (1785–1789) in Baltimore is provincial in character. Small did give serious consideration to the acoustics of the assembly rooms. He arranged seating octagonally facing a podium, a solution adopted in the House of Commons of the Irish Parliament House, completed in 1767 (Fig. 16; Cat. 36.1).[11]

Little is known about the second of the three Maryland entrants, Philip Hart of Taneytown, who also submitted three designs (Cat. 37). All are compact in their massing, are three stories tall, and have high balustrades masking steep roofs. Their overall forms and details, especially wide molded window frames, bespeak a carpenter steeped in the Georgian style

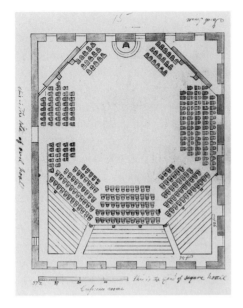

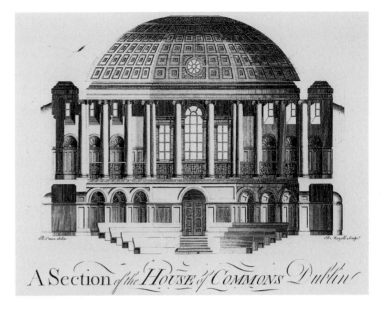

Fig. 15. Jacob Small. "Conference Roome," 1792. Maryland Historical Society.

Fig. 16. Rowland Omer. "A Section of the House of Commons, Dublin," 1767. Courtesy of the National Library of Ireland, Dublin.

Fig. 17. Robert Goin Lanphier. "Elevation for the Capitol," 1792. Maryland Historical Society.

popular a quarter- to a half-century earlier. Although Hart was obviously not academically trained as a draftsman, his drawings do convey through their intense linearity a sense of architecture as a three-dimensional and spatial experience. In addition, he recognized the need to convey the Capitol's special meaning, decorating the half-dome above the main entry of his simplest design with thirteen stars. The symbolic intention of full-scale standing figures atop the balustrades of Hart's two more complex entries is difficult to decipher due to the crudeness of their drawing. If they are indeed as they appear to be, male figures clothed only in loincloths, they may represent the Twelve Labors of Hercules.[12]

Robert Goin Lanphier (1765–1856) was born in Alexandria, Virginia, the son of an Irish immigrant builder employed by Washington on his renovations at Mount Vernon during the 1770s (Fig. 17; Cat. 38). Little is known of the younger Lanphier's career, but he did advertise his services as a carpenter in 1806. By 1830, he was in business on Pennsylvania Avenue in Washington as a "Manufacturing Jeweler & Seal Engraver." His Capitol submission is noteworthy for its unusual arrangements and combinations of architectural elements and its complex symbolic sculpture. Both indicate that Lanphier had received a substantial education and may have aspired to architecture as a profession rather than a craft. Although only 220 feet wide, his four-story, rectangular Capitol has one and possibly two imposing oval domes, obelisks marking each corner, and a wide colonnade surrounding the whole. His plans indicate two similar oval rooms on the second floor to accommodate the Senate and the House of Representatives. On the ground level, wide arched passageways separate the central core from four rectangular rooms isolated in each corner. Lanphier's colonnade supports porticoes on each facade and would shade people beneath it as well as provides a walkway on its roof accessible from all second-story rooms, principally the legislative chambers.[13]

To ornament and give meaning to his Capitol design, Lanphier chose accepted American symbols and a range of allegorical figures that echoed popular conceptions of the benefits the country was to enjoy under the Constitution. His intentions are preserved because he wrote the description of his sculptural program directly on his elevation drawing. The Great Seal eagle is above the central second-floor door leading from the colonnade's roof to the House chamber; Liberty and Justice are in the pediment of the portico in front of this entry. Six figures were to stand at the base of an octagonal dome: "Cornucopia offering the horn of plenty to Industry, Wisdom holding forth her precepts to Justice and Fame offering a wreath of laurel to Bel[l]onia (Military Science)." The cupola lighting the dome supports a monumental eagle with its wings spread.

It is not known if Joseph Clark (ca. 1753–1799), architect of the second dome on the Maryland State House, formally entered the competition. His background is problematical, as his common name and the variety of skills that eighteenth-century immigrants by necessity had to have make it difficult to identify him. He first advertised as an "Architect, Builder and Surveyor, [who] Composes designs, draws plans, elevations, and sections of buildings of all kinds of civil architecture" in the *Maryland Gazette and Baltimore Advertiser* on April 7, 1785. On April 11, 1792, Clark wrote to the commissioners in response to the competition advertisement offering his opinion on the size of the proposed rooms and his services as a superintending architect:

> The line of my duty on which I now offer you my services, on an agreed for annual Salary, is to appropriate the whole of my working time from 9 to 3 o'clock solely to the service of the commissioners, for the purpose of making Designs, drawings, Estimates, Particulates of labor and Materials, Drafts of contracts, and Supervising the different contractors for the Building and their appendants; according to the direction, advice, and consent of the commissioners in all cases.

No actual drawings by Clark survive, but it is believed that he submitted a city plan directly to Washington early in 1791.[14]

Architect-Builders

Drawing ability, sophistication of historical sources, and careful thought about the spatial needs and symbolic function of the Capitol distinguish the designs of three talented and well-trained architect-builders who competed for the Capitol's design.

The education, background, and subsequent career of the Irish-born architect James Diamond (?–1797) is unknown, as is the date when he immigrated to America and settled in Somerset County, Maryland. On April 29, 1785, the *Maryland Gazette and Baltimore Adver-*

tiser carried an advertisement for a surveying instrument invented by Diamond, evidence of an advanced education borne out by his submissions to both the Capitol and President's House competitions. For the Capitol, he designed three elevations to fit square, two-story plans with open internal courtyards, a common building shape for Renaissance palaces, including English Elizabethan ones. Diamond's designs range from plain to complex, with elaboration of window treatments and wall surfaces creating more or less distinguished (and expensive) buildings. For his two more ornate versions, Diamond suggested substantial octagonal wood domes atop truncated entrance towers, one having a massive eagle, apparently to serve as a weathervane.[15]

Diamond's "Plan No. 1" is the smallest and simplest of his proposals, with thirteen bays on each 200-foot side (Cat. 39). These facades are competent compositions of simple Georgian architectural details and proportions, notable only for having no basement level. Eliminating basements or half-basements was a recent innovation that allowed for more immediate interaction between buildings and their natural and man-made environments. Bay windows in three octagonal courtyard towers would have admitted copious light into each assembly room: the Senate, hall for the House of Representatives, and conference room. In the 1793 renovation of Philadelphia's Congress Hall, an octagonal bay was added to the west wall and the speaker's podium was placed in front of it, a solution analogous to the one Diamond was suggesting a year earlier.

Diamond's more elaborate elevations for two designs based on 300-foot square plans are an interesting mixture of Italian Renaissance forms and articulation and English Renaissance entrance towers instead of classical porticoes. The simpler has a blind arcade formed of engaged (attached) columns to frame arched windows on the ground story and simple pedimented windows on the second story (Cat. 40). Diamond's third elevation is remarkable for having ten bays of Palladian windows on both stories of all sides (Fig. 18; Cat. 41). This elaborate window type, consisting of a tall, central arched window flanked by lower, narrow rectangular windows, was popular in fine American Georgian buildings; Washington had one built to light his dining room at Mount Vernon during the 1770s. An entire building lit by Palladian windows was, however, unprecedented in America. Andrea Palladio's Basilica (1545–1580) in Vicenza, well known from its illustration and description in his *Four Books of Architecture,* provided Diamond with an appropriate prototype (Fig. 19; Cat. 42). Ancient basilicas, according to Palladio, were assembly places for public business, including the administration of justice. Palladio noted that although Renaissance basilicas had raised basements, ancient ones did not, another authority for Diamond's

Fig. 18. James Diamond. "An Elevation for a Capitol for Plan No. 2," 1792. Maryland Historical Society.

Fig. 19. Giacomo Leoni, after Andrea Palladio. "Basilica, Vicenza." *The Architecture of Palladio in Four Books,* 1742. Library of Congress.

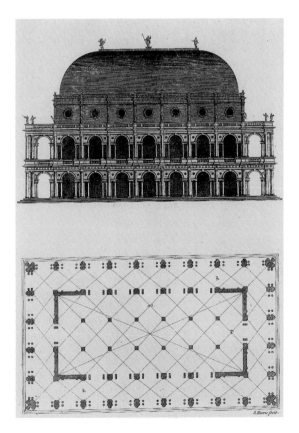

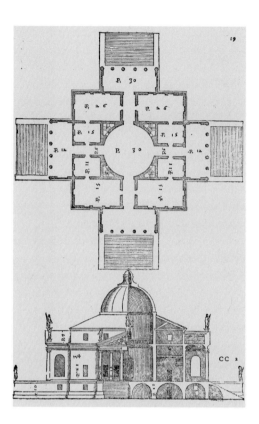

Fig. 20. Samuel Dobie. "No. 2 of Saml. Dobie invt & del. for a Capitol to be built Det. in the City of Washington," 1792. Maryland Historical Society.

Fig. 21. Andrea Palladio. "Villa Rotunda," *I Quattro libri dell'architettura,* 1601. Library of Congress.

elimination of the basement level. Diamond's most elegant Capitol submission was doubly sanctioned by antiquity and the great Renaissance architect and theorist read and used by Jefferson in his own architectural works. For Diamond to seek a source for the Capitol in Palladio reveals a highly educated architect-builder who had access to, and perhaps owned, a copy of the *Four Books of Architecture.*

Samuel Dobie (1730–?), listed in the 1790 census as a chemist, had an alternative career as a supervising architect, and perhaps a designer, of many public buildings in Richmond, Virginia. His advertisement offering to design or build in a "neat, plain, or elegant style, in the newest European taste" first appeared in the *Virginia Gazette or the American Advertiser* on October 25, 1786, suggesting that he may have been a recent immigrant. His most famous job was as the superintendent in charge of constructing the Virginia State Capitol. Like Diamond's, Dobie's national Capitol submission closely follows a Palladian model, the Villa Rotunda, illustrated in the *Four Books of Architecture* (Figs. 20 and 21; Cats. 43, 44.1, and 45). Variations on Palladio's villa, a cube house dominated by a large central dome with double-story porticoes that provide entry on each facade, had been popular among English Georgian country-house architects.[16]

Dobie's reason for choosing an Italian Renaissance villa as the model for the Capitol is suggested by the allegorical figures he selected for its decoration. Three statues atop the pediments on Dobie's elevation drawing can tentatively be identified by their attributes, the symbolic implements they carry, or their dress. Winged Fame blows a horn; Ceres or Abundance carries a cornucopia and possibly stalks of corn; and Liber Pater (an early Roman variant of Bacchus, the god of agriculture) holds a staff, or thyrsus, and what appears from their large size to be tobacco leaves. Allegorically, Fame announces the benefits of the federal union;

Ceres or Abundance represents America's agricultural richness; and Liber Pater, the god of fertility, promotes the country's leading export commodity. Liber Pater's female counterpart, Libera, was linked to Ceres, the goddess of grain; Dobie may have intended the Ceres-like figure to be Libera. The root of the names of the Roman god and goddess is, of course, the same as that for "liberty," underlining the ancient Roman link of land ownership and cultivation with freedom, a recurrent theme in Revolutionary America. Like most of the other competitors, Dobie used the Great Seal eagle in his pediment to identify his building as the Capitol.

Dobie's decision to transform a Renaissance farmhouse into the United States Capitol may have been intended to reinforce a belief held by Jefferson and others that agriculture should be the basis of American commercial and domestic life. The most immediate precedent for adapting an ancient building type—a religious temple—to a modern civic function was the Virginia State Capitol. To Dobie, using a farmhouse model for the Capitol to represent a nation composed predominantly of farmers may well have seemed as appropriate an architectural conversion as changing a religious to a civic one.

One of the architect-builders who competed for the Capitol's design stands apart as an exceptionally talented designer and craftsman. Samuel McIntire (1757–1813), descended from a family of Massachusetts housewrights, designed and built most of the finest Federal-style buildings in Salem. His talent as a carver in wood was not limited to the graceful and correct architectural details that ornamented his buildings' exteriors and interiors, but extended to carved furniture, ship's mastheads, and portrait sculpture, including busts of Voltaire and Washington. McIntire's submission to the Capitol competition was preceded by a letter from Senator George Cabot, also a native of Salem, dated June 14, 1792. Cabot noted that although McIntire's circumstances "confined him to labor in a small sphere," he was believed capable of "producing a plan for a National Edifice not wholly unworthy the consideration of the Commissioners."[17]

McIntire's lack of a formal education in architecture and background that did not include travel in Europe (and perhaps even in America) limited his knowledge of monumental buildings to those illustrated in architectural treatises. As did most of his contemporaries in similar circumstances, McIntire followed his sources fairly closely. The model for the main facade of his Capitol design is Colen Campbell's unexecuted design for Wansted House, illustrated in Campbell's *Vitruvius Britannicus* (1715), a rare and expensive book, but known to be available in private American libraries as early as 1741 and at Harvard College library by 1790 (Figs. 22 and 23; Cats. 46 and 47). The formula of a flat-roofed, rectangular building bisected by a classical portico was a common architectural form in Georgian architecture found throughout Great Britain. In fact, a smaller version provided James Hoban with the model for his winning design in the President's House competition. Campbell's design for Wansted House is unusual in its overall length, with six bays on either side of the central five bays behind a hexastyle portico. The Wansted House design is also a full three stories tall with a rusticated basement level above ground.

McIntire closely imitated the Wansted model, but eliminated rustication except as frames for ground-level windows. He elaborated on Campbell's design by having triangular and curved pediments above main-floor windows and balustrades beneath them. In addition, he framed the two end bays with pilasters that help to visually shorten the exceptional width of his Capitol design. McIntire provided entries through a central ground-level door or via two monumental imperial, V-shaped staircases that lead to a shallow portico. The opposite side, which he designated "Facade of the Back Front," differs from the east front by having no end pilasters, framing all the windows with segmental, or curved, pediments, and eliminating the

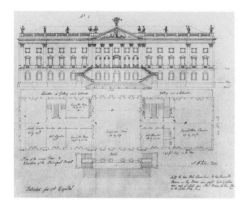

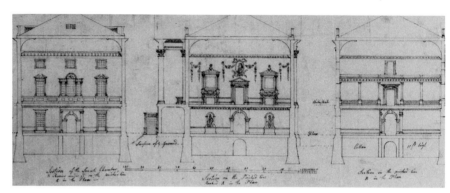

Fig. 22. Samuel McIntire. "Plan of the Second Floor & Elevation of the Principal Front," 1792. Maryland Historical Society.

Fig. 23. Colen Campbell. "The First Design of the West Front of Wansted." *Vitruvius Britannicus,* 1715. Library of Congress.

Fig. 24. Samuel McIntire. "Sections for the Capitol Design," 1792. Maryland Historical Society.

elaborate staircase (Cat. 48). Two separate single-story, projecting colonnades composed of double columns span the width of each wing. Presumably, they provide a raised outdoor gallery accessible from the two legislative chambers on the second story as well as a covered loggia below.

The distribution of major and minor rooms within McIntire's Capitol is similar to that in Charles Bulfinch's Massachusetts State House, for which the design was submitted in 1787, although construction did not begin until 1795 (Cat. 49b). McIntire placed a nearly square "Representative Chamber" in the north wing and a long rectangular "Senate Chamber" in the south. He provided the House chamber with two visitors' galleries, but the Senate with none because its debates were not open to the public until 1795. McIntire's section drawings indicate that his most ornamented room was to have been the central two-story conference room-cum-entrance hall (Fig. 24; Cat. 49a). Elaborately carved fireplace surrounds and overmantels are supplemented by swags that continue around the room above arched windows. Similar carved and paneled fireplaces were planned for the House and Senate chambers and would have utilized to the fullest extent McIntire's considerable talents as both designer and sculptor. The framed oval portrait above the door appears to be of Washington. Below in the entry hall, the architect planned four niches to contain statues, the subjects of which cannot be identified from the drawings.

McIntire was probably the only architect among the entrants who had had actual experience as a sculptor in the round rather than solely as a carver of architectural ornament. Thus his inclusion of exterior allegorical figures was not entirely motivated by fashion, but was sculpture he hoped to execute himself. The central figure of his east pediment is Liberty standing beneath a rising sun and flanked by what seem to be scenes of agriculture (harvest?)

and commerce (ships). Winged Fame stands atop the pediment and is flanked by Ceres (agriculture) and Justice on the south and Bellona (military science) and an unidentified figure on the north. The Great Seal eagle, accompanied by double rows of fourteen stars, fills the west pediment. (Vermont, the fourteenth state, entered the union in the spring of 1792.) The remaining standing figures along the top of the balustrade may have been intended as portraits of America's civic and military heroes, because some appear to be dressed as Revolutionary War soldiers. The figure immediately to the north of the west pediment can be identified as a Native American carrying a bow and arrow.

The consistency of the sculptural themes among the builders and architect-builders suggests not just the influence of published views of Federal Hall, but widely held ideas of how to express American social and political circumstances.

Gentlemen-Amateurs

Four gentlemen-amateur architects are known to have competed for the Capitol's design, but drawings by two of them—Boston businessman Samuel Blodget, Jr., and Judge George Turner—are lost. In a letter to the commissioners written on July 10, 1792, Blodget described his design as a variant of the Maison Carré, a Roman temple in Nîmes, France, to which he had appended a dome. In 1793, Blodget was hired by the commissioners at Washington's suggestion to superintend the day-to-day operations of the construction of the federal city, as their own monthly meetings proved to be inadequate. Turner, who had been appointed by Washington in 1789 to a judgeship in the Northwest Territory, also submitted a classically inspired design "with a semicircular projection at the end" that the president liked, although he suggested that Turner's building would be improved by the addition of a colonnade surrounding it.[18]

According to his obituary in the *National Intelligencer* on July 23, 1827, Andrew Mayfield Carshore (ca. 1757–1827) was "a foreigner by birth, educated in one of the first universities of Europe." In 1792, Carshore was working as a schoolmaster at the Washington Seminary in Claverack, New York, a career he followed throughout his life in the United States. His entries in both the President's House and Capitol competitions included single-point-perspective drawings (Cat. 50). That for the Capitol exaggerated the proportional relationships among the three masses of his C-shaped building in an attempt to visualize its sculptural qual-

Fig. 25. William Thornton. "East Elevation, 'Tortola' Plan for a Capitol," 1792. The Prints and Drawings Collection, The Octagon, The Museum of the American Architectural Foundation, Washington.

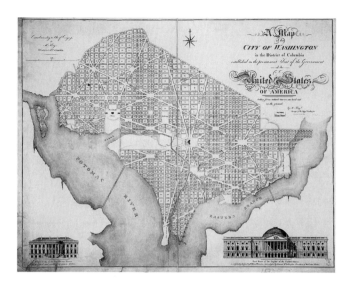

Fig. 26. Robert King. "A Map of the City of Washington in the District of Columbia," 1818. Library of Congress.

ities. Carshore's drawing gives the overall impression of an academic exercise rather than a carefully thought-out architectural solution to the Capitol's unique spatial and symbolic needs. For instance, both projecting wings contain offices rather than the House and Senate chambers, as one might suppose; Carshore placed all three assembly rooms at the back of the building, along its main spine. In its presentation, plan, massing, steep roofs, and surface simplicity, Carshore's design harks back to late-seventeenth- and early-eighteenth-century English models. Its plainness may have been a statement about "republican simplicity" as much as a reflection of the designer's personal taste. A large number of Americans were critical of ostentation in public architecture, considering the extra expense of architectural ornament wasted on nonessentials inappropriate in a republican society.[19]

The fourth and most important amateur competitor, William Thornton, was an English-educated physician living on his native Tortola in the West Indies when he learned of the Capitol competition (Cat. 71). In the fall of 1792, he journeyed to Philadelphia, where he lobbied vigorously for his designs. Thornton's initial plan, begun on Tortola, was never actually submitted for official consideration, but when compared with the second design he produced soon afterward, it demonstrates Thornton's range of knowledge and flexibility. His magnificent drawings of the "Tortola" plan for the Capitol are for a five-part building based on grand English Georgian country houses (Fig. 25; Cats. 60 and 61). A wide, two-story portico approached by an imperial staircase is the focus of its main front. To observers standing in front of the east facade, the eagle and shield of the Great Seal in the pediment would have identified Thornton's Tortola design as the Capitol. More significantly, its public nature could be determined from a distance by a small classical tempietto in the center of the roof; it also functioned as a cupola to light a central space within. On the west facade facing the Mall, Thornton planned a large triple-bay projection to contain the conference room mandated by the competition guidelines.[20]

Two-story office wings are connected to the central mass by single-story screens. Thornton drafted alternative designs for the wings by changing their mode of entry, offering either single- or double-story porticoes reached via small imperial staircases. This design's grandeur and obvious expense, as well as its decidedly English manner, would have argued against it had Thornton formally submitted it for consideration as the American Capitol.

Thornton's second design, given to Washington in January 1793 by the painter John Trumbull, is entirely different in character—a single, compact building with a low dome and east-facing portico derived from the Roman Pantheon (Fig. 26; Cats. 62 and 63). A semicircular projection on the west front covered by a low dome or coved ceiling encloses the circular or semicircular conference room. A presidential waiting room located between the two rotundas was designed to be a few steps higher than both, a remnant of royal architectural spaces. The elevated waiting room was eliminated at least by the mid-1790s, when Thornton produced a revised design with a tall colonnaded tempietto above the conference room (Cat. 74). With this design, the plan of which closely resembles the footprint of L'Enfant's Capitol shown on published maps of the city, Thornton was judged the winner of the competition. However, his involvement can be understood only in the context of the contributions made by the only contestant known to have been educated primarily to be an architect.

A Professional Architect

A Parisian by birth, Stephen Hallet immigrated to America about 1790. His formal education as an architect is unknown, yet the 1785 *Almanach royal* listed him as an "architect experienced in middle class buildings" and the 1786 *Almanach des bâtiments* as a "qualified architect licensed by the city of Paris." Hallet's first known professional association in America was as L'Enfant's draftsman in Philadelphia in 1791, when he prepared a reduced copy, now lost, of L'Enfant's plan of Washington for the engravers. Sometime during 1791, Hallet gave Jefferson his first design for the Capitol, thus beginning his complex four-year involvement as competitor and superintending architect in charge of constructing Thornton's design. In total, Hallet did five separate designs for the Capitol, each reviewed by Washington, Jefferson, or the commissioners, all of whom made suggestions for their improvement. All his surviving drawings demonstrate that Hallet was an excellent architect. Finely proportioned, balanced, and detailed facades and complex internal organization reveal Hallet's extensive knowledge of the French classical tradition; inventive allegorical schemes pertinent to American history suggest that he was advised about an appropriate iconography for the Capitol.[21]

Hallet's precompetition design established the basic form that the Capitol was eventually to take: a central dome flanked by wings containing legislative chambers, symbolically separate yet part of a single architectural unit (Fig. 27; Cat. 51). It was dubbed his "Fancy Piece" by the commissioners in October 1792 because of its elaborate nature. The rotunda and dome of Hallet's first design are notable for both their architectural lineage and the unusual way they function. He modeled the dome's exterior—a high drum with alternating arched windows and double pilasters—on the seventeenth-century dome of the chapel at the Collège des Quatre Nations in Paris (Cat. 52). The school had been founded by the statesman and cleric Jules Mazarin (1602–1661) to educate sixty sons of leading citizens from the provinces along France's oft-disputed borders with Spain, Italy, Germany, and Belgium. His intention was to instill in these young men a lasting sense of being French citizens; the school's dome thus came to symbolize France's geographic and political union.

The dome of the Collège des Quatre Nations was appropriate as a symbol of America's national union because of France's crucial participation in the American Revolution. Early in January 1793, the commissioners of the District of Columbia wrote to officials of the city of Bordeaux, France (accompanied by a letter from Hallet), seeking French workmen to construct and ornament Washington's public buildings. They said that they wished

> to express in some Degree in the Stile of our Architecture, the sublime sentiments of Liberty which are common to Frenchmen and Americans. We wish to exhibit a grandure of conception,

Fig. 27. Stephen Hallet. "Elevation of Precompetition Design," Plan B2, 1792. Library of Congress.

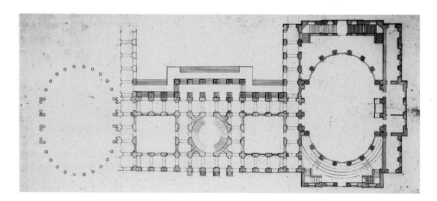

Fig. 28. Stephen Hallet. "Plan of Precompetition Design," 1792. Library of Congress.

a Republican simplicity, and that true Elegance of proportion which corresponds to a tempered freedom. . . . Our Country is young in Arts—from whence may we better expect Assistance than from the only nation who think and act as America on the End of Government and the rights of man.[22]

Hallet's Capitol rotunda was to stand isolated in the center of a series of vaulted loggias that connect the legislative wings (Fig. 28; Cat. 53). The openness of this central section would have given visitors approaching from either the east or the west glimpses of the cityscape through multiple arcades and entry into the rotunda. Although French on the exterior, the interior of Hallet's rotunda was derived from an American source, Joseph Clark's treatment of the octagonal rotunda and dome (1789) of the Maryland State House as part-steeple, part-belvedere. In Hallet's design for the Capitol, a circular staircase was to wind upward to a viewing platform at the base of the dome from which the layout of L'Enfant's city—6,100 acres in extent—could be seen in its entirety. In addition to making the organization of L'Enfant's radiating state avenues more immediately comprehensible, this bird's-eye view would have offered panoramic vistas of an extensive and picturesque landscape. Hallet's appreciation of the region's natural beauty is expressed in a short essay, "Observations upon the prospect East of the Capitol," that he wrote in November 1794: "The Capitol from its elevated Seat commands almost the whole of the western part of the City the most Important for its vast Extent; the appropriations it includs and, the natural disposition of the Ground which affords already a Magnificent prospect Surrounded with Hills that terminate the horison very Pittoreskly for almost the whole Semi Circle."[23]

The shape of the legislative chambers was a second conscious link that Hallet's design would have forged between American and French political systems via the architecture of the Capitol. They are in the form of the Roman hippodrome—a rectangle with two deep semicircular ends. This is the same spatial arrangement adopted in August 1789 for seating the French National Assembly to improve audibility and visibility in the rectangular Mênus Plaisirs at Versailles (Cat. 54).

While the interiors of Hallet's legislative chambers are French in inspiration, the facades of the House and Senate wings are modeled on the facade of Federal Hall, identified specifically by its recessed balcony. Federal Hall's balcony, where Washington was inaugurated in 1789, stood outside the Senate chamber used by the First Federal Congress; future inaugurations and public proclamations would have taken place on Hallet's balconies. Hallet retained the Collège des Quatre Nations dome and Federal Hall's recessed balconies on two of his subsequent designs, as he sought to combine historically meaningful French and American architectural features for the Capitol.

The complex sculptural program for Hallet's precompetition design cast Revolutionary-era ideas of American national identity in a synthesis of European and American iconographical imagery. His American symbols are primarily the eagle and stars of the Great Seal in the pediment, but he also included a column, probably a liberty pole. Liberty poles had been erected in many American communities after 1766, when the "Pillar of Liberty" was erected in Dedham, Massachusetts, in protest against the Stamp Act.[24]

Hallet proposed four allegorical figures as visual support for the eagle pediment. On the left, Liberty or Minerva, carrying a shield and spear or pike, is Americanized by her garb, a feather skirt and headdress (or perhaps a liberty cap). Ceres, the Roman goddess of agriculture, identified by the sickle she carries, was to stand next to Liberty-Minerva, followed by Justice carrying a sword and scales. Hallet's fourth figure, Mercury, wearing a winged cap and carrying a caduceus, is emblematic of commerce. Hallet's allegorical meaning seems to be the ideal promised by the Constitution: that agriculture and commerce will flourish under the conditions of liberty and justice.

Hallet's pedimental sculpture planned for the House and Senate wings depicts busts of Franklin and Washington being crowned with laurel wreaths, the ancient symbol of immortality. Franklin (who had died in 1790) is shown associated with the dawn of a new age in the arts and sciences, represented by the traditional emblems of globe, lyre, triangle, and books. Washington's personifications and attributes depict war and peace, the two arenas in which he was the national leader. Mars, the classical god of war who crowns Washington, is shown wearing military garb; cannon and cannonballs stand nearby. Mercury, representing commerce, a major benefit of peace, is accompanied by a figure who is bailing what appears to be a hogshead of tobacco next to a dock piled with bundled goods. The frontispiece of W. D. Cooper's *The History of North America,* published in London in 1789, depicts America as Liberty flanked by portraits of Washington and Franklin accompanied by attributes similar to those used by Hallet.

Hallet submitted a design entirely different from his precompetition one to the official competition in July 1792 (Cat. 55). His second proposal was for a peripteral classical temple, probably prompted by Jefferson's Virginia State Capitol of 1784 (Cat. 56). Although his design was not immediately chosen, Washington asked that Hallet's temple plan be enlarged, but the columns of this altered design would have been 50 feet tall and the whole too expensive an undertaking. There was also a strong consciousness that the national Capitol should be a unique architectural expression; the resemblance of Hallet's second design to the Richmond capitol may have been a factor in its rejection.

Fig. 29. Stephen Hallet. "Elevation of Fourth Design for the Capitol," 1793. Library of Congress.

When none of the competition entries met with the unqualified approval of Washington and Jefferson, the commissioners requested from Hallet a simpler and less expensive version of his precompetition design to exhibit at the second sale of city lots scheduled for October 8, 1792 (Plate 3, Cat. 57). Hallet responded with a brick building with white stone trim in which architectural and emblematic decoration is held to an absolute minimum: fifteen stars in the entablature and a national clock in the pediment. Balancing the budget, yet choosing a design appropriate for the Capitol, was the quandary the commissioners faced. They wrote to Washington in March 1793:

> In our Idea the Capitol ought in point of propriety to be on a grand Scale, and that a Republic ought especially not to be sparing of expense on an Edifice for such purposes, yet under the uncertain State of our funds depending altogether on opinion, though the current Sums to be gaining Strength, we cannot but feel a degree of anxiety for the Event of Expensive undertakings, when According to the Candor of the World our Characters will be judged, not on present Circumstances but on efficiency or want of funds when the Fact is disclosed. However we are willing to Act on your and our Ideas of Propriety regarding the destined use and Circumstances of the United States, risking in some measure the efficiency of the Funds.[25]

On October 14, 1792, the commissioners reported to Jefferson that Hallet's third design did not "meet altogether with our approbation, nor does it appear to be agreeable to his own taste, and judgment." Hallet himself confided to Jefferson that he had "surpassed the views on economy that were recommended to me."[26]

Hallet met with Washington before executing his fourth design (Fig. 29; Cats. 58 and 59). Washington came to the meeting with either a drawing or a print ("un dessin," in Hallet's words) that the president found "convenable au sujet," or appropriate for the purpose. As a result of this meeting, Hallet fused his first two designs, combining the outward forms of his precompetition domed plan with the classical temple of his competition entry. The result, judged against Thornton's winning scheme in January 1793, is a cross-shaped building with a double-porticoed temple facing east–west and elongated lateral wings spreading out to the north and south. A tall belvedere dome (based on that at the Collège des Quatre Nations) marks the intersection of the four wings. Hallet's impressive fourth design answered all the functional and symbolic purposes of the proposed Capitol, but would have been vastly expensive to build.

The sculpture that Hallet planned for this penultimate design focuses on expressing emblematically the aspirations and organization of the new government. He used allegorical figures drawn from ancient history and mythology, previously suggested as appropriate symbols for America, to express the structure and benefits of the Constitution. Washington in the guise of the Roman senator Cincinnatus was to occupy the central pediment and to be accompanied by six toga-clad figures. To Revolutionary-era Americans, Cincinnatus was the exemplar of selfless patriotism, having set aside his personal agricultural affairs to answer the military needs of Rome, as Washington had done for his country. In 1783, Washington had been elected the first president of the Society of the Cincinnati, the brotherhood of Revolutionary War officers who initially banded together to thwart mutiny in the Continental Army and to care for needy veterans or their widows and orphans.[27]

The pedimental sculpture of Hallet's fourth design depicts Washington-cum-Cincinnatus resting with fasces (symbol of civic authority as well as union) at his feet; two trees (Liberty Trees?) separate him and six attendants from a plowed field on the left and sheaves of wheat on the right. The six figures probably were intended to represent the six original cabinet officers: the vice president, secretary of state, secretary of the treasury, secretary of war, attorney general, and postmaster general. On another level, Hallet may have meant them to allude to the six purposes of the Constitution, outlined in its Preamble: "We the People of the United States, in Order to form a more perfect Union, establish Justice, insure domestic Tranquility, provide for the common defense, promote the general Welfare, and secure the Blessings of Liberty to ourselves and our Posterity, do ordain and establish this Constitution for the United States of America."

Each wing of Hallet's fourth design is decorated with three sculptural panels. On the north wing (probably intended to contain the conference room), a winged figure appears in all the panels and may represent the Genius, or spirit, of the Constitution or perhaps the Genius of America. The main figure in the left panel, probably allegorically representing Revolutionary War patriot-soldiers, is a seated nude warrior who has set aside his armor. The same figure in the right panel seems to be felling trees—that is, clearing the wilderness for the coming of civilization. In 1794, Congressman Richard Bland Lee noted:

> In travelling through various parts of the United States, I find fields a few years ago waste and uncultivated filled with inhabitants and covered with harvests, new habitations reared, contentment in every face, plenty on every board; confidence is restored and every man is safe under his own vine and fig tree, and there is none to make him afraid. To produce this effect was the intent of the Constitution, and it has succeeded.[28]

The iconography of the panels decorating the south wing (which was to contain the House of Representatives) is derived from the most powerful ancient god, Jupiter, and the strongest ancient hero, Hercules. In the central panel, a single standing figure (representing either collective American patriots or Washington) takes an oath before the seated Jupiter (bearded, with his eagle by his side), king of the gods in Roman mythology, and his consort, Juno. A long-necked goose stands alert at Juno's feet; geese guarded the Roman Capitol. Oaths in ancient Rome were taken at the Temple of Jupiter Optimus Maximus, located on the Capitoline hill. Washington's oath as president, required by Article VI of the Constitution, was taken at Federal Hall on April 30, 1789. The Oath Act was the first law enacted under the Constitution, signed by Washington on June 1, 1789. It was commemorated on the House wing pediment because the legislation had been initiated in the House, bill HR-1.

On February 1, 1793, Jefferson reported to the commissioners that he and Washington

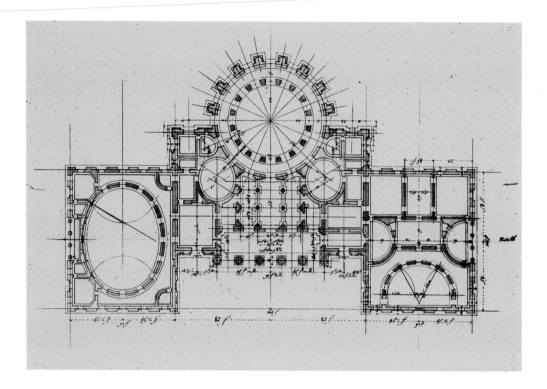

Fig. 30. Stephen Hallet. "Conference Plan for the Capitol," July 1793. Library of Congress.

preferred Thornton's plan, as it was "simple, noble, beautiful, excellently distributed, and moderate in size." Thornton's premiated drawings have been lost, but Robert King's engraved view of the east front, published on his 1818 map of Washington, depicts Thornton's winning design. On March 11, 1793, the commissioners gave Thornton's submission their official imprimatur. In recognition of Hallet's diligence, particularly in changing his designs at their request, they awarded him a premium equal in value to what Thornton received, £100 (the value of a lot of land) and $500 (the announced first prize money). In addition, Hallet, a trained architect, was placed in charge of constructing Thornton's plan.[29]

On March 15, after being notified of Thornton's success, Hallet sent Jefferson a description of his fifth design (Cat. 65; Plate 4, Cat. 66). He wrote that it was the first of his projects that truly reflected his own ideas about what the Capitol should be, rather than a design prompted by others, and he asked that it be considered before a final decision was made. Its similarity to Thornton's winning plan—both are low, compact buildings, with large Pantheon-inspired rotundas projecting from their west facades—suggests that Hallet's design was influenced by that of his successful rival. Hallet's fifth design differs from Thornton's in having a square recessed central courtyard that faces east (Cat. 67). Its emblematic ornament consists of relief-sculpted panels set into the rotunda walls above the arcaded entrance level. They are scenes depicting the discovery, exploration, and settlement of America by different European peoples, the aspect of America's history that Hallet considered to be of greatest lasting import.[30]

At Washington's suggestion, Jefferson convened a conference in Philadelphia on July 15, 1793, after Hallet, Samuel Blodget, Jr., and James Hoban (architect of the President's House) seriously criticized Thornton's successful entry. Its major faults were restricted light and air to the wings because of its dense central section and structural faults in supporting the dome of the House chamber. The outcome of the conference was that Thornton's elevations were to be married to Hallet's plan (Fig. 30; Cat. 68). The latter was to be revised with a project-ing portico added on the east to balance the rotunda on the west; internally, the Senate cham-ber was to be a semicircle rather than a hippodrome (Cat. 69). Jefferson, Washington, Thorn-ton, and the commissioners regarded the so-called conference plan as an alteration to Thornton's winning design; Hallet considered it to be the adoption of his modified plan. Hal-let was hired as the superintending architect. The Capitol's foundations were laid in August and September 1793 according to the conference plan; Hallet's name appeared as architect on the cornerstone, laid on September 18.[31]

The architects and builders who submitted designs to the Capitol competition repre-sented the entire range of design and building talent available in America in the late eigh-teenth century and probably replicated the approximate proportions of each group among the architectural community. One of the most surprising aspects of the design competition is the unknown fate of most of the entrants. Only McIntire and Thornton are known to have had subsequent productive architectural careers, while the Capitol competition drawings are the only evidence of the architectural careers of many of the other contenders.

Designing the Capitol demonstrated the imperceptible merging of architectural and polit-ical interests in 1792 and 1793. Washington's and Jefferson's involvement attests to the Capi-tol's significance in their eyes: it must express America's political ideals while fulfilling Con-gress's legislative needs. Interaction of the country's most important political leaders with the architects who implemented their joint ideas continued into the Capitol's construction phase, as successive presidents monitored the work of those charged with carrying out the Thorn-ton-Hallet design.

~ III ~

"The Temple of Justice and Faith"

The Capitol's East and West Porticoes, Dome and Rotunda

Revisions to William Thornton's winning design for the Capitol, agreed to at the July 15, 1793, conference convened by Washington and Jefferson, ought to have determined the Capitol's final exterior form. Solutions to architectural problems, however, are often fluid in the minds of creative designers. The size, shape, and details of Thornton's wings were built essentially as he designed them because the north wing was begun immediately after the conference and the south wing was built to correspond to it a decade later. The "center building," as it was called—containing at various times the conference room, crypt, domed Rotunda, and Library of Congress—was the last section to be built. This phased construction provided several successive architects with the opportunity to redesign the Capitol's most visible elements: the east and west entrance porticoes and the dome. When Charles Bulfinch's wood and brick double dome was finished in 1826, the Capitol's exteriors represented a composite of ideas suggested by at least five of its seven architects: Thomas Jefferson, William Thornton, George Hadfield, Benjamin Henry Latrobe, and Bulfinch.

DOMES FOR AMERICA'S SECULAR TEMPLES

To plan a dome as the Capitol's central element implied that the building was to serve a quasi-religious function—indeed to be a civic temple. (Domes were generally reserved for pagan temples in antiquity and for churches in the Christian world.) During the American Revolution, several actual or metaphorical secular "temples" had been invented, designated, or erected, each extolling some aspect of the young country's purpose and history or the conduct of American patriots. The surrender of British troops at Yorktown, Virginia, on October 19/20, 1781, took place on the surrender field near Washington's tent, which was called the "Temple of Glory." "The Temple of Virtue," a combination chapel, meeting hall, and recreation center, was erected in January 1783 at the Continental Army's headquarters in Newburgh, New York. It was the site on March 15 of Washington's famous rebuttal of an attempted mutiny, in which he exhorted his officers to maintain their reputation as selfless patriots despite grievances against Congress.[1]

These temple-like structures were deemed appropriate because liberty was a new secular religion in Revolutionary America. On September 11, 1787, jurist and signer of the Declaration of Independence James Wilson, in an address before the Pennsylvania legislature, prophesied that the new federal government would "lay a foundation for erecting temples of liberty in every part of the earth." Washington observed in his first inaugural address that the "preservation of the sacred fire of liberty, and the destiny of the republican model of government, are justly considered as deeply perhaps as finally staked, on the experiment entrusted to the hands of the American people."[2] In his essay "The New Roof," published in at least fifteen newspapers in 1787 and 1788, signer of the Declaration of Independence Francis Hopkinson used an architectural structure as an allegory for the states united under the federal government:

> The intention really was to make a firm and substantial roof by uniting the strength of the 13 rafters; and that this was so far from annihilating the several rafters and rendering them of no use individually, that it was manifest from a bare inspection of the plan, that the strength of each contributed to the strength of the whole, and that the existence of each and all were essentially necessary to the existence of the whole fabric as a roof.[3]

Actual images of classical temples or colonnades to express the federal union were published widely in Federalist newspapers to promote ratification of the Constitution. The Constitutional Convention, which concluded its work in September 1787, required the legislatures of nine states to vote for, or ratify, the Constitution in order that the federal government be established. Throughout 1788, the *Massachusetts Centinel,* published in Boston, promoted ratification with rhetorical texts and poems accompanied by woodcuts of a colonnade joined by arches ornamented with stars (Fig. 31; Cat. 20). The columns were inscribed with the names of the states in the order in which they ratified the Constitution, thus vigorously promoting competition among the states. Many other newspapers quickly followed suit, with the columns arranged in various ways, including a circular tempietto: a small domed and open temple (Cat. 21).[4]

Of the numerous parades, or "federal processions," to celebrate passage of the Constitution held in American cities between February and July 1788, Philadelphia's was particularly significant. Half of the city's population, 17,000 people, attended the Fourth of July event. Decorations were elaborate, ranging from colorful banners carried by guild members to horse-drawn floats. Painter and inventor Charles Willson Peale designed a circular temple 10 feet in diameter and 23 feet, 6 inches high to allegorically represent national union (Cat. 23). Peale referred to it as the "Temple of Immigrants," but Francis Hopkinson called it the "Grand Federal Edifice" in a lengthy description published in the July 1788 issue of the *American Museum:*

> The dome [is] supported by thirteen Corinthian columns, raised on pedestals proper to that order; the frieze decorated with thirteen stars; ten of the columns complete, and three left unfin-

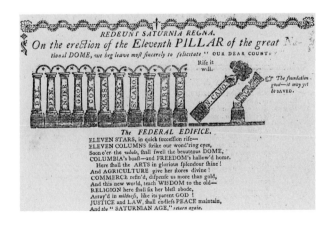

Fig. 31. "Federal Pillar." *Massachusetts Centinel* (Boston), August 2, 1789. Library of Congress.

ished: on the pedestals of the columns were inscribed, in ornamented cyphers, the initials of the thirteen American states. On the top of the dome, a handsome cupola surmounted by a figure of Plenty, bearing her cornucopia, and other emblems of her character.[5]

"In union the fabric stands firm" was inscribed around the base of the temple. During the parade, representatives of the ten states that had ratified the Constitution sat under the dome. Replicas of Peale's Grand Federal Edifice were built for reenactments of Philadelphia's federal procession in 1888 and a century later (Cat. 22).[6]

Although many American statehouses had cupolas, only one was planned with a dome. The low, octagonal wood dome on the Maryland State House (1769–1773), designed by Joseph Horatio Anderson, was replaced in 1788 by a taller one designed by the English-born and -trained architect Joseph Clark. The second dome's height (60 feet higher than Anderson's) and form proved to be a carpenter's masterpiece, as it rose 200 feet through nine successive, ever-diminishing stages to tower over the town of Annapolis. Clark's dome was essentially an octagonal tower that functioned both as an important object on the skyline and as a belvedere; a staircase filling the rotunda led to an exterior platform. In September 1790, Jefferson and Madison in the company of Thomas Lee Shippen "passed 3 hours on the top of the [Maryland] State House steeple from which place you descry the finest prospect in the world, if extent, variety [of] Wood and Water in all their happiest forms can make one so."[7] This experience seems to have left a significant impression on Jefferson; perhaps at his suggestion, Stephen Hallet included belvedere domes on three of his designs for the Capitol.

PIERRE CHARLES L'ENFANT'S CAPITOL

Pierre Charles L'Enfant designed Washington's first Capitol, known from only a plan on engraved maps of the city. Its most notable features were its large scale and a circular room, undoubtedly a domed rotunda, that overlooked the city's great public park, the Mall. L'Enfant's Capitol was integral to his city plan, which he regarded as a microcosm of the country, "this vast Empire." Accordingly, he designed the city on an unprecedented scale and arranged the state avenues to reflect the geography of the United States and the history of its national union. He located state squares, as well as every kind of public building (from cathedral to market halls), on topographically prominent sites, then laid out direct state avenues between them, and finally arranged an irregular grid of streets as an underlying infrastructure—the whole a unique city-in-the-country plan.

L'Enfant made the entire city a symbol of national union by the interrelationships he created between the state avenues and key public spaces. The avenues named for the New England states are grouped in the northern section of the city, those for the central states are near the city's geographic center, and those for the southern states are on Capitol Hill. Their lengths reflect both the size of each state and the importance of its contributions during the Revolutionary era. The three longest avenues, representing the largest states, traverse the city: Massachusetts Avenue is north of Pennsylvania Avenue, which lies above Virginia Avenue. Pennsylvania Avenue was connected to both the Capitol and the President's House because of the importance of the military and civic events that took place in Pennsylvania. The Continental and Confederation congresses met in three of the four states whose avenues bisect the Capitol grounds: Maryland, Pennsylvania, and New Jersey. The fourth avenue, Delaware, represents the first state to ratify the Constitution. L'Enfant's city was intentionally larger and more complex than any European city, a new kind of plan in which natural and man-made elements were totally in harmony and together acted as a meaningful symbol of union under the Constitution.[8]

L'Enfant's intense interest in embodying America's size, history, and national union in its capital city reflected his own background and interests as well as those of President Washington. In April 1791, shortly after showing Washington his preliminary plan for the city, L'Enfant wrote to his friend Alexander Hamilton that he "gave imagination its full Scope" and "was fortunate enough to see [his ideas] meet with [Washington's] approbation." In his first report to Washington, dated March 26, 1791, L'Enfant noted that the public buildings should be placed on hills so that they might offer commanding views and "might be seen From Twenty mile off." Three months later, on June 28, L'Enfant explained that reciprocal vistas linked to existing landscape conditions were a fundamental consideration for the siting of public buildings. He placed the Capitol, which he called the "Congress House," on the west end of Jenkins Hill, "which stand[s] as a pedestal waiting for a monument." With an "eminent Italian sculptor" (probably Giuseppe Ceracchi), L'Enfant planned for the foot of Capitol Hill an important emblematic sculptural group, *Liberty Hailing Nature out of its Slumber*. As Liberty founded the country and the federal city, it was appropriately located near the Capitol.[9]

On February 29, 1792, commissioner Thomas Johnson wrote to Jefferson:

I have never heard whether Majr. L'Enfant has prepared Drafts [drawings] of the Capitol Palace and other public Buildings or any of them from the places marked [out on the map]. . . . The Capitol seems to me [from the map] to be on a very extraordinary Scale and I suspect that the Concentration of the Streets and Avenues is calculated accordingly so that it must either proceed or a good deal of the Work must be done over again.[10]

Jefferson's reply confirms that if L'Enfant had drawings of the Capitol, he showed them to none but his closest confidants. Jefferson wrote to Johnson on March 8: "Majr. Lenfant had no plans prepared for the Capitol or government house. He said he had them in his head. I do not believe he will produce them for concurrence." The previous January, however, L'Enfant's assistant Isaac Roberdeau had overseen the digging of trenches on Capitol Hill, and the commissioners had noted in their proceedings on January 7, 1792, that the laborers were following "a plan of the intended work drawn by Mr. Roberdeau."[11]

In 1795, the anonymous "Essay on the City of Washington" was published as a pamphlet in French and serialized in English in several American newspapers. It opened with the statement "To found a City in the center of the United States, for the purpose of making it the depository of the acts of the Union . . . is [to create] a temple erected to liberty." The Capitol's location was in the center of Washington, "as the city is the center of the American empire," with its streets "directed towards every part of America, to enlighten its inhabitants respecting their true interests." L'Enfant's entire plan, especially the central public spaces and buildings, was presented in the essay as an allegory of good government:

Each street is also an emblem of the facility, with which the Capitol may be approached, in every respect, and at all times, by every individual, who shall live under the protection of the Union. . . . The capitol and the President's house are so situated, that the President may have continually in his view, the temple where are deposited the laws, the execution of which is committed to him; and it seems, that by the multiplicity of the streets and their diverging direction, it was intended to remind him constantly of the importance of directing his official views to the most distant parts of the Empire; and this ingenious allegory, in its inverted sense, will call to his mind, at the same time, that his actions, are continually and unavoidably open to general inspection.[12]

THOMAS JEFFERSON'S CAPITOL

While L'Enfant's Capitol depicted on published maps certainly influenced some entrants in the competition, Jefferson's promotion of a domed Capitol had the more decisive influence. Jefferson expressed his preferences in a famous letter he wrote to L'Enfant on April 10, 1791. He wanted America's Capitol to be based on "some one of the models of antiquity which have the approbation of thousands of years," while the President's House might be modeled on a modern building (Cat. 31).[13]

All of Jefferson's drawings associated with the Capitol incorporate domed rotundas. His most developed sketch is for an enlarged version of the Roman Pantheon, a choice he made for symbolic as well as didactic reasons. Within a rotunda 162 feet in diameter (compared with 142 feet for the ancient building), Jefferson designed a series of oval rooms, labeling three of them "H. of Representatives," "Senate," and "Courts of Justice" (Fig. 32; Cat 32). By the summer of 1791, the decision had been made to provide a separate building for the Supreme Court, but insufficient funds dictated that the judiciary be housed temporarily with Congress.

Jefferson's bias in favor of Roman architecture seems to have been based partially on his education, steeped in ancient history and literature, and partly on Neoclassical aesthetic beliefs. In reaction to the exuberance of the Baroque period, many Neoclassicists maintained that ancient architecture provided correct principles of structure, form, and decoration, canons that had been slowly eroding since the Renaissance. Because of its great size, Jefferson's Capitol probably could not have been roofed with a dome either framed in wood or vaulted with brick or stone, yet the grandeur of his conception and his idea of a Pantheon-inspired dome was crucial to the Capitol's future development.

The Roman Pantheon was known to Jefferson through a variety of engraved sources, including any of the four editions of Andrea Palladio's *Four Books of Architecture* that he owned. However, on March 16, 1791, Jefferson directed his secretary, William Short (who was in Paris), to acquire for him "a compleat set of Piranesi's drawings of the Pantheon, and especially the correct design for its restauration as proposed by I forget whom which was not executed, and of which I have heard you speak. I wish to render them useful in the public buildings now to begin at Georgetown. To this I wish Frouillé [a Parisian bookseller] would add Desgodetz's ancient buildings of Rome (Fig. 33; Cat. 33).[14]

Designed by the Emperor Hadrian and built in A.D. 117, the Pantheon simultaneously represented Roman

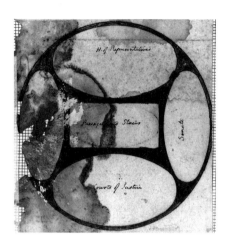

Fig. 32. Thomas Jefferson. "Study for the Capitol, Plan," ca. 1792. Massachusetts Historical Society.

Fig. 33. Antoine Desgodetz. "Elevation de la face du Panthéon, à Rome." *Les Edifices antiques de Rome,* 1779. Library of Congress.

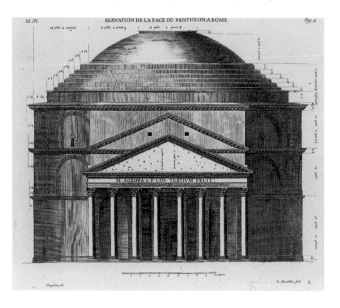

civic virtues, typified the rationality and coherence of ancient architecture, and provided a meaningful architectural form to express the union of the states. The hemispherical geometry of the Pantheon's dome represented unity, as did its function as the temple dedicated to all the Roman gods; Jefferson's Capitol was to represent all the American people.

Jefferson's adoption of a rectangular Roman temple as the basis for the Virginia State Capitol in Richmond gave America a model of what he called "cubic" architecture; a national Capitol derived from the Pantheon would give a model of "spherical" architecture. One of Jefferson's major concerns in all the public-building projects in which he was involved was to provide actual exemplars derived from great historical architectural prototypes for his compatriots to emulate. He hoped thereby to improve the taste in architecture of American builders unable to visit Europe and to educate all Americans about their place in Western history and culture. His design for the University of Virginia (1803–1826) is his most successful expression of this didactic notion; its central building, the rotunda library, is an amplification of his Pantheon-inspired design for the Capitol. Architectural quality was joined to his other objectives when Jefferson directed the Capitol competition and advised on the early form, spaces, and details of the Capitol. In 1803, during his presidency (1801–1809), he selected the finest architect in the United States known to him to complete the Capitol, probably not realizing how significant their collaboration was to be. Jefferson hoped to ensure that the Capitol would be properly expressive of sober republican civic virtues as well as America's unique political system and that it would be a great work of architecture.[15]

STEPHEN HALLET'S THREE DOMES

Between 1791 and 1793, Jefferson worked closely with Stephen Hallet while the French architect was developing a series of designs to submit to the Capitol competition. Hallet experimented with a modern dome typology ultimately derived from Renaissance ones that had high colonnaded rotundas. The outward appearance of Hallet's tall domes was borrowed from a Parisian example, that for the chapel of the Collège des Quatre Nations, probably chosen for symbolic reasons. Their function as belvederes may have been suggested to Hallet by Jefferson, who had recently viewed the town of Annapolis from the Maryland State House dome. Hallet's tall domes would have provided bird's-eye views of L'Enfant's city plan, the true complexity and meaning of which could be appreciated only from such a high vantage point. Charles Dickens in his *American Notes* recognized the natural reciprocal relationship between the city plan and the Capitol: "It is sometimes called the City of Magnificent Distances, but it might with greater propriety be termed the City of Magnificent Intentions; for it is only on taking a bird's-eye view of it from the top of the Capitol that one can at all comprehend the vast designs of its projector, an aspiring Frenchman."[16]

On August 15, 1807, the Architect of the Capitol, Benjamin Henry Latrobe, complained to Jefferson that the "constant walking by visitors over the roof" to see the view was contributing to leaks.[17] By the 1830s, Washington guidebooks frequently described the view from the Capitol's roof. Robert Mills in his *Guide to the Capitol and National Executive Offices* directed visitors to the north stairway, which led to the roof:

> [T]hose fond of picturesque and panoramic scenery will be fully repaid for ascending to the giddy summit of the great dome. Those more timid will be satisfied to view the landscape from the general level of the roof; . . . from the galleried apex of the dome, you can take a bird's eye

view embracing the whole horizon. In whatever direction here the vision is cast, there is something interesting to be seen. On one hand a rising city, with its numerous avenues, branching off in all directions, like radii from a centre, its splendid public buildings, and hum of active life; on the other hand, the noble Potomac. . . . To the North stretches a range of high lands, with varied scenery of groves and buildings; to the East the native forest terminates the view, opened here and there by the rail and turnpike roads to Baltimore; on the South-east lies the Navy Yard and Marine Barracks, City Asylum and Congressional Burying-Ground; on the South and West, the Arsenal and Penitentiary; on the West, the public mall with its progressive improvements, the Smithsonian building, and the Washington National Monument; further on the National Observatory lifts its revolving dome, and beyond this are seen the heights of Georgetown, with its cluster of buildings rising in bold relief.[18]

WILLIAM THORNTON'S CENTER BUILDING

During the fall and early winter of 1792, while Hallet was revising his designs following suggestions by Washington, Jefferson, and the commissioners, the physician and amateur architect William Thornton was preparing two designs for the Capitol. The first was begun on Tortola in the West Indies before Thornton was fully cognizant of the Capitol's functional and symbolic needs, as well as the financial limitations imposed on its construction. The scale of this Capitol design and a tempietto on its roof would have identified it as an important public building. Thornton may have intended the tempietto to serve a symbolic purpose at the same time as it functioned as a cupola to admit light into a major room below. Small circular temples commemorating liberty or fame were part of an active English Georgian iconography during the latter half of the eighteenth century, the tradition from which Thornton's "Tortola" plan was drawn. Thornton's later suggestions for the decorative and symbolic adornment of his winning Capitol design demonstrate his wide-ranging knowledge of the language of symbols and his intense interest in formulating or transforming symbols to express the Capitol's national function.

Thornton's second design for the Capitol, given to Washington in January 1793, was entirely different in character: a low, compact building with probably two large circular rooms spanning the circular or semicircular conference room and a central hall. Both were probably domed, but the early loss of Thornton's premiated design drawings leave the exact nature of the original west front uncertain. Robert King's 1818 map of Washington illustrates Thornton's original design, which is identified by the inscription "East Front of the Capitol of the United States as originally designed by William Thornton, and adopted by General Washington, President of the United States" (Cat. 62). Its middle third was a low, hemispheric dome and rotunda entered via a giant Corinthian portico in conscious emulation of the Roman Pantheon.

Thornton's description written in April 1793 outlined the interior and exterior features of his Capitol. Its dome was to be constructed of wood and sheathed in copper. Thornton planned a figure of Atlas carrying a globe—"an allusion to the members assembled in this house bearing the whole weight of government"—to be associated with the dome, but its intended placement is unclear.[19]

Thornton filled the east front pediment with an American eagle accompanied by the Latin motto "Justitice fides sacrum" which he translated variously as "Sacred to Justice & Faith (national) or The Temple of Justice and Faith." At the apex of this pediment, he placed the "Farnese Hercules (who has obtained the Fruits of his labour) alluding to the happiness which America enjoys, as its reward, for the labours of past years." Standing figures in niches flanking the entrance to the rotunda seem to be Ceres and Mercury, figures to represent America's farmers and merchants (Plate 5, Cat. 72).

Thornton had a clear vision of how the interior of his domed, 112-foot-diameter rotunda should look. He knew that light-brown Aquia sandstone from Virginia was being quarried for the Capitol and suggested that his rotunda's ring of 30-foot-high Corinthian columns be executed in white Italian marble to provide a subtle color contrast. In proposing such an elegant design, Thornton was not unmindful of the limited resources—financial as well as technical— of the young country. However, writing in April 1793, he conceived of the Capitol as representing America for centuries to come:

> If the expense of white marble Columns could possibly be objected to, we ought to consider it the house of the people which they are meant to decorate; a house which is meant to serve them for many Centuries, and which the richest people in the world cannot surely hesitate to erect in a manner worthy of their dignity: If the external be magnificent their representants will not fail to give a high finish to the chambers intended for their Councils, and the Statues and other ornaments on the Balustrades pediment &c will be much more correspondent: These may be finished and put up by degrees.[20]

Thornton recommended placing a white marble equestrian statue of Washington in the center of the rotunda. This sculpture expanded the Capitol's function from solely the meeting place of Congress to a public monument, a pilgrimage place with the rotunda functioning as a great public space open to all. Thornton reinforced the Capitol's purpose as a secular temple by suggesting a "great repository," probably a burial crypt in the tradition of European churches, but one destined for America's civic and military heroes. Although he was still living, Washington's deification was well under way by 1793.[21]

A decade earlier, on August 7, 1783, Congress had voted to erect a bronze equestrian statue of Washington, in "Roman dress," "where the residence of Congress shall be established." Its marble pedestal was to have relief-sculpted panels showing the four greatest military actions of the Revolution that Washington had commanded. L'Enfant planned such a statue to be placed at the west end of the Mall, where the central axes of the President's House and Congress House cross. Equestrian statues to commemorate great military heroes were a Roman tradition carried through the Renaissance to modern times. Such figures typically were located in great public squares, not within buildings. Thornton's placement of an equestrian statue of Washington in the Capitol's rotunda expanded the building's purpose and multiplied its rich historical content.[22]

WILLIAM THORNTON'S WEST FRONT

From 1990 to 1994, architect Don Alexander Hawkins reconstructed Thornton's west front based on written descriptions of the original plan as well as later modifications of it. A series of double columns outlined the projecting conference room, which overlooked the Mall, but the height of the building's dome is uncertain. In April 1793, Thornton described part of his west front's decorative and emblematic scheme: "[O]ver the pairs of columns [at the ends of the circular portico] in the west front there ought to be pairs of figures, emblematical, which may be chosen thereafter. Over the Balconies of the West Front are meant to be placed two supporters—on one side a Buffaloe and Indian; on the other an Elk, or a moose Deer, and an Indian; the rest of the Front ornamented with Urns or other Decorations."[23]

About 1797 or 1798, Thornton revised the Capitol's west front to include an expansive,

Fig. 34. William Thornton. "Sketch of Section of Monument and Conference Room," ca. 1797. Library of Congress.

open "Temple of Fame" or "Temple of Virtue" to commemorate the Revolution's civic and military heroes (Fig. 34; Cat. 75). He replaced the native animals he had proposed in 1793 with emblematic sculptural figures. Thornton's drawing of the revised west front shows fourteen traditional allegorical figures standing atop the balustrade of the conference room colonnade (Plate 6, Cat. 73). Each is in classical garb; those who can be identified by their various implements include Mars carrying a shield, Justice with scales, Abundance with a cornucopia, Hope with an anchor, and History with a mirror. Thornton also planned massive relief-sculpted panels to decorate the walls flanking the conference room colonnade. The scene sketched in for the north wall—figures in a coastal landscape with ships at sea—may represent the discovery of America or may be an allusion to peacetime trade with Europe. It is not known what prompted Thornton to eliminate Native Americans and indigenous animals from his iconographic scheme to concentrate on European allegories to express European achievements in America.

WASHINGTON'S MONUMENT

Washington's unexpected death on December 14, 1799, prompted a great outpouring of national sentiment. Congress responded nine days later with a resolution: "That a marble monument be erected by the United States in the Capitol at the city of Washington; and that the monument be so designed as to commemorate the great events of his military and political life."[24] On January 22, 1800, Thornton wrote to John Marshall, chairman of the congressional committee charged with deciding how George Washington should be memorialized. The architect recommended that Washington's tomb be placed "in the Center of that National Temple which he approved of for a Capitol." Thornton realized that the country's response to Washington's death would be a "very great inducement to the completion of the whole Building, which has been thought by some contracted Minds, unacquainted with grand works to be upon too great a Scale."[25]

Thornton described his design for Washington's monument, a tomb to hold both the Washingtons, in a letter to an unknown correspondent published in the *National Intelligencer* nearly a year later, on December 8, 1800:

> The most suitable, in my opinion, would be a fine group of figures on a well composed massy rock, the whole executed in white marble. The figures to consist of Eternity, leading him [Washington] to the pinnacle, and pointing upward, ready to take flight, while Time is left below in a posture as if inviting him to stay; attended by Independence, by Victory, by Liberty, by Peace, Virtue, Prosperity and Fame— all but the two first Figures would be in lower region of the rock, and they ought not to be crowded.— . . . The bodies of the general and his [wife, Martha,] may be deposited in a place prepared in the rock, in the region where [T]ime and the rest of the figures are grouped, signifying that though Time has taken possession of his body yet Eternity has taken his spirit out of the reach of Time. . . .
>
> Pedestals with brass relief figures and mottos will do very well in common cases, but in the present case there is nothing common, and we may rise as high in our representation as mortals ought to go.[26]

Years later, on March 18, 1819, Benjamin Henry Latrobe, the Architect of the Capitol for more than a decade and Thornton's avowed rival in matters concerning the Capitol, recalled

Thornton's description of this monument and his own amusing spoof of its convoluted iconography:

> Some Years ago Dr. Thornton of Washington described in a large company the Allegorical group which it was his intention as Commissioner of the city of Washington to place in the center of the Capitol around the Statue of the General.
>
> "I would," said he, "place an immense rock of Granite in the Center of the dome. On the top of the rock should stand a beautiful female figure to represent eternity or Immortality. Around her neck, as a Necklace, a serpent, the Rattlesnake of our country, should be hung, with its tail in its mouth, the ancient and beautiful symbol of endless duration. At the foot of the rock another female figure stretching her hands upwards, in the attitude of distressful entreaty[,] should appear ready to climb the steep. Around her a group of children representing agriculture, the arts and sciences, should appear to join in the supplication of the female. This female is to personify time, or our present state of existence. Just ascending the rock, the noble figure of General Washington should appear to move upwards, invited by immortality; but also expressing some reluctance in leaving the Children of his care. There," said he, "Mr. Latrobe, is your requisite in such works of art; it would represent *a matter of fact*, a *truth,* for it would be the very picture of the Generals sentiments, feelings, and expectations, in departing this life: Regret at leaving his people, but hoping and longing for an immortality of happiness and of fame. You yourself have not ingenuity sufficient to pervert its meaning, and all posterity would understand it."
>
> The Doctor was so full of his subject, that I was unwilling to disturb his good humor. But, I said, that I thought his groupe might tell a very different story from what he intended. He pressed me so hard that at last I told him: that supposing the name and character of General Washington to be forgotten; or at least that the group being found in the ruins of the Capitol, the learned Antiquarians of 2,000 Years hence were assembled to decide its meaning. I thought then, that they would thus explain it.
>
> Here is a beautiful woman on the top of a dangerous precipice, to which she invites a man, apparently well enough inclined to follow her. Who is this woman? Certainly not a very good sort of a one, for she has a snake about her neck. The snake indicates assuredly her character, cold, cunning, and poisonous. She can represent none, but some celebrated courtisan of the day. But there is another Woman at the foot of the rock, modest and sorrowful, and surrounded by a family of small Children. She is in a posture of entreaty and the man appears half inclined to return to her. She can be no other than his wife. What an expressive groupe! How admirable the art which has thus exposed the dangerous precipice to which the beauty and cunning of the abandoned would entice the virtuous, even to the desertion of a beautiful wife and the mother of a delightful groupe of Children. I was going on, but the laughter of the company, and the impatience of the Doctor stopped my mouth. I had said enough and was not easily forgiven.[27]

By May 8, 1800, after considerable debate about the nature and location of Washington's monument, Congress resolved "That a mausoleum be erected for George Washington in the City of Washington." The original congressional bill had stipulated that the mausoleum, or tomb, be "of American granite and marble, in a pyramidal form, one hundred feet square at the base, and of a proportionate height." Representative Willis Alston of North Carolina suggested that the pyramid be placed inside the Capitol, but the final vote favored a separate structure.[28]

None of the early proposed monuments to Washington was even begun, and his remains were never removed from his tomb at Mount Vernon, where his will stipulated that he be buried. Numerous later attempts to erect a statue of Washington or entomb him in the Capitol Rotunda or crypt resulted in minor alterations to the building. In 1824, Charles Bulfinch, the Architect of the Capitol who built the Rotunda and dome, left a circular opening about 10 feet in diameter in the center of the Rotunda for visitors to view a statue of Washington proposed for the crypt below. The hole was closed in 1828 because of rising dampness. Two years later, a select committee of the House of Representatives proposed placing Washington's actual coffin in a vault located in the sub-basement, an empty marble cenotaph in the crypt, and a standing figure of Washington in the Rotunda, all in the center of the building.

In 1832—the centennial of Washington's birth—Congress commissioned the American sculptor Horatio Greenough to execute a statue of Washington for the Capitol Rotunda. When Greenough's seated marble figure was installed a decade later, the foundations of first the crypt and then the Rotunda had to be strengthened to support its weight of 30 tons. In 1843, the statue was moved to the Capitol grounds on axis with the east portico, but damage due to exposure to the elements led to its being removed to the Smithsonian Institution in 1908.

THREE ROMAN PANTHEON-INSPIRED DOMES

After Hallet was informed of Thornton's success in February 1793, he asked permission to submit a final design that would reflect his own ideas of the organization of the Capitol's exteriors and interiors and the appropriate symbolic decoration. The striking resemblance between Hallet's fifth proposal and Thornton's winning plan has led some scholars to assume that Hallet was taking advantage of Thornton's success. The vast differences between Thornton's Tortola and winning designs suggest that he had arrived at his final version after consultation with some knowledgeable persons who advised him about the expected nature of the building. Hallet, in his fifth design, adapted his own ideas of wall treatment and symbolic program to a general format known to have been approved by Washington and Jefferson. Moreover, the resemblance of both Thornton's and Hallet's plans, done early in 1793, to the footprint of L'Enfant's Capitol on the engraved maps first published in March 1792 suggests the last as a common source.

If the actual Capitol's plan resembled in outline the building depicted on the published city plans, it would promote confidence in the entire endeavour. The plans were being used in the auctions of land sales; public trust in their veracity was crucial for the success of the city. Hallet's third design had been displayed at the first public auction of city lots in October 1792. Sales were disappointing because public skepticism about the federal city's future was widespread, an attitude that might have been fueled by the great differences between Hallet's proposed Capitol and the one whose plan was shown on the printed maps.

Like Thornton's winning design, Hallet's fifth design has a domed, west-facing conference room that was derived ultimately from the Roman Pantheon, but it is a freer, less archaeologically correct interpretation than Thornton's. In a version of his fifth design drawn in 1794 to 1795, Hallet planned an altar to liberty to stand in the center of an open, square courtyard, rather than a second rotunda, as Thornton proposed. Hallet's altar was to be surrounded by female figures representing the union of states, while statues of the Founding Fathers would have stood around the perimeter of the courtyard; the whole would have been remarkably Roman in its general appearance.[29]

In a report to Congress on January 21, 1796, on the status of the construction of the federal city's public buildings, Commissioner Alexander White noted that the Capitol's "grand vestibule may, or may not, be covered with a dome—architects differ in opinion, with regard to covering it. If it should not be covered, it will consist only of an arcade, twenty feet high, and ten feet wide; and over that, a colon[n]ade sixteen feet high, affording a communication from the grand stair case to all other parts of the building."[30]

Washington appointed Thornton as one of three commissioners of the District of Columbia on September 15, 1794, ensuring that the Capitol's winning architect could exercise control over the execution of his design. On November 15, Hallet was dismissed "because he had altered the intended Dome in the centre."[31] Hallet did remain at work until January 1795, when James Hoban began acting as an interim architect until the English architect George Hadfield took over Hallet's responsibilities on October 15, 1795.

GEORGE HADFIELD'S PROPOSED REVISIONS TO THORNTON'S CENTER BUILDING

Immediately after Hadfield examined the drawings and existing fabric of the Capitol, he proposed changes because of defects he perceived in Thornton's design. Although Hadfield's drawings and papers are lost, two unsigned and undated elevation drawings, formerly attributed to Hallet, are probably Hadfield's suggestions made before November 18, 1795, of how to reconcile the existing foundations dug at Hallet's order with Thornton's design (Fig. 35; Cats. 81a and 81b). On that date, the commissioners reported to Washington that Thornton and Hoban were opposed to Hadfield's suggested changes to the Capitol's design. These two drawings indicate that the English architect wanted to modernize the design by eliminating the high basement—in fact, to reconcile it with internal changes being carried out at Jefferson's suggestion. Hadfield's drawings show the Capitol's two Pantheon-type domes, with the east-facing one entered at ground level through a giant hexastyle Corinthian portico and the conference room rotunda outlined by giant Ionic columns that framed a series of arches, probably a carriage entrance under the conference room.[32]

A watercolor done by the New York architect Alexander Jackson Davis about 1831 to 1834 purports to be a copy of a drawing by Hadfield showing other recommended alterations (Fig. 36; Cat. 79). In addition to bringing the main story to ground level, he wanted to widen the east portico by adding two columns and introduce a broad east front staircase. His revisions would have made the Capitol more visually inviting and physically accessible and been more in keeping with its isolated setting; arcades implied a continuous urban infrastructure.

Fig. 35. Attributed to George Hadfield. "East Elevation of the Capitol," ca. 1795. The Historical Society of Washington, D.C.

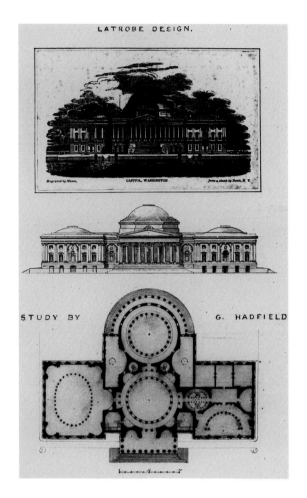

Fig. 36. Attributed to Alexander Jackson Davis, after George Hadfield. "Plan for the Capitol, Washington, by George Hadfield, first Arc. 1795," ca. 1831–1834. The Historical Society of Washington, D.C.

By lowering the wing masses, Hadfield's design threw the center into greater prominence; he gave it further emphasis by inserting an octagonal drum between the saucer dome and the roof. Three of these four ideas were in embryo changes actually instituted by Hadfield's successor, Benjamin Henry Latrobe.

A third and entirely different solution by Hadfield for the Capitol's center building appeared two decades after he resigned as superintending architect. On February 2, 1819, an engraved vignette, a perspective view of the Capitol's east facade, was published in the *Washington Gazette* as the heading for local news (Cat. 80). The editor introduced it by crediting the Capitol's original design to Hadfield. The error was corrected in the next issue, and on February 6 the newspaper published a letter from Hadfield discussing his involvement:

> As respects your vignette, it appears to me to have been copied from an impression of the fifty dollar note of the Bank of the Metropolis for which I made a perspective drawing: and Doctor Thornton is welcome to the credit of the design, except the management of the dome with an attic, which I claim as my introduction in said drawing; as believing it more consistent with good architecture, although differing from the engraving of the capitol, in the city plan lately published by Mr. Robert King, and acknowledged to be Dr. Thornton's design of the capitol.[33]

Hadfield's third solution, radically modern in its spare and abstract geometry, may never have been officially considered. He proposed a solid, undecorated cube for the center building to which separate architectural pieces were to be attached: Thornton's wings with their innermost receding bays, Thornton's arcaded east portico, but Hadfield's exceptionally broad and expansive saucer dome that sat directly on top of the central cube and extended to its edges. Why the Bank of the Metropolis put an inaccurate view of the Capitol on its notes is unclear; seemingly, the Capitol's convoluted design history was by 1819 already confused in the public mind.

BENJAMIN HENRY LATROBE'S CENTER BUILDING

The redesign of the center building was next addressed when in 1803 Jefferson hired Benjamin Henry Latrobe to oversee the completion of the Capitol (Cat. 84). The north wing was finished and had been occupied by the Senate and Supreme Court since November 1800. In 1801, a temporary House chamber had been erected on the south wing site. The conference room to accommodate both houses of Congress had been eliminated sometime after 1803 because of the rarity of joint sessions. After a thorough survey of the entire Capitol, including the foundations, Latrobe outlined internal changes he felt were necessary because of faulty construction. His ideas for finishing the exterior were presented to Jefferson in their final form on a perspective watercolor done in 1806 (Plate 7, Cat. 88). He placed a low, Pantheon-inspired dome set on an octagonal drum in the center of the building's mass, simplifying Thornton's eccentric double-domed profile. Latrobe's major contribution to the Capitol's exterior was a grand and impressive east portico and staircase, the result of an important collaboration with Jefferson. Latrobe spanned the 154-foot distance between the House and Senate wings with a wide, giant colonnade set on a basement arcade, the whole projecting in front of the wings. He then placed a six-columned Corinthian portico in the center of the colonnade, the whole approached by a monumental staircase deep enough to accommodate a covered carriageway passing beneath it.

In a letter to Jefferson dated December 7, 1806, Latrobe credited the president with suggesting an ancient portico "said to be of *Dioclesian*['s reign]" as the model for the Capitol's east portico. During the latter part of Jefferson's presidency, two pictures, "a small one on the Dioclesian Plan, and the Dioclesian Portico," hung with Latrobe's 1806 watercolor view of the Capitol in the White House. Robert Wood's reconstruction of the entrance portico to a building he identified as the Temple of the Sun, illustrated in *The Ruins of Palmyra* (1753), may be the Roman building that so impressed Jefferson (Fig. 37; Cat. 88.1). Latrobe's transformation of Wood's conjectural restoration resulted in a striking and effective portico-colonnade combination that, while faintly echoing the famous east front of the Louvre (begun 1667) in its pairing of a pedimented portico with a colonnade, is nonetheless a unique modern entrance for the Capitol. Stephen Hallet's postconference design, although known only from plans, had a hexastyle projecting east portico that bears comparison with Latrobe's design. Hallet's portico was to be raised just above ground level, with a carriage drive passing through its center (leading to a square courtyard); multiple shallow stairways between the columns would have led to separate vestibules for each wing.[34]

Latrobe's east portico totally changed Thornton's approach to the Capitol, making entry into the central Rotunda an important event. Its staircase visually and physically draws visitors into the Rotunda, in contrast to Thornton's pedestrian and carriage entries hidden behind an arcade. Latrobe's solution is more appropriate for a free-standing building in a large open square; Thornton's would have functioned best in a dense architectural ensemble of many interconnected buildings. Most important, Jefferson's and Latrobe's east portico focuses enormous architectural energy on the Capitol's Rotunda, perceived by them to be primarily a place of public assembly and secondarily a vestibule to the House and Senate chambers.

On a floor plan dating about 1806, Latrobe labeled the Rotunda "Hall of the People," echoing Thornton's idea of the Capitol as the people's "house" (Fig. 38; Cat. 118). By 1815, Latrobe identified the Rotunda, which had not yet been built, as the "Grand Vestibule, Hall of Inaugurations, of impeachments, and of all public occasions," clarifying its intended use as a room for organized functions rather than simply a place for Americans to visit. Accordingly, Latrobe designed the Rotunda as a civic museum, its walls to be decorated with niches, four large rectangular ones in which to hang paintings, and twenty-four small semicircular ones to shelter portrait statues. Broad semicircular staircases behind the large niches led down to the crypt and Washington's proposed mausoleum (Fig. 39; Cat. 161). The large niches were centered in the walls between the Rotunda's four doors, the entire arrangement spatially analogous to the Roman Pantheon's alternating rectangular and semicircular niches, which sheltered altars. Thornton's final dimension for his rotunda had been 120 feet in diameter, 22 feet less than the Roman Pantheon; Latrobe designed his to be 96 feet, the dimension as built.

In a split partial-elevation, partial-section drawing that Latrobe made of the west portico and the dome late in 1808 or early in 1809, he contemplated introducing semicircular thermal windows (so-called because they had been used in Roman baths, or thermae) to light the rotunda (Cat. 89). Located on a second, upper level of the octagonal drum, these eight windows would have replaced the central oculus and cupola, flooding the room below with indirect, diffuse light. Latrobe continually sought to enhance the Capitol's classical allusions while creating new Neoclassical solutions to architectural problems.

About 1810 or 1811, Latrobe made a second perspective watercolor of the Capitol's north and east facades (Fig. 40; Cat. 90). He had by 1806 wholeheartedly accepted the Roman Pantheon's saucer-dome type for the Capitol, but with Hadfield's suggested modification of an octagonal drum. Five years later, Latrobe refined its proportions and oculus details and added a frieze of relief sculpture on the drum. No written description of this sculpture survives, but Latrobe's drawing shows groups of standing figures in classical garments, presumably allegories of American historical events. The dress and poses of Latrobe's figures recall the famous Parthenon frieze, which depicts the Panathenatic Procession, the most famous annual civic event in Athens. Lord Elgin, British ambassador to Constantinople, removed most of the Parthenon's sculpture between 1801 and 1806, but detailed engravings had appeared in the second volume of James Stuart and Nicholas Revett's *Antiquities of Athens* (1788) (Cat. 91).[35] Lord Elgin's removal of some of the Parthenon's sculpture may have inspired Latrobe to strengthen the Capitol's associations with the ancient temple most associated with Greek democracy. Latrobe's frieze would have been both an elegiac memorial to the Parthenon and an affirmation that the spirit of democracy and civic responsibility had been reborn in the New World.

Fig. 37. Robert Wood. "Temple." *The Ruins of Palmyra, Otherwise Tedmor in the Desart [sic].* 1753. Library of Congress.

Fig. 38. Benjamin Henry Latrobe. "Plan of the Principal Story of the Capitol, U.S.," 1806. Library of Congress.

Fig. 39. Benjamin Henry Latrobe. "Ground Story of the Capitol, U.S.," 1806. Library of Congress.

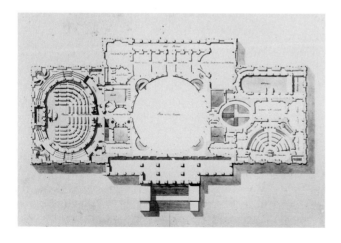

Fig. 40. Benjamin Henry Latrobe. "Perspective View of the Capitol from the Northeast," 1810. Maryland Historical Society, Baltimore.

Thornton did not approve of Latrobe's new design for the dome or the general appearance of the Capitol's emerging roofline. On April 13, 1820, he wrote to the commissioner of public buildings, Samuel Lane:

> The Dome of the Building as now intended, standing in the centre of two other Domes [over the Senate and House wings], surrounded with all kinds of fantastic ornaments, will be so ridiculous in the Eye of a chaste Architect that he will be involuntarily reminded of the old fashioned Tea Cannisters, Bobea at one end, Green Tea at the other, and in the centre the large Sugar Dish. It is a matter of great regret that such innovations should ever be permitted without consulting or making an Engineer, or the author of the Design, who with these unavailing regrets, can only now offer this solumn protest against such barbarisms.[36]

Contemporaneous with his revised dome, with its decidedly Greek frieze, Latrobe proposed a propylaea (classical gateway in the form of a temple) as the entrance to the Capitol from the west (Cats. 92 and 93). Latrobe's propylaea was a six-columned Greek Doric portico flanked by cubic guardhouses, his Greek Revival rendition of the Athenian Acropolis's Propylaea, through which one passes to visit the Parthenon. Latrobe's proposed alterations which hellenized the Capitol's exterior, date just after Jefferson's retirement from the presidency in 1809. They were in concert with many Greek architectural elements that he had begun introducing into the interiors as early as 1803.

Because of his choices of the prototypes for the Virginia State Capitol and the federal Capitol and the contents of his architectural library, Jefferson's preference among ancient architectural traditions has always been supposed to be for the Roman Republic. Perhaps because of Latrobe's influence, however, Jefferson came to appreciate the aesthetic, in addition to the political, implications of ancient Greek history and culture for America. After the construction of the Capitol was halted during the War of 1812, he wrote to Latrobe: "I shall live in the hope that the day will come when an opportunity will be given you of finishing the

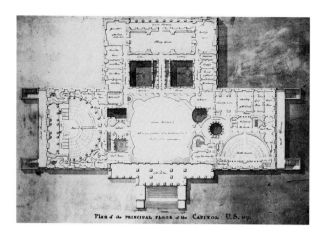

Fig. 41. Benjamin Henry Latrobe. "Plan of the Principal Floor at the Capitol, U.S.," 1817. Library of Congress.

middle building in a style worthy of the two wings, and worthy of the first temple dedicated to the sovereignty of the people, embellishing with Athenian taste the course of a nation looking far beyond the range of Athenian destinies."[37]

Latrobe's design for the Capitol's west facade portico, which faces the Mall, was consistent throughout his first building campaign. His watercolors of 1808 to 1809 and 1810 to 1811 show it as an unpedimented colonnade standing on an arcade, the whole spanning the entire width of the slightly projecting west portico (Plate 8, Cat. 95). The declivity of Capitol Hill dictated the absence of a pediment, because its triangular form would have obscured the view of the dome from the west (Plate 9, Cat. 94). Latrobe substituted a monumental statue on a stepped plinth, shown in his drawing of the west elevation as a toga-clad figure holding a pike, wearing an elaborate headdress, and accompanied by an eagle—presumably America as Liberty (Plate 10, Cat. 96). A separate watercolor of a monumental classical figure may represent the development of Latrobe's thinking about the sculpture for the west front of the Capitol. It is a female figure who raises her left arm in an oratory gesture while resting her right hand on a tablet, probably meant to represent the Constitution. She wears a liberty cap and two garments: a toga over an inner tunic decorated with a composite Apollo-Medusa head. Apollo was the symbol adopted by Louis XIV and thus may represent France; a Medusa head was worn on a breastplate by the Greek Athena, whose Roman equivalent was Minerva. Latrobe may have intended this figure to synthesize several allegorical concepts key to the Capitol's iconography, an updated and Hellenized version of Giuseppe Ceracchi's *Minerva as the Patroness of American Liberty,* which had been executed in 1792 for Philadelphia's Congress Hall. This interpretation strengthens his vision of the Capitol as a synthesis of Roman and Greek political and artistic principles. Athena had been the mythical founder of Athens; her temple had been the Parthenon. "Liberty" had founded the United States as well as the city of Washington; her temple was the Capitol.

On August 24, 1814, the Capitol was burned by British troops under the command of Admiral Sir John Cockburn, which made it necessary to rebuild the wing interiors before construction of the center building could be considered (Cats. 97 and 98). Latrobe took advantage of the fire to redesign or enlarge interior spaces and to propose his third project for the center building. In 1815, in response to increased and projected space needs, he replaced the propylaea with a deep west wing that changed the Capitol's footprint from I-shaped to cross-shaped with one truncated arm (Fig. 41; Cat. 119). He retained his west facade from 1810 to 1811, with the portico in antis—that is, set within the end walls (Plate 11, Cat. 119). Latrobe's resignation on November 20, 1817, jeopardized his entire center building because its construction was in a preliminary phase.

CHARLES BULFINCH'S CENTER BUILDING

This rich array of metaphorical domes and paper designs contributed to the Capitol's first actual dome, constructed between 1822 and 1826. Charles Bulfinch, appointed as the fourth Architect of the Capitol on December 12, 1817, eventually redesigned as much of the center building as was yet unbuilt (Cats. 99 and 162). Bulfinch noted in his first report to Commissioner Samuel Lane on February 5, 1818, that he was preparing drawings of several alternative solutions for submission to President James Monroe "from which he may select the one he may most approve for completing the building." These drawings are lost, but two of them may have been used by the English architect Charles A. Busby, who in 1819 visited Washington and copied Bulfinch's elevations and plans. Busby engraved two of his drawings and published them in London in 1823. His east front elevation indicates that Bulfinch intended to reinstate Thornton's central octastyle portico atop an arcade, the whole projecting in front of single-bay recesses that attached the center building to the wings (Fig. 42; Cat. 102). Surviving correspondence and reports do not indicate why Bulfinch finally executed Latrobe's east staircase, but it was completed by 1824 and was immediately considered to be one of the Capitol's most magnificent architectural elements.[38]

Within a few months of studying the building and the drawings Latrobe left, Bulfinch outlined a major change to the west front, the insertion of a subbasement beneath the portico in order to gain twelve much-needed committee rooms. He sketched this idea in a letter sent to painter John Trumbull on April 17, 1818 (Cat. 100). In contrast to Latrobe's recessed west portico, he proposed projecting the portico beyond the main body of the west wall and adding a shallow pediment. A slightly revised version without the pediment was engraved by W. I. Stone and published in the *National Calendar* for 1821 (Cat. 101). One notable change from Latrobe's design was a Bulfinch trademark used on many of his earlier public buildings: two sets of double columns at the portico's edges flanking two single central columns. Double columns were a common Baroque and Neoclassical device for defining edges of porticoes, just as double pilasters were often used on wall corners, but two sets framing single columns were unusual. Bulfinch's articulation of the north and south walls of the west wing also broke from accepted practice. He placed sets of paired pilasters on the inside corners, but used single pilasters on the outside edges next to the portico, a solution that defied the canons of classical architecture and resulted in an odd imbalance with the adjacent wing walls. Presumably this was a pragmatic means of strengthening a physically weak join of the west wing to the north and south wings, but it marred the overall harmony of the west front.

The Rotunda and dome were Bulfinch's most significant contributions to the Capitol's development. In February 1822, Bulfinch did comparative estimates for a wood ($19,745), brick ($24,988.90), or stone ($60,870.25) dome (Fig. 43; Cat. 103). By December 9, he reported to the new commissioner of public buildings, Joseph Elgar:

> The principal labor of the season has been devoted to raising the dome of the centre. For this purpose, the interior walls of the rotunda were con-

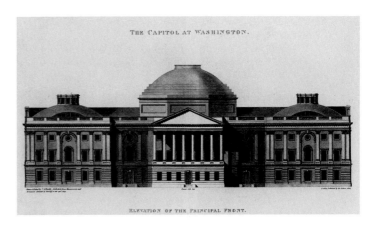

Fig. 42. Charles A. Busby. "The Capitol at Washington. Elevation of the Principal Front," 1823. Library of Congress.

Fig. 43. Charles Bulfinch. "Alternative Designs for the Capitol Dome," ca. 1824. Library of Congress.

tinued: as soon as appropriations were made in the spring, they were raised to the full height, and covered with the entablature and blocking course. The exterior walls were carried up with stone, formed into two large pannels, and crowned with a cornice and four receding gradins; about two thirds of the interior dome is built of stone and brick, and the summit of wood. The whole is covered with a wooden dome of more lofty elevation, serving as a roof. . . . It will be finally crowned with a ballustrade, to surround a sky-light of twenty-four feet diameter, intended to admit light into the great rotunda. This work has required a great effort to complete it, from the mass of stone and other materials employed in it, and raised and secured at so great a height.[39]

The outer dome's unusually high profile was at the request of James Monroe and John Quincy Adams, who wished that the Capitol be visible from some distance (Plate 12, Cat. 113). Its bulbous profile was based on a stilted arch, one whose curve begins above the impost line where the dome emerges from the roof (Cat. 105). Few considered the form of Bulfinch's dome an aesthetic success. He himself was unhappy with the result because he recognized that it distorted the profile of the Roman Pantheon dome favored by all the Capitol's architects, including Jefferson (Cat. 106). In 1833, an English visitor found that the "chief architectural ornament of Washington" was "surmounted by a lofty but heavy dome."[40] In the same year, Godfrey T. Vigne felt that Bulfinch's dome "would look a great deal better if it were deeply fluted, like the dome of St. Paul's; at present it would be much better out of the way, as it gives a general appearance of heaviness, to what would otherwise be deservedly thought a very fine building."[41] Bulfinch's dome was sheathed in copper but never gilded, as the dome for his Massachusetts State House (1795–1797) had been (Cat. 104).

Bulfinch must have completed Latrobe's design for the crypt, for which the drawings are lost, as its scenographic spatial qualities and the daring engineering of the slender columns that carry the Rotunda floor speak directly of Latrobe's sensibility. The crypt's forty unfluted Greek Doric columns, arranged in two circles with the outer ring composed of double columns, support airy elliptical groin vaults (Cat. 166). This concentric arrangement, as well as the crisp profiles of the column entablatures, recall the crypt of St. Paul's Cathedral (1675–1711) in London. Such an ecclesiastical model was appropriate because the Capitol's crypt was designed and built with the expectation that it would one day either be Washington's burial place or contain a major monument honoring him; St. Paul's crypt serves as both burial vault and memorial. Undated sketches by John Trumbull show that Bulfinch considered a major spatial interconnection between the crypt and the Rotunda to highlight Washington's monument or cenotaph (Cat. 164). Busby's 1823 engraved plan after a lost Bulfinch drawing depicts a large hole in the center of the Rotunda floor framed by a wide, circular double staircase (Fig. 44; Cat. 163). Busby labeled the Rotunda "Grand Vestibule for Great Public Occasions," indicating that Bulfinch intended to combine Thornton's and Latrobe's proposed functions for the Rotunda. A marble compass rose, set in the center of the crypt's granite floor, now marks the point from which the city's quadrants originate and recalls that the Capitol once served as the place from which state lines were measured.[42]

The architectural merit of Bulfinch's Rotunda derives from its elegantly decorated surfaces, rather than from the exploitation of its spatial and lighting possibilities, as Latrobe had proposed (Cat. 165). During the summer of 1822, while the Rotunda walls were under construction, Bulfinch planned their ornamentation. As he had done previously, the architect prepared at least two alternative designs, offering President James Monroe and the Congressional Committee on Public Buildings a choice. Only his drawing labeled "No. 2"—a cross section of the crypt, Rotunda, and dome—survives (Cat. 167). It shows the railing around the hole left in the Rotunda floor, the division of the Rotunda walls by pilasters into vertical segments, sketches of John Trumbull's Revolutionary War paintings, a frieze of wreaths, and paneled coffers in the dome modeled on those of the Roman Pantheon. The drawing corresponds closely to how the Rotunda was decorated, with the exception of a sculptural panel above the door depicting Roman fasces topped by an American heraldic eagle. On July 8, 1822, Bulfinch wrote to the Italian sculptor Enrico Causici:

> I have long considered that it would be suitable to the purposes of the building, to have 2 tablets in the interior of the Rotundo, in the panel over the east & west doors, one to represent, either the discovery of America by Columbus, or which I should prefer, the landing of Capt. Smith in Virginia; & the other the Declaration of Independence, or the adoption of the Federal Constitution. These bas reliefs would be about 7 feet wide & 10 high.[43]

Bulfinch's introduction of pre-Revolutionary American historical events signaled the passing of the vision of the Capitol's dome and Rotunda as a symbol of national union, the primary preoccupation of Washington and Jefferson. Its new function was to mark the place where the concept of Manifest Destiny was codified. As Euro-Americans moved westward, they justified the displacement of Native Americans on the grounds that they were bringing "civilization" to a savage, untamed world.

Trumbull's four history paintings (eight were originally planned) had been commissioned in 1817 and recount the great civic and military events of the Revolution (Fig. 45; Cat. 168). From the outset of his appointment as architect, Bulfinch corresponded with John Trumbull about the proper placement, framing, and ventilation of the painter's history paintings. Trumbull, himself an amateur architect, had been dismayed that Latrobe's Rotunda was not totally oriented toward his paintings and suggested to Bulfinch several schemes for the architectural division of both the crypt and the Rotunda. The paintings, which measure 12 by 18 feet, were finished over a five-year period: *Declaration of Independence* (1819), *Surrender of Lord Cornwallis at Yorktown* (1820), *Surrender of General Burgoyne at Saratoga* (1822), and *Washington Resigning his Commission* (1824).

The four vertical historiated panels over the doors commissioned by Bulfinch complement Trumbull's paintings. They portray events in pre-Revolutionary American history: *Preservation of John Smith by Pocahontas* (Antonio Capellano, 1825), *Landing of the Pilgrims* (Enrico Causici, 1825), *William Penn's Treaty with the Indians* (Nicolas Gevelot, 1827), and *Daniel Boone Fighting*

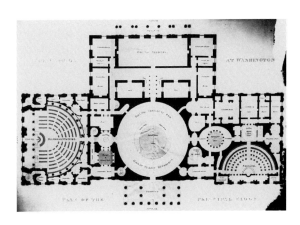

Fig. 44. Charles A. Busby. "The Capitol at Washington. Plan of the Principal Floor," 1823. Library of Congress.

Fig. 45. Alexander Jackson Davis. "Perspective View of Capitol Rotunda," ca. 1832–1834. Avery Architectural and Fine Arts Library, Columbia University in the City of New York.

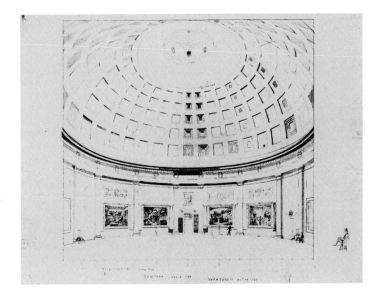

the Indians (Causici, 1826–1827). Between 1840 and 1855, four additional paintings depicting pre-Revolutionary events were placed in the Rotunda: *Baptism of Pocahontas at Jamestown, Virginia, 1613* (John G. Chapman, 1840), *Discovery of the Mississippi by De Soto, 1541* (William H. Powell, 1853), *Embarkation of the Pilgrims at Delft Haven, Holland, July 22nd, 1620* (Robert W. Weir, 1843), and *Landing of Columbus at the Island of Guanahani, West Indies, October 12th, 1492* (John Vanderlyn, 1847). Four of the eight decorative panels above the paintings contain portraits by Francisco Iardella of early explorers who visited North America: John Cabot, Christopher Columbus, René-Robert de La Salle, and Sir Walter Raleigh.[44]

On May 6, 1825, Bulfinch called on President John Quincy Adams with about thirty-six designs submitted by sculptors and architects for the east front tympanum. Adams declined to make a decision because he found none of the entries acceptable. Adams suggested that a jury of three judges be appointed. Members William Thornton, the Washington painter Charles Bird King, and Colonel George Bomford of the Army Ordnance Department decided that no individual entry was worthy of the premium. On May 31, 1825, Adams recorded in his diary:

> Bulfinch and the sculptor [Luigi] Persico came at one o'clock, and we discussed the new design, which was a personification of the United States standing on a throne, leaning upon the Roman fasces, surmounted with the cap of liberty, with Justice at her right hand, blindfolded, holding the suspended balance, and in the other hand an open scroll, and Hercules at her left, seated on a corner of the throne, embracing the fasces, and emblematical of strength; to which were added, separately drawn, and to fill up the space, Plenty seated with her cornucopia, in one corner, and Peace, a flying angel, extending a garland of victory towards America with one hand, and bearing a palm in the other.
>
> These two last figures I advised should be discarded, as well as the Roman fasces and the cap of liberty. The Hercules had also too much of the heathen mythology for my taste, and I proposed to substitute in his place a figure of Hope, with an anchor—a Scriptural image, indicating that this Hope relies upon a Supreme Disposer of events; "which hope we have as an anchor to the soul, sure and steadfast." Instead of the fasces I proposed a pedestal, with 4th July, 1776, inscribed on its base, and 4th March, 1789, upon its upper cornice. The whole design then would represent the American Union founded on the Declaration of Independence and consummated by the organization of the General Government under the Federal Constitution, supported by Justice in the past, and relying upon Hope in Providence for the future. (Fig. 46; Cat. 115)[45]

In 1848, architect Robert Mills evaluated Persico's *Genius of America,* quoting an unnamed source to help explain its meaning:

> The centre figure represents the Genius of America, modestly attired in full drapery, standing on a broad plinth, and holding in her hand an oval shield, inscribed with the letters U.S.A. in the centre, surrounded with a glory. This shield rests on a pedestal, ornamented on the front with an oaken wreath in bas-relief, encircling the words July 4, 1776. Behind the figure rests a spear, and at her foot an eagle, with its wings partially expanded. The head of the Genius, crowned with a star, is inclined in a listening attitude, over her left shoulder, towards the figure standing in this direction, which represents *Hope,* who appears to be addressing the Genius; her right hand and arm being elevated toward the Genius, her left apparently resting on the stock of an anchor, and the hand grasping a part of her drapery. The eager gaze and delighted smile she gives the Genius indicate her earnest plea for the glory and prosperity of the Union. The Genius, however, instead of catching her enthusiasm, points, with sober dignity, to the object standing on her right hand. This is *Justice,* with stern and icy countenance, her eyes lifted

Fig. 46. Luigi Persico. *Genius of America,* 1825–1828. Architect of the Capitol.

towards Heaven, and holding in her right hand a scroll partly unrolled, and displaying, in letters of gold, the words "Constitution of the United States." Her left hand elevates and sustains the scales; neither bandage nor sword are associated with this American Justice; "for, in our free and happy country, justice is clear-sighted, and stands with open countenance, respecting and weighing equally, the rights of all; and it is in this, rather than in her punitive energies, that she is the object of veneration of freemen."

"A moral is intended to be conveyed in this group, that however Hope may flatter, the American people will regard only the prosperity which is founded on public right and the preservation of the Constitution." The figures are all highly finished, unnecessarily so for their great elevation; their execution does great credit to the artist, but the design is *outre;* the idea too complex, difficult to be understood, and not adapted to the place, which requires unity, boldness, and withal, a subject that would be fully comprehended at the first glance of the eye.[46]

By 1834, Persico had also sculpted over-life-size figures of *War* and *Peace* for niches flanking the east entrance to the Rotunda (Cats. 116 and 117). Both were Roman in attire and inspiration—the armor-clad *War* based on Mars and the toga-clad *Peace* modeled on Ceres—personifications that replaced the olive branch and arrow emblems of the Great Seal. Neither figure in either dress or attributes made any specific reference to America. Whereas the subtle implications of Persico's *Genius of America* were perhaps not easily understood by all, the militant and pacific natures of his *War* and *Peace* were obvious, as well as being more readily seen by the Capitol's visitors. Two later sculptural groups placed on the cheek blocks of the east staircase, Persico's *Discovery of America* (1837–1844) and Horatio Greenough's *Rescue* (1837–1853), had overt nationalistic content, as both depicted the on-going racial conflict with Native Americans. They continued the concept of Manifest Destiny begun in 1822 with the pre-Revolutionary themes of the Rotunda's relief sculpture, soon to be reinforced by four new history paintings of America's discovery and settlement.[47]

The Capitol Rotunda has served as the locus for many of America's great national events, particularly those commemorative in nature. The first marked the Marquis de Lafayette's triumphal fortieth anniversary tour of the United States. Lafayette represented a living link between the Revolution, George Washington, and the Capitol. On December 9, 1824, he

Fig. 47. Charles Burton. "View of the Capitol," 1824. Lent by the Metropolitan Museum of Art, New York. Purchase, Joseph Pulitzer Bequest, 1942.

addressed the Senate, and the following day, the House of Representatives. George Washington Parke Custis lent Washington's Revolutionary War tent, which was erected on the Capitol's east portico. Washington mayor Roger C. Weightman began his address honoring Lafayette with the words: "In beholding you again in our country, after a lapse of forty years, and in the Capital of our Nation, on the vestibule of this magnificent temple dedicated to its liberty, and at the door of the tent which, for eight year, formed the principal habitation of the achiever of our freedom . . . the citizens of Washington feel emotion beyond the power of utterance."

For the preliminary version for a leaf in an album of watercolors of the buildings in which he spoke in 1824 that was presented to Lafayette, Charles Burton chose to illustrate the Capitol's west facade (Fig. 47; Cat. 109). He framed it with the double rows of poplars that lined Pennsylvania Avenue between the Capitol and the President's House, destined to be one of the most popular early vantage points because it gave the impression that the Capitol was the focal point of a thriving metropolis (Cat. 237). In reality, there were still log cabins along the perimeter of the Capitol grounds in the late 1820s (Cat. 110). In 1828, Timothy Flint, writing in the *Western Monthly Review,* noted the contrast between the Capitol's splendid architecture and its unkempt setting: "Unenclosed and naked pastures, looking for all the world, like New-England blueberry swamps, spread almost from the foot" of the Capitol.[48]

Gardener John Foy had been hired in 1817 to superintend the "ornamental work on Capitol Square" designed by Latrobe, but by 1832 the landscaping was unfinished, and Foy wrote that if "it is left to me, [it] will be one of the handsomest Squares in the Fashionable World." During the 1830s, the Capitol grounds were transformed by James Maher, the public gardener whose nursery supplied congressmen with flowers. Maher gradually graded, turfed, enlarged, and densely planted the grounds with trees, shrubs, and flowers in a wide variety of specimens, a precursor to proposals in the 1840s to landscape the Mall as a botanical garden (Plate 13, Cat. 112; Cat. 114). Washington had proposed such a garden for the federal city in 1796, and in 1820 one was begun under the auspices of the Columbian Institute on 5 acres at the foot of Capitol Hill. By the winter of 1823, two ponds, a fountain, flower beds, and gravel walks had been laid out, the genesis of the present United States Botanical Garden. Full landscaping of the Mall did not begin until 1851 when Andrew Jackson Downing's proposal for a picturesque design for the Mall and President's Grounds was given presidential approval.[49]

– IV –

"To throw the labor of the artist upon
the shoulders of the President of the United States"

The House and Senate Wings

Much of the interior of the Capitol was designed to be open to the public (Cat. 85). For the legislative chambers, this meant two-story rooms with public galleries overlooking the proceedings on the floor below. The crypt, intended as a pilgrimage place—either Washington's monument or his mausoleum—had to be capable of accommodating crowds while providing support for the Rotunda floor above. The Rotunda itself was perceived from the beginning as a place set apart for specifically public purposes, a "Hall of the People." The connective tissue between these large spaces—vestibules, staircases, hallways—served as a circulation system as well as a buffer between the public and the offices and committee rooms. Beginning in 1808, Benjamin Henry Latrobe used the Capitol's ancillary spaces to create such symbolically significant places as the corncob vestibule and the tobacco-leaf rotunda. Architecturally, he made them directional indicators, but more important, he increased their apparent size through a number of visual devices in order to make the entire Capitol seem larger and more impressive than it really was in comparison with contemporary European public buildings. Multiple entries that led to specific areas, such as two on the south wall that opened directly into staircases going up to the House gallery, contributed to the aggrandizement of the Capitol.

EARLY EVOLUTION OF THE LEGISLATIVE WINGS

Following Renaissance-inspired Anglo-Palladian palace facades, William Thornton's winning design for the exterior walls of the Capitol's wings was a grid of three stories by five bays, arranged hierarchically with the greater importance of the second story indicated by larger, pedimented windows (Cat. 76). His wall pattern within this paradigm was particularly light and elegant, with the center of each five-bay segment on the east and west sides framed by an arch with a round, rather than square, attic window (Plate 14, Cat. 83). Thornton chose for the Capitol's exterior pilasters and columns the rich Corinthian order, with three rows of acanthus leaves beneath central and lateral volutes illustrated by Sir William Chambers in *A Treatise on Civil Architecture* (1759) (Cats. 77 and 78). Throughout the many challenges to Thornton's design during the Capitol's tumultuous early history, this basic wall-window pattern prevailed because Thornton helped oversee the construction of the north wing beginning in 1794, when he was appointed one of the commissioners.

Credit for the idea of dividing the Capitol into three nearly equal zones, with the legislative chambers separated by a politically neutral space, cannot be determined from the textual records, surviving drawings, or competition guidelines. Bilateral wings were the obvious architectural response to the organization of Congress as a bicameral body. Common sense and American traditions probably influenced Washington in his directions to Pierre Charles L'Enfant and Jefferson in his to Stephen Hallet; both architects designed three-part capitols. An architecturally clear separation of the House of Representatives and the Senate continued the tradition of bicameral legislatures in colonial statehouses. Those at Philadelphia and Annapolis had two chambers within a single block divided externally by either tower or dome and separated internally by large central halls. More significantly, Williamsburg's "capitoll," the oldest purposely built statehouse in America, was designed by Governor Francis Nicholson in 1699 and rebuilt in 1751 to have separate, visually distinct wings. The House of Burgesses met on the ground story of the east wing and the Governor's Council on the second story of the west. They were connected by a conference room for joint sessions located on the second story above an arcaded loggia open at ground level. Understandably, the Virginia Capitol provided an important model for Washington and Jefferson, both Virginians whose varied public service often had taken them to Williamsburg before the capital was moved to Richmond in the spring of 1780.

Two features of the Capitol in Williamsburg may have influenced Jefferson in his guidance of the national Capitol's early designs: Hallet's loggias of his precompetition plan of 1791, and the conference room mandated by the competition guidelines. Neither of these was realized, but a third important architectural and symbolic idea, ground-story legislative chambers like those at the House of Burgesses—were built at Jefferson's suggestion. Ground-story halls made the Capitol more accessible, perhaps intentionally reflecting the responsive nature of the national legislature. Jefferson's recollections on April 14, 1811, to Architect of the Capitol Benjamin Henry Latrobe reveal a French source for his thinking:

> Another principle of conduct with me was to admit no innovations on the established plans, but on the strongest grounds. When, therefore, I thought first of placing the floor of the Representative chamber on the level of the basement of the building, and of throwing into its height the cavity of the dome, in the manner of the Halle aux Blèds at Paris, I deemed it due to Dr. Thornton, author of the plan of the Capitol, to consult him on the change. He not only consented, but appeared heartily to approve of the alteration.[1]

The timing of Jefferson's decision is unclear, for the call for legislative rooms of "full elevation" was stated in the competition guidelines. Most competitors responded with two-story buildings, but Thornton's winning design was three stories tall, with the double-story chambers spanning the second and third floors. Although Thornton's original drawings are lost, Don Alexander Hawkins has reconstructed their general character from Thornton's description written in April 1793 and from correspondence between Thornton and Jefferson and between Jefferson and Washington in July. Alterations in 1794 at Washington's suggestion to

James Hoban's design for the President's House eliminated the full-height basement story, with the former second story lowered to just a few steps above ground level. Pragmatic issues of cost and stylistic ones of a new architectural taste may have been joined by the desire to make the federal government's two important structures physically, visually, and symbolically more accessible.[2]

Thornton's chambers were rectangular rooms with large semicircular apses projecting from the north and south ends of the building (Fig. 48; Cat. 64). That in the House was to contain the rostrum and may have provided the precedent for the renovated legislative chambers in Philadelphia's Congress Hall, where apses for speakers' podiums were added in 1793 and 1794. Thornton filled the entire envelope of the Capitol's north wing with his hall for the House of Representatives. Its suspended U-shaped public gallery facing the Speaker's dias was very spacious, a reflection of the popularity of House debates. Thornton's Senate chamber, in the south wing, had no gallery because Senate debates were not open to the public until 1795. Thornton did, however, plan that a small gallery could eventually be built above the Senate's north door.

As a result of the conference convened by Washington on July 15, 1793, Thornton's interiors were replaced by ones designed by his chief rival, Stephen Hallet. The shape of Hallet's chambers was one of several French-inspired aspects of the Capitol's design. For his earliest designs, Hallet planned a colonnade inside rectangular chambers to define a central hippodrome-shaped floor or rostrum, with stepped seating to rise in tiers behind the columns. A similar speaking-and-seating plan had been adopted in August 1789 by the architect Pierre Adrian Pâris to accommodate the French National Assembly in an existing rectangular room at Versailles. The Roman hippodrome, or circus—formed by semicircles added to the long ends of a rectangle—was currently fashionable in French architecture. Its political use in antiquity had been the subject of a series of lectures by the Abbé Brothier delivered in Paris between 1780 and 1784 and published in 1793. This shape was modified to an elliptical room for the House chamber and a half-ellipse for the Senate in the conference plan.[3]

Contrary to Thornton's scheme, Hallet allocated the north wing for the Senate and the south for the House of Representatives, probably to take advantage of the light and heat of the southern exposure for the larger room. Two surviving sections by Hallet for his third and

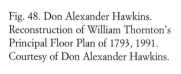

Fig. 48. Don Alexander Hawkins.
Reconstruction of William Thornton's
Principal Floor Plan of 1793, 1991.
Courtesy of Don Alexander Hawkins.

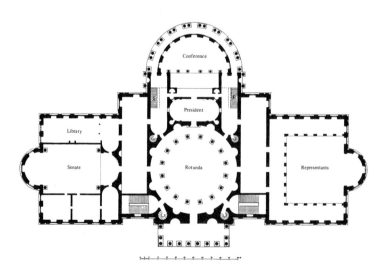

fourth competition designs, done in October 1792 and January 1793, show that he placed the legislative halls at ground level. Yet both of Hallet's elevations that match these sections maintain the traditional three-story organization of basement, main story, and attic. He solved this architectural solecism in his fifth design, which was made after Thornton was declared the competition winner. Hallet introduced a fourth story, a sub-basement, and sandwiched two main floors between it and the attic story. He thus satisfied the rules of architectural propriety by having the exterior reflect the relative importance of interior spaces: two main stories encompassed the double-level legislative chambers, the lower reserved for congressmen, the upper for the public.

Thornton, writing to Washington on November 2, 1795, called on his own knowledge in citing an important instance of ground-level chambers in an Irish Palladian building: "Mr. Hoban & I have made no material Alteration that can affect the Sections of the principal Rooms made by Mr. Hallet, indeed a Section of the Irish Parliament Hall would give a sufficient Idea to any Man conversant with Architecture of the intention of the Halls."[4] Such a section had been engraved by Rowland Omer and published in 1767 (see Fig. 16). The House of Commons was an octagonal chamber buried in the center of the Irish Parliament House (1728–1739), designed by Edward Lovett Pearce. Like Hallet's Senate and House chambers, it was a domed room that rose through two stories, with an arcade on the ground level supporting a colonnade above. Seating on the entry level for the members of the House of Commons was stepped, as in theaters; balconies behind the colonnades accommodated visitors. The ground-level House of Commons matched the exterior of the building, the ground story of which was its main level.

Thornton's reference was to an Irish example, but the room was designed by Hallet and argues for a parallel French source. Among France's great Neoclassical buildings, Jules Hardouin Mansart's chapel at Versailles (1678–1689) initiated in France the motif of a double-story gallery with columns supported by an arcade. The upper gallery of the chapel was specifically reserved for the king; those in the Capitol's legislative chambers provided seating for the public. It is likely that Hallet, and possibly Jefferson, knew about the chapel's spatial and social divisions.

Jefferson was too knowledgeable about architectural theory and practice to ignore the traditional exterior emphasis of important floors by large, more elaborately framed windows. One therefore supposes that he intended the second-story galleries to be read from the exterior as the Capitol's most important spaces, areas specifically reserved for the American people. If this supposition is correct, his ground-level chambers were one of Jefferson's many statements about America's new political and cultural system to be expressed by the Capitol's architecture. His ability to break free of conventional architectural thought at the conceptual level of planning, yet to strictly adhere to correct classical ornamental details, characterized his other architectural designs, both public and private.

Two professionals who followed Hallet as the Capitol's superintending architect questioned the relationship of the building's exterior to its interior. John Trumbull, who suggested George Hadfield as Hallet's replacement in 1794, had only the highest praise for the young architect's talents. He wrote to his brother Jonathan Trumbull on September 23, 1794, from London: "Before He went abroad He was considered as possessing Talents & Knowledge in Architecture superior to any of the young men his contemporaries; He has not misimprov'd his time in Italy; & is now considered by Mr. [Benjamin] West the President of the Academy, as well as by others, to possess the *Theory of Civil Architecture,* more perfectly than any young man in England."[5]

Hadfield's unhappy three-year tenure as the supervising architect of the Capitol is the least well understood because of the paucity of written and visual records. In 1806, Latrobe recorded in his journal:

> Too young to possess experience, and educated more in the room of design, than in the practical execution of great works, he was no match for the rogues then employed in the construction of the public buildings, or for the charlatans of architecture who had designed them. All that he proposed however proved him a man of correct taste, of perfect theoretic knowledge, and of bold integrity. He waged a long war against the ignorance, and the dishonesty of the Commissioners and of the workmen. But the latter prevailed, for General Washington, led by his feelings, and possessing no knowledge of this subject sided against him. Thus has Hadfield lost the most precious period of his life, that of the practical study of the profession in the first Works he might have executed, and loiters here, ruined in fortune, in temper, and in reputation. Nor will his irritable pride, and neglected studies ever permit him to take the station in the Art, which his elegant taste, and excellent talents ought to have obtained.[6]

On assuming his position in October 1795, Hadfield immediately proposed lowering the Capitol's elevation a half-story to reflect on the exterior the floor level of the House and Senate chambers. He suggested replacing Thornton's east front portico, which consisted of columns topped by a pediment and set above an arcade, with a broad flight of stairs leading to a lower and wider portico. He proposed inserting an octagonal drum between the dome and the roof and suggested pushing above the cornice line the smaller domes covering the congressional halls, domes that Jefferson wanted contained within the building's mass. Hadfield's changes reflect the thinking of a well-trained professional architect concerned with the volumetric realities of interlocking the Capitol's plans with its facades and sections.

Another set of unsigned and undated drawings of the Capitol's east and west facades, probably made by Hadfield, show another possibility of how to express on the Capitol's exterior walls the reality of its interior spaces, while conforming to the existing foundations (see Fig. 35). This solution was to eliminate all rustication that indicated "basement" and to elaborately frame the ground-story windows while treating those on the second and recessed third stories more plainly. Latrobe's two-story tobacco-leaf rotunda, erected between 1815 and 1817 adjacent to the Supreme Court and Senate chambers, is a circular colonnade set on an arcade, the only echo of the unusual architectural arrangement of the first Senate chamber (Cat. 128; Plate 15, Cat. 131).

FIRST SENATE CHAMBER

While most of the changes to the Capitol's exterior remained speculative paper designs, its more numerous interior alterations were real (Cat. 87). The Capitol's north wing, finished by November 1800, was completed first because its number and variety of rooms could "accommodate both Houses of Congress, during the present state of representation." Elevation, plan, section drawings, and sketches of details have not survived to show how the original Senate chamber and its ancillary rooms really looked. Rather, its appearance has to be pieced together from fragmented descriptions, passing remarks, and reference to architectural traditions and contemporary practice.[7]

The only descriptions of the first Senate chamber are newspaper accounts and official progress reports: Hallet's are nonexistent; Hadfield's are cursory; but Hoban's are more informative. On November 18, 1799, Hoban reported on the status of the semielliptical room:

The Senate Chamber, 86 by 48 feet, and 41 feet high, with its lobby and gallery are floored; the door-ways are trimmed with framed jamb-linings, soffits and architraves; the windows, straight and circular, are trimmed with backs, elbows, soffits and architraves; the sashes are fitted to run double, with brass pullies, metal shieves and patent fastenings; the arcade piers, on a semi-ellip-tic plan, are trimmed with panelled work, and the columns raised on the arcade, sixteen in num-ber with two semi-pilasters to correspond, of the ancient ionic order, two feet three inches in diameter; the entablature is finished with stucco, ornaments, and the walls and ceiling finished, two coats of mortar floated, and one coat of stucco; the sulley seats are framing, to form an amphitheatre one hundred and ten feet in circumference.[8]

Latrobe described the Senate in 1808 before he dismantled it as having a public gallery supported by a plastered wood and brick arcade "placed in [an] irregular curve, partly elip-tical, partly circular." The Ionic columns of the gallery were plastered wood, and wood pan-eling decorated the floor-level walls. Almost certainly, some allegorical decorations existed, but no record of their subjects survives. The Senate wing's north-south axis contained in its center a double flying staircase that survived until 1814, when British troops burned the Capi-tol. It was set within oval walls that now enclose Latrobe's tobacco-leaf rotunda, the only important interior space that dates before Latrobe began rebuilding the north wing in 1808.[9]

BENJAMIN HENRY LATROBE'S NORTH (SENATE) WING

Latrobe brought an advanced and sophisticated Neoclassical taste, as well as a profound knowledge of the history and tectonics of architecture, to the task that Jefferson set before him on March 6, 1803. Although Latrobe, like his predecessors, believed that the Capitol commission would bring him renown, near the end of his life he repeated his initial evalua-tion: that he had merely supervised the realization of another's design. He believed that he had managed only to overcome innumerable difficulties rather than make his own positive architectural contribution. Posterity disputes Latrobe's assertion, as the changes he wrought in the Capitol brought coherence and meaning to its interiors and focused attention on the central rotunda and dome with his unusual and compelling east portico.

On April 4, 1803, within a month of being hired, Latrobe wrote Jefferson a lengthy report in which he proffered his evaluation of the Capitol's design. Like Hadfield and Hoban, Latrobe considered the contradictory relationship between the exterior elevations and the legislative chambers to be a grave error in architectural taste and propriety. Latrobe acknowl-edged, however, that construction was too far advanced to correct the fault. Due to a variety of circumstances, he did eventually rebuild the interiors of both wings, raising the legislative chambers to the second floor; his ground-floor Supreme Court is the permanent reminder of one of the Capitol's earliest executed politico-architectural ideals.[10]

In early May 1803, John Lenthall, Latrobe's clerk of the works, completed a survey of the north wing, which revealed that the 108- by 84-foot rectangle was 16 inches out of square; windows and pilasters on its east and west facades were not opposite each other, as they should have been. Latrobe's reaction was to plan the west face of the proposed south wing to correspond with the west face of the existing north wing, and then to match the south wing's east face to its west one. Thus the irregularity between the two wings would have been visible only on the east front, barely noticeable because Latrobe's elaborately sculptural east staircase and portico was to draw attention away from the wings. Lenthall's survey also revealed that the north wing's unlit and unventilated cellar had produced rotting timbers, and numerous roof leaks had seriously damaged walls and ceilings. Much of the 1803 building season was occupied with emptying the cellar of rubble and constructing furnaces to heat the Senate chamber.[11]

As early as August 31, 1805, Latrobe reported to Jefferson that the north wing "must some day or other be compleatly *gutted,* and solidly constructed in the interior." Cracking plaster on the wood columns in the Senate chamber apparently prompted Jefferson to suggest to Latrobe that the two-story Senate be divided horizontally by placing a floor between the arcade and the colonnade. By mid-August 1807, Latrobe was redesigning the north wing's interiors, "pursuing the *eventual* plan" Jefferson had approved. Earlier in the year, large sections of rotting roof and floor timbers had had to be replaced. Latrobe urged the president to "present to congress fair drawings of the Senate Chamber, as proposed to be executed" in order to stimulate interest in and approval of the extensive changes. On September 8, 1807, Jefferson wrote to Latrobe that Congress "will consent to nothing more than vaulting the floor of the N. wing, making a floor of the Senate in the level of their present gallery, and heightening and decorating the room." When work began, however, Latrobe found that dry rot had invaded many supporting timbers, requiring that large sections of the interior be replaced.[12]

In the spring of 1808, Latrobe began renovating the old Senate and its adjoining hallways, locating the Senate on the upper story and the Supreme Court below. On April 26, Jefferson ordered him to "leave the present Senate chamber exactly in it's [*sic*] present state [and] lay a floor where the gallery now is to be the floor of the future Senate chamber." Jefferson wished to "prevent the possibility of a deficit of a single dollar this year." (In 1807, Latrobe had overspent congressional appropriations by $51,500 in order to ready the south wing for occupation by the House of Representatives.) Jefferson admonished Latrobe: "It is so contrary to the principles of our government, which make the representatives of the people the sole arbiters of the public expence, and do not permit any work to be forced on them on a larger scale than their judgment deems adapted to the circumstances of the nation."[13]

Latrobe's estimates of time and money to complete various portions of the building were continually being adjusted, to the dismay of Jefferson and Congress. Throughout his first decade as the Architect of the Capitol, Latrobe was repeatedly plagued by the lack of suitable building materials or had great difficulty in procuring them either in the United States or from Europe. Added to this was an unreliable labor force resulting from uncertain congressional funding and a general shortage of workmen, particularly trained stonemasons for whose services architects of stone buildings in Baltimore, Philadelphia, New York, and Albany were in constant competition. These continual problems with the north wing added to the Capitol's already considerable expense.

These vexations were trivial compared with the tragedy that struck the Capitol on September 19, 1808, when a section of the main arch in the Supreme Court chamber fell and killed Lenthall (Cat. 122). Throughout the summer, new arched and vaulted rooms had been erected on each floor. The Supreme Court's unusual vaulted construction contributed to the misfortune. A week before the accident, Latrobe wrote to Jefferson: "I will observe that the two domes of the Court room and Senate chamber, with the cylindrical additions, would cover the Hall of Representatives within a few feet in length and that the whole work is by far the most solid and on the largest scale that I have ever seen of modern attempts at vaulting, exclusive of bridges."[14] To save time and expense, Lenthall had used an alternative method of constructing the room's complex brick vaults and stone arches than that stipulated by Latrobe. When the wood centering supporting the main arch was removed, the arch twisted and fell.

Fig. 49. Benjamin Henry Latrobe. General View of the Supreme Court, ca. 1976. Architect of the Capitol.

Latrobe's first courtroom was divided into three separate areas: the semicircular main space, with a span of 60 feet; a curved passage behind it; and the long rectangular retiring room along the east wall, which was 56 feet long. After the accident, the single barrel vault along the east wall was replaced by the present arrangement: three small barrel vaults supported on their open ends by six massive stone Greek Doric columns (Fig. 49; Cat. 120). The passage at the back of the room is separated from the courtroom by plain curved piers from which spring stone ribs that converge on a semicircular rib; shallow butterfly vaults between the ribs contribute to a multifaceted and remarkably light and airy ceiling. The columns and moldings were Greek in inspiration and the vaulting Roman, but the principle of stone ribs was medieval (Plate 16, Cat. 123). Latrobe's willingness to combine three distinct traditions to create unique rooms at the Capitol was integral to his interpretation of Neoclassicism as eclectic historicism.

Latrobe's greatness as an architect is particularly evident in the Supreme Court and its surrounding hallways. He repeatedly used layered and interpenetrating spaces, coupled with varied ceiling shapes, to achieve monumentality and spaciousness within the Capitol's relatively small interiors. The Supreme Court vestibule, a small rectangular room with one semicircular end, is subtly divided into several units defined by half-domes, domes, and barrel and groin vaults (Fig. 50; Cat. 129). These separate ceilings are carried by the six famous corncob and -stalk columns, which stand in front of unfluted pilasters (Cat. 130). This layering creates the illusion that the walls are receding rather than the columns intruding into the room. Archways instead of doors and varied ceiling shapes and heights increase the sense of continuously flowing space, giving the impression of a monumentally scaled building. The Supreme Court chamber and corncob vestibule exemplify Latrobe's dictum that "a graceful and refined simplicity is the highest achievement of taste and of art," addressed to Congress on November 28, 1806. With great economy of surface ornament, Latrobe achieved the most magnificent suite of rooms then existing in America primarily through their shapes and spatial arrangements.[15]

Fig. 50. Benjamin Henry Latrobe. "Corn Capital Vestibule to the Supreme Court of 1808," ca. 1976. Architect of the Capitol.

Fig. 51. Benjamin Henry Latrobe. "Details of the Upper Columns in the Gallery of the Entrance of the Chamber of the Senate, U[nited] States," 1809. Library of Congress.

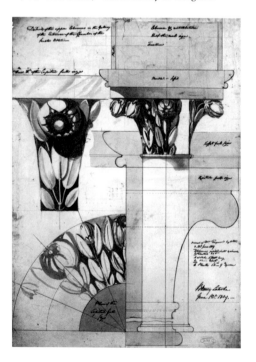

The Capitol's famous American orders were designed by Latrobe as a counterpoint to the European tradition of national orders. The ancient Doric, Ionic, and Corinthian orders carried place names that the Roman architectural writer Vitruvius in the *Ten Books of Architecture* associated with the character of the Greek locales (and peoples) for which they were named. During and after the Renaissance, national symbols or emblematic devices were incorporated into national orders, such as the cock, France's national bird, and the globe, in recognition of Spain's explorers. Latrobe, perhaps at Jefferson's urging, revived the ancient practice of using native plants as the basis of his three American orders.

Latrobe's choice of uniquely American plants—corn, tobacco, and magnolia—probably went beyond simply expressing the country's agricultural richness, but followed Vitruvius's interpretation of the orders as expressions of peoples as well as places. Both corn and tobacco had been domesticated and cultivated by Native Americans and were very important in their cultures. In addition, corn, as a food staple, may have represented American farmers, while tobacco, a commercial crop, symbolized American merchants (Cats. 133 and 134). Jefferson, for instance, referred to the corn order on October 10, 1809, as the "Cerealian capital," in recognition of its nature as a foodstuff. A magnolia was the first American tree to be planted at the Royal Botanical Gardens at Kew near London in 1740 (Fig. 51; Cat. 139). It may have been added to the triad of indigenous American plants to represent America's arts and sciences. Latrobe probably recognized that for most Americans these native plants were potentially more meaningful allusions than were the classical personifications of Ceres to represent agriculture and Mercury for commerce proposed by many of the entrants in the Capitol competition in 1792. The beauty and uniqueness of each of these botanical specimens may also have been planned as permanent parts of the Capitol to answer some European naturalists who maintained that the flora and fauna of the New World were inferior to European species. In his *Notes on the State of Virginia* (1785), Jefferson had heatedly refuted Georges Buffon's assertion in his *Histoire naturelle* (1749–1788) that "nature is less active, less energetic on one side of the globe than she is on the other."[16]

The corn order for the Supreme Court vestibule was Latrobe's first design, carved in 1809 by Giuseppe Franzoni, one of the two Italian sculptors imported from Italy in 1808 at Jefferson's suggestion to execute the Capitol's decorative and emblematic sculpture. The corncob vestibule was undamaged by the fire of 1814, but Latrobe's successor, Charles Bulfinch, altered its picturesque sequence of openings by cutting a second arch opposite its east door. On August 28, 1809, Latrobe sent

Jefferson, now retired to Monticello, a model of the corncob capital and suggested that the former president use it as the base for a sundial. Seven years later, on August 27, 1816, Jefferson sent Latrobe a sketch of the corncob capital supporting a globe that he had designed to serve as the sundial. In 1881, Latrobe's son, John H. B. Latrobe, recalled: "In 1832, I saw it, not in plaster, but in the freestone of which the old Capitol is built. It was then in a sort of loggia that extended from the main building at Monticello." Its whereabouts is unknown.[17]

Latrobe's substitution in 1816 of the double-story tobacco-leaf rotunda for the north wing's flying staircase brought to its central circulation spine a spatially exciting interlude that recalled the colonnade-above-arcade motif of the first Senate chamber. Tobacco leaves had been used in America as both decoration and symbol. Original plaster ceilings at Drayton Hall (1738), near Charleston, South Carolina, are decorated with a design of tobacco leaves, perhaps one of many tobacco-growing plantations to be so ornamented. A banner carried in Philadelphia's federal procession in 1788 was decorated with "a tobacco plant with thirteen leaves, ten in perfection, three not finished (signifying the states which had not yet ratified the Constitution)." Latrobe designed the tobacco-leaf and -flower order for the sixteen rotunda columns, he wrote to Jefferson, to have "an intermediate effect approaching the character of the Corinthian order"; the rotunda is located adjacent to the Ionic Senate. (The corn cob capital's outline is similar to that of ancient Doric orders; Latrobe's corn order on the ground floor is located next to the Doric Supreme Court.) The tobacco-leaf capitals were sculpted by the newly arrived Italian sculptor Antonio Iardella because Franzoni had died in 1815. Latrobe planned to paint their leaves "faint brown." Latrobe sent a model carved in stone of the tobacco order to Jefferson at Monticello, where it is extant.[18]

Latrobe did not ignore the power of allegorical sculpture to convey important abstract ideas, although he often expressed doubt about its ability to convey its correct meaning to the common man. In 1809, he agreed to pay Franzoni an extra $200 to model a figure of Justice for the Supreme Court, the work to be done on Sundays and in the evenings. After Giuseppe Franzoni's death in 1815, his brother Carlo carried out the commission; two preliminary sketches survive, but none for the executed work (Fig. 52; Cats. 125 and 126). Carlo Franzoni's plaster relief was placed in the semicircular lunette on the west wall of the Supreme Court in May 1817. It is a seated figure of Justice holding scales and leaning on a sword, accompanied by an eagle guarding law books and a winged youth holding a tablet inscribed "The Constitution of the U.S." crowned by a rising sun. Robert Mills did not find the design acceptable, identifying what was probably meant to be the Genius of the Constitution as Fame. In 1848, he wrote, "This design is in bad taste, and should be corrected by obliterating the caricature figure of Fame, with its Sun; then the figure of Justice will appear to some advantage, and the design be passable."[19]

Latrobe planned additional sculpture for the Supreme Court, but it is not certain if it was executed: "In the Court room was a symbolical figure of Justice, and on the block of the Columns was a head of Minerva (wisdom) to the right and of Justice (blinded) to the left." Latrobe's drawing of September 26, 1808, of details of the Supreme Court vaults, shows scales of justice decorating the impost blocks above the Doric columns.[20]

While Latrobe was rebuilding the Senate chamber in 1808, he had the long rectangular room on the west side of the north wing redecorated by the painter George Bridport for the interim accommodation of the Senate. Bridport's watercolor shows a brilliantly colored room ornamented with several of America's widely accepted symbols (Plate 17, Cat. 152). Wreaths

Fig. 52. Guiseppe or Carlo Franzoni. *Justice,* ca. 1809–1815. The Historical Society of Washington, D.C.

enclosing the state seals were in the lower entablature, and stars in the one above the gallery; fasces topped by liberty caps flanked the rostrum.

Latrobe was justly proud of his first Senate chamber. It was decorated with his magnolia-flower order, which was eliminated when the room was enlarged (Plate 18, Cat. 137). Although part of the arch in the Supreme Court had fallen in September 1808, the corresponding one in the new Senate, above the Supreme Court, remained firm. At the urging of the workmen, however, Latrobe consented to take down about one-third of the Senate's half-dome while repairs were under way on the ground story. By September 8, 1809, the upper dome had been rebuilt, and Latrobe boasted to President James Madison: "This vault is one of the most extraordinary ever attempted, as to *span* and *altitude,* being a segment of a Dome 110 feet diameter supported by less strength of walling than any other arch, in modern or ancient times with which I am acquainted."[21] Latrobe's pride in this achievement was short-lived. He described the damage to the north wing wrought by the August 1814 fire in a letter to Jefferson dated July 12, 1815: "In the North wing the beautiful Doric Columns which surrounded the supreme Court room have shared the fate of the Corinthian Columns of the Hall of Representatives and in the Senate Chamber the Marble polished Columns of 14 feet Shafts in one block are burnt to lime and have fallen down. All but the Vaults is ruined. They stand a most magnificent ruin."[22] Latrobe deeply regretted that the enlargement of the Senate chamber meant dismantling the brick half-dome. However, forty-four seats were needed to accommodate the senators from the sixteen states and those to come from the Michigan, Illinois, Indiana, and Mississippi territories entering the union as well as from future states.

Latrobe intended in 1815 to erect another permanent brick vault over the Senate chamber, but he was forced to build a half-dome framed in wood with plaster coffers (replaced by cast steel in 1901) (Fig. 53; Cat. 135). The wood dome did allow him to experiment with ways to bring more light into a domed room than that admitted through a cupola, yet avoid the hazards of skylights. His solution was to design a new hemispherical ceiling punctured by a series of small circular windows that formed a half-ring around a large semicircular window. Light from an east-facing lay light, an upright semicircular window, and from the large cupola in the center of the dome entered obliquely through a series of vertical windows rather than horizontally through one concentrated central oculus, or eye. The natural light that once flooded the Senate would have been abundant, but softly diffused by this ingenious double shell.

In rebuilding the Senate, Latrobe followed the same basic semicircular pattern as in his earlier rooms, with a screen of columns separating the chamber itself from a retiring area, or private lobby, along the east wall. The column shafts were of mottled gray Potomac breccia, a rich, striking limestone that resembles marble found in Loudoun County, Maryland, that Latrobe had quarried specifically for the Capitol in 1815. Their Ionic capitals in white Carrara marble were carved in Italy and modeled on those of the Erectheum, on the Athenian Acropolis, one of many examples in the Capitol of Latrobe's preference for Greek architectural details (Cat. 136).

For his first Senate, Latrobe had designed six caryatids, female figures used as columns, to support the back of the public gallery along the east wall. At least some were executed in stone by Giuseppi Franzoni, who carved them during the congressional recess in the summer of 1812. Franzoni's proposal, dated July 21, 1812, estimated the cost of each figure, apparently in relation to the ornateness of its insignia: Bellona, $125; Agriculture and Commerce, $150 each; Science, $175; Minerva, $200; and Art, $400. They were destroyed in the fire of 1814. Latrobe noted in a letter to Thomas Law, husband of Washington's adopted granddaughter Eliza Custis, on November 10, 1816, that these Senate caryatids had represented "arts, Commerce, Agriculture, Science, Military force, and civil government: representations in matter, of Spiritual essences. Personifications of immaterial qualities, and operations."[23]

When Latrobe began the enlargement of the Senate chamber in 1816, he was free of Jefferson's restraining hand and changed both the position and the meaning of the caryatids. In his design, they were brought forward to form a balcony rail for the upper of two public galleries along the east wall, and their number increased to at least thirteen, perhaps as many as seventeen. In reply to Law's criticism of them, Latrobe defended the new caryatids as representations of the states because the Senate was the "assembly of the states," in contrast to the House of Representatives, the body that directly represented the people. Latrobe went on to enumerate historical examples of "national decoration," concluding:

Fig. 53. Benjamin Henry Latrobe. "Old Senate Chamber," 1815–1817. Architect of the Capitol.

> If then it is the intention of architectural writing to record events, or to perpetuate sentiments, national customs, or private manners, and it is admitted, that such records are worthy of the expense they may occasion, the consideration of the *Character,* in which the record shall be written and of the style is the only one before us. It may indeed be said that as good Laws may be made in a Wigwam, as in the Capitol, and that all decoration is useless, and all history mere idle amusement. You however who admit Corinthian columns without Censure will not, I presume make that assertion.[24]

In 1842, former Librarian of Congress George Watterston described these second caryatids, sculpted by Carlo Franzoni, in *A New Guide to Washington:* "[T]he emblematic figures of the old thirteen States, decorated with their peculiar insignia, and the models were actually prepared by one of the Italian artists whom he had engaged to come to this country: but a neglect or refusal on the part of Congress to make the necessary appropriations defeated his designs, and the plaster models were afterwards thrown aside and destroyed."[25] Latrobe's son, prominent Baltimore lawyer John H. B. Latrobe, recalled in 1881 some of the details of the caryatids representing the states: "figures of North and South Carolina, represented as sisters, the arm of one around the neck of the other; also, Massachusetts and Maine,—a mother leading her child—for Maine was as yet a district only."[26]

THE LIBRARY OF CONGRESS

The Library of Congress was housed in the Capitol until a separate building was opened in 1897. In the original north wing, it was located on the second floor overlooking the Mall. In 1808, Latrobe redesigned the library to be a two-and-a-half story room sunk 5 feet below the second floor (Fig. 54; Cat. 140). Its southern end was semicircular, and stacks were located on balconies around its perimeter. The library's expansive size and shape would have contributed to the Capitol's spatial fluidity and internal grandeur, two of Latrobe's primary architectural goals. In addition, his major underlying symbolic purpose would have been furthered by the library's exotic decoration. It was the first example in America of the Egyptian Revival style, designed just six years after Dominique Vivant Denon's illustrated *Voyage dans la Haute Egypte pendant les campagnes du général Bonaparte* was published in Paris. In Latrobe's library, lotus and papyrus columns complemented wall panels and fireplaces with battered (sloping) sides and cavetto (concave) cornices (Cat. 141). He adopted the Egyptian style about the same time he designed the corn order; the variety of Egyptian floriate capitals may well have stimulated Latrobe to think specifically about American orders based on its wide variety of unique native trees and plants.

Fig. 54. Benjamin Henry Latrobe. "Design of the Library of Congress of the United States, North Wing of the Capitol," 1808. Library of Congress.

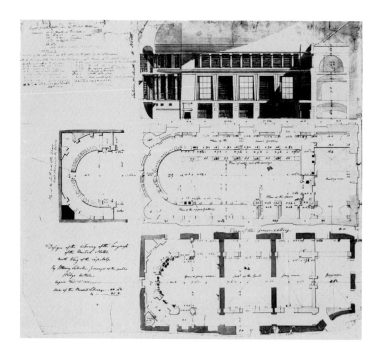

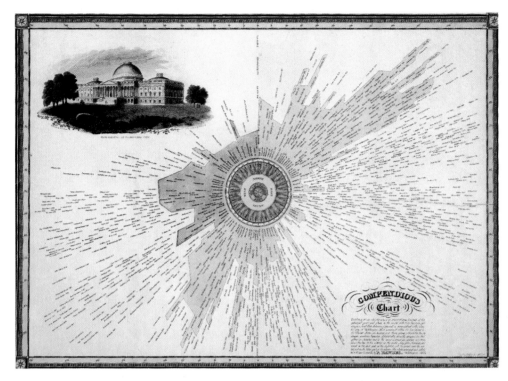

[Plate 1]

225 Thomas Doughty. "Compendious Chart" (Washington, D.C.: P. Hawkes, 1827). Map. 21 ⅜ x 30 ⅜ in. Geography and Map Division, Library of Congress.

[Plate 2]

108 John Rubens Smith. [West Front of the Capitol with Gatehouses], ca. 1828. Watercolor on paper. 15 ½ x 21 in. John Rubens Smith Collection, Prints and Photographs Division, Library of Congress. Gift of the Madison Council and Mrs. Joseph Carson.

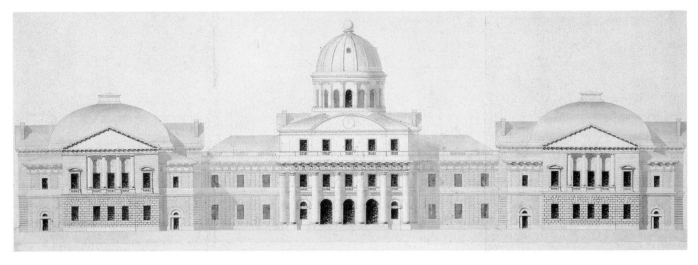

[Plate 3]

57 Stephen Hallet. [Elevation of Third Design for the Capitol], 1792. Ink and watercolor on paper. 14 ⅝ x 45 ½ in. Neg. nos. LC-USZ62-13234, LC-USZC4-221. Prints and Photographs Division, Library of Congress.

[Plate 4]

66 Stephen Hallet. [Cross Section Through the Conference Room of Fifth Design for the Capitol], 1793. Watercolor on paper. 19 x 27 ¾ in. Neg. no. LC-USZC4-1094. Prints and Photographs Division, Library of Congress.

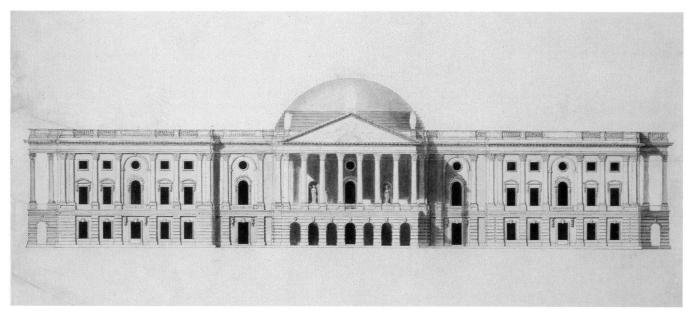

[Plate 5]
72 William Thornton. [Revised East Elevation, Capitol Design], 1795–1797. Watercolor on paper. 14 ¾ x 24 ⅜ in. Neg. no. LC-USZC4-112. Prints and Photographs Division, Library of Congress.

[Plate 6]
73 William Thornton. [Revised West Elevation of the Capitol], ca. 1795–1797. Watercolor on paper. 15 x 24 ¼ in. Neg. nos. LC-USZ62-4712, LC-USZC4-113. Prints and Photographs Division, Library of Congress.

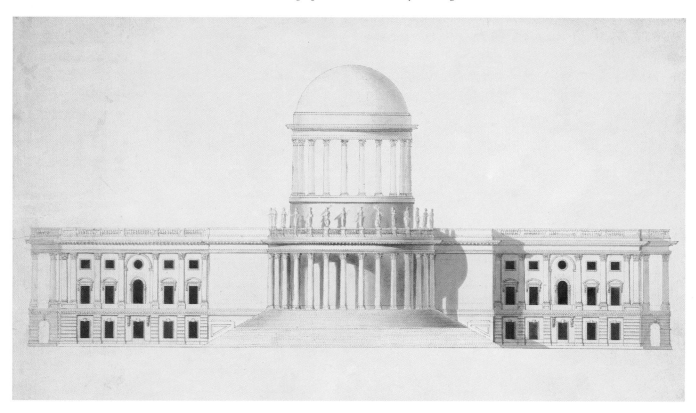

[Plate 9]

94 Benjamin Henry Latrobe. [South Elevation of the Capitol with Propylaea], ca. 1811. Watercolor on paper. 19 ¼ x 30 ⅛ in. Neg. nos. LC-USZ62-4710, LC-USZC4-197. Prints and Photographs Division, Library of Congress.

[Plate 10]

96 Benjamin Henry Latrobe. [Figure of Athena as American Liberty], ca. 1811. Watercolor on paper. 27 ¹¹⁄₁₆ x 18 ¹¹⁄₁₆ in. Neg. nos. USZ62-20860, LC-USZC4-153. Prints and Photographs Division, Library of Congress.

Opposite page

[Plate 7]

88 Benjamin Henry Latrobe. [General View of the Capitol from the Northeast], 1806. Watercolor on paper. 19 ⅜ x 27 ¼ in. Neg. no. LC-USC4-1090. Prints and Photographs Division, Library of Congress.

[Plate 8]

95 Benjamin Henry Latrobe. [West Elevation of the Capitol with Propylaea], ca. 1811. Watercolor on paper. 19 ⅜ x 29 ⅞ in. Neg. nos. LC-USZ62-13241, LC-USZC4-276. Prints and Photographs Division, Library of Congress.

[Plate 11]
111 John Rubens Smith. [West Front of the Capitol], ca. 1828. Watercolor on paper. 15 ½ x 21 in. Neg. no. LC-USZC4-3579. John Rubens Smith Collection, Prints and Photographs Division, Library of Congress. Gift of the Madison Council and Mrs. Joseph Carson.

[Plate 12]
113 Russell Smith. "Capitol from Mr. Elliot's Garden," ca. 1839. Oil on paper. 8 ½ x 11 ¾ in. Architect of the Capitol. Donated by U.S. Capitol Historical Society.

[Plate 13]
112 John Rubens Smith. [East Front of the Capitol], ca. 1828. Watercolor on paper. 16 ½ x 23 ¼ in. John Rubens Smith Collection, Prints and Photographs Division, Library of Congress. Gift of the Madison Council and Mrs. Joseph Carson.

[Plate 14]
83 William Birch. "View of the Capitol," 1800. Watercolor on paper. 8 ⅜ x 11 ¼ in. Neg. no. LC-USZC4-247. Prints and Photographs Division, Library of Congress.

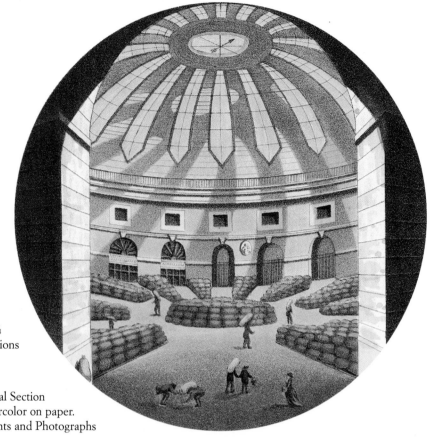

[Plate 20]
150 "Halle aux Bleds." Opposite page 21
in *Picturesque Views of Public Edifices in
Paris* (London: Gale, Curtis, Fenner, and
Samuel Leigh, 1814). Aquatint in book. 4 ⅜
in. diameter. Rare Book and Special Collections
Division, Library of Congress.

[Plate 21]
144 Benjamin Henry Latrobe. [Longitudinal Section
of the Hall of Representatives], 1804. Watercolor on paper.
13 ⅝ x 22 in. Neg. no. LC-USZC4-225. Prints and Photographs
Division, Library of Congress.

[Plate 22]
253 "The National Tobacco Company,"
1868. Tobacco label. 16 ½ x 11 ¼ in.
Neg. no. LC-USZC2-1879. Prints and
Photographs Division, Library of
Congress.

[Plate 23]
171 Alexander Jackson Davis. "Basement Plan of the Capitol," 1832. Watercolor on paper. 14 ¼ x 19 ⅞ in. Neg. nos. LC-USZC4-250, LC-USZ62-20464. Prints and Photographs Division, Library of Congress.

[Plate 24]
178 Alexander Jackson Davis. "Hall of Representatives, Wash.[ington], D.C.," 1832. Watercolor on paper. 10 ⁷⁄₁₆ x 11 in. I. N. Phelps Stokes Collection, Miriam and Ira D. Wallach Division of Art, Prints and Photographs, The New York Public Library, New York. Astor, Lenox, and Tilden Foundations.

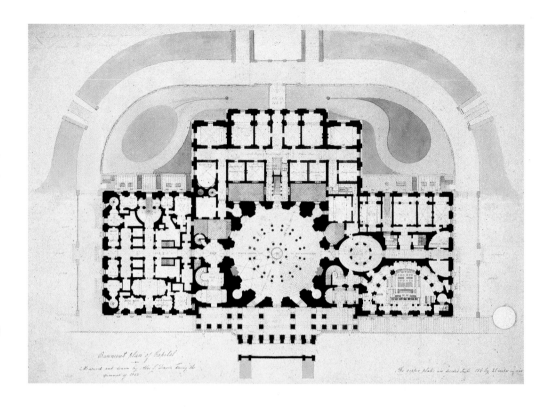

[Plate 25]

184 Thomas U. Walter. [Design for the Extension of the Capitol], 1851. Watercolor on paper. 30 x 53 in. The Athenaeum of Philadelphia.

[Plate 26]

186 Thomas U. Walter. [Design for the Extension and New Dome of the United States Capitol, Washington, D.C.], 1855. Watercolor on paper. 29 ½ x 50 ¼ in. The Athenaeum of Philadelphia.

[Plate 27]
206 Johannes A. Oertel. [Delaware
State Seal from the House of Representatives Chamber Ceiling], ca. 1856. Oil on glass.
20 ¾ in. diameter. Delaware State Museums, Dover.

[Plate 28]
204 Thomas U. Walter. "Details of Gallery in Hall of Representatives," 1856, detail. Ink and watercolor on paper. 33 ⅜ x
53 ½ in. Architect of the Capitol.

195 Thomas U. Walter. "Details of Senate Chamber, U.S. Capitol Extension," 1855. Ink and watercolor on paper. 20 x 26 in. Architect of the Capitol.

[Plate 30]
209 Thomas U. Walter. "Section Through Dome of U.S. Capitol," 1859. Ink and watercolor on paper. 42 ⅝ x 24 ⅞ in. Architect of the Capitol.

Had Latrobe's Library of Congress been completed, the Capitol's north wing would have contained Egyptian decorative and structural details, Greek Doric and Ionic columns, Roman vaults, medieval-inspired ribs, and the three American orders, all contained within a Renaissance-derived external shell. In totality, the Capitol's north wing was an architectural history museum symbolically linking the United States to the roots and main limbs of Western civilization. By choosing the library as the locus for his Egyptian component, Latrobe was also participating in the Enlightenment theory of associationism, connecting past and present time through the replication of historical artifacts. The greatest library of antiquity was that of Ptolemy Philadelphus, founded at Alexandria, Egypt, in 305 B.C.; America's greatest library was that assembled for the use of Congress.

Following the 1814 fire and the decision to enlarge the Senate chamber, Latrobe relocated the library to his newly proposed west wing. It is uncertain if Latrobe intended to retain its Egyptian character, but its construction fell to his successor, Charles Bulfinch, who designed the library in a sedate classical vocabulary (Plate 19, Cat. 142). Bulfinch's library was a long, narrow room overlooking the Mall with double-story alcove recesses ranged along both sides. He decorated the ends of the bookcases with the simple Greek proto-Corinthian pilasters adapted from the Athenian Tower of the Winds. Four columns of the same order framed a small vestibule that led onto the west portico balcony. This room housed Thomas Jefferson's private library, some 6,700 volumes purchased by the government for $23,950 after the books composing the first library were destroyed in the 1814 fire. Bulfinch's Library of Congress was itself the victim of a localized fire in 1851, and was soon replaced by a cast-iron room designed by Thomas U. Walter. In 1900 to 1901, after the Library of Congress building was completed, Walter's library was dismantled and the space replaced by offices.

BENJAMIN HENRY LATROBE'S
SOUTH (HOUSE OF REPRESENTATIVES) WING

Special attention was always accorded the hall for the House of Representatives because it was the meeting place of the legislative body most directly representing the American people. In 1801, James Hoban submitted three designs for the House and oversaw the erection of an elliptical House chamber 94 feet long by 70 feet wide independent of the south wing's exterior walls, which were to be built later. Hoban enumerated its basic facts on completion: "The Eliptic Room has been carried up 2 feet 8 inches high, 4½ bricks thick, and 16 feet higher, 3½ bricks thick, with 16 niches and 16 arches, to form an arcade. . . . A Gallery, on a semi-eliptic plan, has been put up, 120 feet long, with three rows of seats" (Cat. 143).[27] A description of Hoban's House published in newspapers in December 1801 read, in part:

> The new Representatives chamber is admirably adapted for the deliberations of a popular assembly. Its great extent, being the largest room in America, renders it very commodious to the members, who may have ingress to, or egress from any part of the House, without the least disturbance to others. The gallery is in front of the Speaker's chair, and is sufficiently large for the present population of the city. The voice is heard distinctly throughout the whole area. This desirable result probably proceeds from the lowness of the ceiling, and more than counterbalances, the unpleasant effect upon the eye for the want of architectural proportion. It must, however, be noticed, that the windows, though numerous, are small, and do not admit sufficient light. This inconvenience can be easily surmounted by a sky light.[28]

In addition to being ill-lit, the first House chamber was poorly ventilated and was soon dubbed the "oven" (Cat. 82).

More seriously, within a year of the chamber's completion construction faults began to appear. A committee appointed by Jefferson to inspect the new House chamber composed of George Hadfield and two local builders reported on October 24, 1802, that "if any further marks should appear that the Building is still giving way the walls may be propped up on the outside."[29] A December 1802 newspaper account noted:

> Over all the windows, which are arched, the wall has opened in cracks from the tops of the arches to the roof; the arched dome has settled down considerably upon the east side, and the wall upon the west has been protruded several inches from the perpendicular. There is much reason to fear, that before long, the whole dome and roof, forming an immense weight, will be precipitated, in mass, into the midst of the hall.[30]

Latrobe's survey of the existing Capitol's structure in 1803 revealed that the foundations of the House wing's exterior wall as well as the walls and foundations of the oven were constructed with "bad workmanship and materials"; the wing was dismantled in the spring of 1804.[31]

The form, lighting, and ornamentation of the second House of Representatives were of great interest to Jefferson and became the major focus of his collaboration with Latrobe over the next five years. When offering Latrobe the job of Architect of the Capitol, Jefferson had projected that the $50,000 voted by Congress on March 3, 1803, as well as an additional $50,000 he expected to be appropriated by the next Congress, would be adequate to roof the north wing and complete the south wing by the end of the 1804 building season. Latrobe's insistence that the oven be dismantled and replaced by a second House chamber changed Jefferson's schedule and budget.

Latrobe advised Jefferson against rebuilding an elliptical room for the House of Representatives, citing aesthetic, structural, and economic reasons. Instead, Latrobe suggested replacing the oval room with a semicircular one based on ancient Roman theaters. He argued that such a room would afford better acoustics, accommodate members of Congress and public visitors more comfortably, admit more natural light, and be more economical to build. Jefferson's reluctance to alter so materially the Thornton-Hallet design for the House chamber led Latrobe to seek an interview with Thornton in February 1804. He reported to Jefferson on February 18:

> I judged very ill in going to Thornton. In a few peremptory words, he, in fact, told me, that no difficulties existed in his plan, but such as were made by those who were too ignorant to remove them and though these were not exactly his words, his expressions, his tone, his manner, and his absolute refusal to devote a few minutes to discuss the subject spoke his meaning even more strongly and offensively than I have expressed it. I left him with an assurance that I should not be the person to attempt to remove them, and had I had immediate possession of pen, ink, and paper, I should have directly solicited your permission to resign my office.[32]

In his report to Congress on February 28, 1804, Latrobe complained that Thornton had given him only a ground plan, that the original designs approved by Washington had been lost during Hadfield's superintendence, and that "no drawings from which the design could be understood or executed" were to be found. Under these circumstances, Latrobe felt that it was unreasonable to compel him to adhere to the chosen design. The most significant change he wished to carry out immediately was to raise the House chamber to the second story in order to place office, committee, and document rooms underneath it. Jefferson realized the practicality of Latrobe's proposal and agreed to it. In April 1804, Thornton gave Latrobe a floor plan with an oval House chamber located on the second floor; Hallet had moved to New York and was no longer concerned with the Capitol in any way (Cat. 86).[33]

Although Latrobe disapproved of oval and elliptical rooms because they are geometrically complex and therefore expensive to build, he was prepared to design and execute a House chamber according to the approved outline. In February 1804, however, Jefferson suggested putting skylights in the hall's elliptical dome (Fig. 55; Plate 21, Cat. 144; Cat. 148). Jefferson greatly admired the grain market in Paris, the Halle aux Blèds, a windowless circular building with a dome composed of long glass panels set between curved wooden ribs (Plate 20, Cat. 150). Latrobe objected to skylights for the House chamber because they would leak, would admit too much glaring light, would allow condensation to drip on the heads of congressmen, and would cause the room to overheat during warm weather.

When Jefferson set aside Latrobe's practical objections to a skylit dome based on his professional judgment and experience, the architect tried to convince him on aesthetic grounds. Writing to Jefferson on October 29, 1806, Latrobe argued that multiple sources of constantly flickering light, rather than a single *"Unity of light"* from a central oculus, would give the House chamber "an air of the highest gaiety" and "destroy the solemnity that is appropriate to the object of the edifice."[34] The architect favored lanterns with vertical windows to illuminate rooms in the wings, as seen on the perspective watercolor he presented to Jefferson in November 1806. Even, diffuse light would fill the legislative chambers and produce a properly sober effect. But as he wrote to Latrobe on September 8, 1805, Jefferson believed that the skylit dome would "constitute the distinguishing merit of the room, and would solely [make] it the handsomest room in the world, without a single exception. Take that away, it becomes a common thing exceeded by many, and even by some corporation buildings."[35]

Yet Jefferson wanted the Capitol to be correct within the dictates of classical architecture; he wrote to Latrobe on April 22, 1807: "It is with real pain I oppose myself to your passion for the lanthern, and that in a matter of taste. I differ from a professor in his own art. But the object of the artist is lost if he fails to please the general eye. You know my reverence for the Graecian and Roman styles of architecture. I do not recollect ever to have seen in their build-

Fig. 55. Benjamin Henry Latrobe. "Sketch of a Section of the Capitol of the United States at Washington, of the Doric Order, Roman," 1804. Library of Congress.

ings a single instance of a lanthern, Cupola, or belfry."[36] This letter prompted one of Latrobe's most famous statements in which he argued that his aesthetic decisions were prompted by function rather than adherence to a single historical style. The result was his synthetic interpretation of Greek and Roman architecture in which he selectively chose principles and details from both traditions, fusing them into his personal version of Neoclassicism.

> In respect to the general subject of cupolas, I do not think that they are *always*, nor even *often* ornamental. My *principles* of good taste are rigid. In Grecian architecture, I am a bigotted Greek, to the condemnation of the roman architecture of Balba, Palmyra, Spalatro, and of all the buildings erected subsequent to Hadrians reign. The *immense size,* the bold *plans and arrangements* of the buildings of the Romans down almost to Consta[n]tine's Arch, plundered from the triumphal arches of former Emperors, I admire beyond tolerance, from the reign of Severus downwards. Wherever therefore the Grecian style can be copied without impropriety I love to be a *mere,* I would say a *slavish* copyist, but the *forms,* and the *distribution* of the Roman and Greek buildings which remain, are in general inapplicable to the objects and uses of our public buildings.[37]

Eclecticism, the conscious combination of stylistic elements from many historical sources, had been adopted in advanced European architectural circles by the mid-eighteenth century. Its use was particularly appropriate for America because eclecticism was a direct cultural expression of the country's heterogeneous population.

Forced to comply with Jefferson's wishes, Latrobe strove to create a beautiful and functional hall to serve the House of Representatives, although he never totally gave up the idea of a permanent stone dome to cover it. In order to erect a wood dome with skylights safely and reasonably economically, Latrobe chose to change Hoban's ellipse to a hippodrome, thus reviving Hallet's original plan (Fig. 56; Plate 21, Cat. 144; Cat. 146). Latrobe was then able to design curved wood ribs for two half-domes for the ends and a barrel vault for the center that could accommodate large skylights (Cat. 149).

Latrobe described the House's completed ceiling in his general survey of the Capitol, written on November 22, 1807, for the Washington newspaper the *National Intelligencer:*

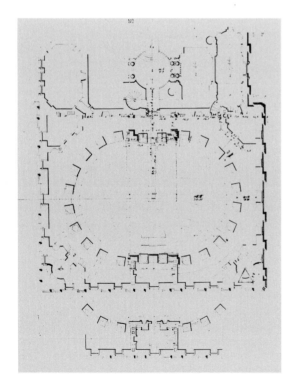

Fig. 56. Benjamin Henry Latrobe. "Plan of the House of Representatives," ca. 1808–1813. Library of Congress.

> The space between the columns and the external wall is covered with a solid brick vault, but the internal area has a roof of timber, which forms a flat dome, rising 12 ft. 6 in. in height. This enormous roof is in thickness only 16 inches and is a very remarkable specimen of excellent carpenters work. It is constructed on the plan of Philibert de l'orme, and is pierced with square lights, five over each intercolumniation. There are 20 tiers or ribs to these lights, in all 100. Each is covered with a single square of plate glass, and the effect is very striking, especially to those who have not seen the Hallaubled or Corn market in Paris, which was lighted on the same principle. This mode of lighting the Hall, forbad[e] the construction of a solid brick dome over the whole building, but every thing is so prepared that it may at any time be solidly domed.[38]

The French Renaissance architect Philibert Delorme had published several treatises on how to build curved wood frames as supports for domes; variants on Delorme's method were used almost exclusively for domes erected in the United States until the mid-nineteenth century. But wood frames are not permanent; they are susceptible to both fire and rot. Part of Latrobe's pride in his stone and brick vaulted Supreme Court and first Senate chamber reflected his desire that the Capitol be of permanent construction, to survive the millennium and be as great a ruin of some future age as those found in Greece and Rome.

Latrobe introduced symbolism into the hall for the House of Representatives through its architectural order and its figural and emblematic sculpture. The wood columns of Hoban's House chamber were apparently Doric, a choice partially prompted by the room's location on the ground story. Traditionally, the simpler orders—Doric and Tuscan—were placed on the lower stories, while the more sculpturally elaborate ones—Ionic and Corinthian—decorated second and third floors. The Doric order may also have been chosen for the first hall of the House of Representatives because it mirrored in an abstract sense the unpretentious republican virtues particularly espoused by Jefferson. He suggested that Latrobe use the Roman Doric from the Theater of Marcellus in Rome (the order used at Monticello) for the new House chamber, although it was to be placed on the second story of the Capitol.

On March 29, 1804, Latrobe submitted to the president two section drawings of the House chamber: a cross section showing the Roman Doric of the Theater of Marcellus, and a longitudinal section depicting the Greek order of the Tower of the Winds. Latrobe suggested that the simple Athenian capitals might be cast in iron, partially to promote a Philadelphia foundry of which he was a partner. Latrobe wrote to Jefferson that the Doric order for the House chamber must be given up on the grounds of propriety, as the ground-level Senate was decorated with Ionic columns. By the end of April, Latrobe had settled on the very elaborate Greek Corinthian order of the Choragic Monument of Lysicrates, too sculpturally complex to be cast in iron (Cats. 159 and 160). Jefferson, however, preferred the Roman Corinthian capital found on the Temple of Castor and Pollux in the Roman Forum, measured and illustrated by Andrea Palladio in the last of his *Four Books of Architecture*.[39]

Jefferson's repeated preference for Roman architectural details has been interpreted as a belief that Roman civic virtues would be promoted among Americans if they had before them examples of Roman architecture. Latrobe preferred Greek ornament because of its simplicity and elegance as well as its greater freedom of expression. On August 5, 1804, Latrobe explained his thinking to his clerk of the works, John Lenthall:

> The rules that determine the proportions of what is called *the orders,* were, no doubt, arbitrary, among the ancients, as to all *matters of detail.* Palladio and his successors and contemporaries endeavored to establish fixed rules for the most minute parts of the orders. The Greeks knew of no such rules, but having established *general* proportions and laws of form and arrangement, all matters of detail were left to the talent and taste of individual architects. . . . Of this license in detail, I think it right to avail myself on all occasions.[40]

Jefferson acceded to Latrobe's wishes. All of Latrobe's many orders in the Capitol—including the Doric Supreme Court, Ionic Senate, and Corinthian House of Representatives—are Greek rather than Roman in derivation. Latrobe's columns in the vestibule of the House of Representatives, modeled on those of the Athenian Temple of the Winds, are the oldest in situ Greek-inspired columns in America.

Latrobe's choice of the Corinthian order for the House of Representatives was the first step toward importing Italian sculptors to carry out the Capitol's decorative and emblematic sculpture. Following Jefferson's orders, Latrobe wrote to Philip Mazzei on March 6, 1805, soliciting his aid in identifying and hiring a *"good Sculptor of Architectural decorations"* to execute the House chamber's twenty-four Corinthian capitals and, for its frieze, an eagle with a wingspan of 12 feet, 6 inches. Latrobe also asked Mazzei, whom Jefferson had befriended during his residence in the United States, to inquire what Antonio Canova, the most venerable of European sculptors then living, would charge for a 9-foot seated figure of Liberty proposed for the House chamber. Pierre Charles L'Enfant had planned to place a figure of Liberty in the same position in the House chamber in Federal Hall in 1789; Giuseppe Ceracchi's terra-cotta bust *Minerva as the Patroness of American Liberty* was actually placed behind the Speaker's chair in Congress Hall in Philadelphia.[41]

By September 1805, Mazzei had contracted with two Italian sculptors: brothers-in-law Giuseppe Franzoni, to do figural work, and Giovanni Andrei, to execute Latrobe's architectural ornament. Canova was unavailable; Mazzei advised on having the figure of Liberty carved in Rome, perhaps by the great Danish sculptor Bertil Thorwaldsen. On April 21, 1806, American painter and scientist Charles Willson Peale sent Latrobe the head and neck of an actual American bald eagle to serve as a model for Franzoni, who was to carve the eagle in the House frieze (Fig. 57; Cat. 145). By May 29, Latrobe reported that Franzoni was capable of carving the figure of Liberty as well as four reclining allegorical figures destined for the House frieze. At some point, "it was contemplated that the *Frieze,* over the Capitals of the Corinthian columns which sustain the dome, should present, in *relievo,* a regular series of the battles which secured our independence." By December 19, 1806, Latrobe was planning a "Groupe of seventeen female figures" for Franzoni to execute after he finished Liberty, probably the allegories representing the states, of which Franzoni's brother Carlo eventually made plaster models for the rebuilt Senate chamber in 1816.[42]

Fig. 57. Benjamin Henry Latrobe. "Eagle in Entablature in Letter to Charles Willson Peale," April 18, 1806. Library of Congress.

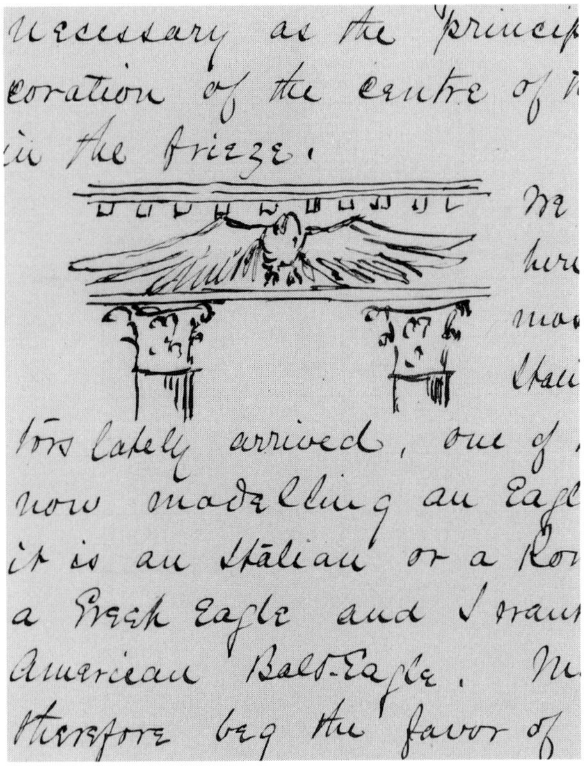

Latrobe and Franzoni collaborated on the insignia to be used for the allegorical figures. Franzoni had chosen a club (an attribute of Hercules) and "doves nestling in a Helmet" to signify war and peace for his first design of Liberty; Latrobe suggested that the traditional pike, or staff, carrying a liberty cap be included. Franzoni's plaster model of his final design was set in place behind the Speaker's chair by September 1, 1807. Latrobe described Franzoni's Liberty in a newspaper article on the Capitol that appeared on November 22, 1807: "The figure, sitting, is 8 ft. 6 in. in height. By her side stands the American eagle, supporting her left hand, in which is the cap of liberty, her right presents a scroll, the constitution of the United States. Her foot treads upon a reversed crown as a footstool and upon other emblems of monarchy and bondage."[43]

Latrobe and Franzoni's Americanization of Liberty predated by two years Franzoni's Justice, also accompanied by an eagle and the Constitution, destined for the Supreme Court. Both allegorical figures retained their traditional identifying insignia—the liberty cap and the scales of justice, respectively—yet each was inexorably identified with America by the addition of some of the country's newly established symbols. Although Latrobe intended that Franzoni's plaster model of

Liberty eventually be carved in Vermont marble, it was not done before the House of Representatives was totally consumed in the August 1814 fire.

Franzoni's four allegorical figures of Agriculture, Art, Science, and Commerce were carved in relief and covered a span of 25 feet of the House chamber's frieze opposite the Speaker's chair. All but Commerce were complete by November 22, 1807, when Latrobe wrote his description of the Capitol for the *National Intelligencer*. Unfortunately, he merely identified their subjects without enumerating their attributes. No other evidence survives to indicate how Latrobe and Franzoni chose to express these allegorical themes, which had been fundamental to the Capitol's iconography since the 1792 competition. Latrobe did report to Jefferson on September 11, 1808, that the figure of Commerce was "entirely new," but not equal in artistic quality to the other three. In December 1808, Latrobe shipped the original plaster models of the House's four allegorical panels to the Pennsylvania Academy of Fine Arts, but they never arrived.[44]

One can only speculate why Latrobe duplicated the four allegories of Agriculture, Art, Science, and Commerce in the Senate and House chambers. The figures in both halls were not free-standing sculpture, but were integral to the Capitol's structural system, caryatids that figuratively supported part of the Senate's ceiling, and reclining figures in the House chamber's frieze that supported its dome. As sculpture, they were literally supports in the Capitol, just as agriculture, art, science, and commerce provided the professional underpinnings of the new nation. The set in the Senate was standing (that is, at work), while that in the House was recumbent (at rest). Latrobe's realization of the same allegorical subjects proposed during the design competition for the Capitol reinforces their validity as expressions of American national identity.

Jefferson's role in choosing the subjects of the Capitol's allegorical sculpture planned by Latrobe is unknown, as no correspondence between the two men discussing it is known. When consulted about the statues of Washington planned for the state capitols in Virginia and North Carolina, Jefferson expressed his preference for Roman togas over contemporary American dress on the grounds that "our boots and regimentals have a very puny effect."[45] Latrobe frequently expressed his own attitude about the use of allegory in America, where he felt classical allusions had to be interpreted for the majority of the people. In 1804, he wrote: "The language of Allegory is like the Indian language of signs. It is *poor* in expression, and to those who do not understand it, appears nothing but ridiculous grimace."[46]

In 1881, Latrobe's son, John H. B. Latrobe, in an address before the American Institute of Architects, described the original House of Representatives as he remembered it:

> I can still recall, among the shadowy impressions of my earliest boyhood, the effect, approaching awe, produced upon me by the old Hall of Representatives. I fancy I can see the heavy crimson drapery that hung in massive folds between the tall fluted Corinthian columns to within a short distance of their base; and I remember, or I think I remember, the low, gilded iron railing that ran from base to base, and over which the spectators in the gallery looked down upon members on the floor. I seem to see, even now, the Speaker's chair, with its rich surroundings, and the great stone eagle which, with outspread wings, projected from the frieze, as though it were hovering over and protecting those who deliberated below. . . . [T]here can be no question that the old Hall of Representatives was a noble room. Even the British officer, who was ordered to destroy it, is reported to have said, as he stood at the entrance, "that it was a pity to burn anything so beautiful."[47]

On July 12, 1815, Latrobe described for Jefferson, who was at Monticello, the nature and extent of the damage to the House after it was burned by British troops on August 24 of the previous year:

> In the house of Representatives the devastation has been dreadful. There was here no want of materials for conflagration. In 1811, when the number of members of Congress was increased the old platform was left in its place, and another raised over it, giving an additional quantity of dry and loose lumber. All the stages and seats of the Galleries were of timber and yellow pine. The Mahagony furniture, desks, tables and Chairs were in their places. At first they fired Rockets through the Roof. But they did not set fire to it; they sent men on it, but it was covered with Sheet Iron. At last they made a great pile in the Center of the room of the furniture, and retiring, set fire to a large quantity of Rocket stuff in the middle. The whole was soon in a blaze and so intense was the flame, that the Glass of the Lights was melted, and I have now lumps weighing many pounds of Glass, run into the Mass. The stone, is like most freestone, unable to resist the force of flame. But I believe no known material could have withstood the effects of so sudden and intense a heat. The exterior of the Columns and entablature therefore, expanded far beyond the dimensions of their interior, scaled off and not a vestige of fluting or Sculpture remained Sound. The appearance of the ruin, was awfully grand when I first saw it, and indeed it was terrific for it seemed to threaten immediately to fall, so Slender were the remains of the Columns that carried the Massy entablature. (Cat. 151)[48]

Immediately after President James Madison reappointed him in March 1815, Latrobe set about planning changes to enlarge and improve the Capitol. One significant administrative change made his job easier: Congress guaranteed a loan of $500,000 to rebuild the Capitol rather than continuing to appropriate uncertain funds on a yearly basis. At the same time, Madison established the Board of Commissioners of the Public Buildings to act as administrators, blocking Latrobe's direct access to the president and thus limiting his influence and authority.

While in the process of dismantling the ruined House of Representatives, Latrobe was planning a new hall, a semicircular auditorium to replace the hippodrome, a scheme he had suggested to Jefferson a decade earlier (Fig. 58; Cats. 153 and 154). The scenographic spectacle of Latrobe's first hall, largely dependent on the movement of broken shafts of light across its majestic colonnade, was much admired, and Latrobe strove to emulate its splendor within a more rational geometric framework for his second House chamber (Cat. 155). Modern semicircular rooms for exposition or assembly, with curved tiered seating derived from ancient theaters, were pioneered in France by Jacques Gondouin in the surgery amphitheater (1784) at the Ecole de Chirurgie. Although often suggested as Latrobe's model for the House of Representatives, more likely sources were French legislative assembly halls, principally Jean-François-Thérèse Chalgrin's Senate chamber erected in the Luxembourg Palace between 1803 and 1807 (Cat. 157). Latrobe's House and Chalgrin's Senate shared hemispherical domes pierced by semicircular oculi that directed light onto their rostra, colonnades across their diameters, and screens of columns along their curved walls that separated ancillary spaces from their main rooms (Cat. 156).

Latrobe used columns much more lavishly than Chalgrin, ranging twenty-two of them along the hall's semicircular perimeter to re-create some of the effect of movement and openness that characterized his first House chamber. They were the same height as the earlier columns—28 feet, 6 inches—and the same order, the rich Corinthian of the Choragic Monument of Lysicrates in Athens. Latrobe intended their unfluted shafts to be monoliths, single pieces of the elegant polychromatic Potomac breccia, but they were finally built with three

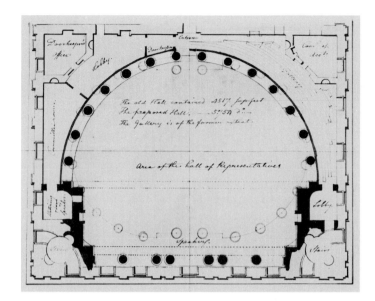

Fig. 58. Benjamin Henry Latrobe. "Sketch of a Design for altering the plan of the House of Representatives in the Capitol U.S. Washington," 1815. Architect of the Capitol.

drums each. Latrobe appreciated that when the mottled limestone is polished, its coloration and patterned surfaces resemble those of the richly veined marbles used so extensively by the Romans. On August 13, 1815, he wrote to the Baltimore lawyer Robert Goodloe Harper that if he were successful in convincing Congress to adopt the breccia, he could say "Cedite Romani [Yield to me, Romans]," confident that another aspect of the Capitol rivaled ancient structures. The intricacy and delicacy of the Corinthian order of the Choragic Monument to Lysicrates prompted Latrobe in August 1815 to send Giovanni Andrei back to Italy to oversee execution of the capitals in white Carrara marble. The color harmonies and subtle textures of the room's materials—warm-brown matte Aquia sandstone; light- to medium-gray, highly polished breccia; and glistening white marble—imparted a particular richness to the House chamber.[49]

Latrobe simplified the sculptural decoration of his second House chamber, retaining an eagle with spread wings in the entablature carved by Giuseppe Valaperta in 1816. By 1819, Enrico Causici's plaster model of a toga-clad figure, wearing a feathered Indian headdress decorated with stars and holding the scrolled Constitution, was placed in the niche above the Speaker's chair. In 1820, Causici petitioned Congress to fund a marble version, which he identified as the *Genius of the Constitution,* the last of a venerable series of allegorical figures of Liberty in some guise planned for or installed behind successive Speaker's chairs. She has her own guardian eagle, and at her side a rattlesnake is wound around a bundle of rods, or fasces, the ancient Roman symbol of civic authority and union. Thus America's first allegorical symbol, Benjamin Franklin's severed snake of 1754, which represented the separate political situation of the colonies, was appropriately shown whole in the Capitol to represent the country united under the Constitution.

Latrobe replaced the allegorical personifications of his earlier frieze with an entirely new conceit. Directly opposite the figure of Liberty above the entrance, he placed the Car of History incorporating a clock, which was carved in marble by Carlo Franzoni in 1819 (Cat. 158). Clio, the muse of History, is in the act of recording America's great events; her car representing time is powered by an eagle's wing and is decorated with a portrait of Washington, whose renown is being trumpeted by Fame.[50]

Jefferson never saw either the completed original chambers or the rebuilt Capitol and depended on Latrobe's letters and drawings to keep him abreast of new developments in their design. On October 10, 1809, in anticipation of the Capitol's completion, the newly retired president wrote to Latrobe: "I think that the work when finished will be a durable and honorable monument to our infant republic, and will bear favorable comparison with the remains of the same kind of the antient republics of Greece and Rome."[51]

CONTEMPORARY EVALUATION OF THE CAPITOL

The Capitol was an immediate popular success. Descriptions in travel accounts beginning in the 1810s often presented it as an accomplished fact, as did the earliest lithographs and engravings (Cat. 229). As soon as Charles Bulfinch's dome was raised, numerous engravings and color lithographs were printed of both facades, but the view from the west was more popular (Cats. 231, 232, and 240). Distant views of Capitol Hill seen from Pennsylvania Avenue or from various elevated sites around the city were more popular in the 1830s and 1840s, as they showed the newly planted trees that covered the grounds and provided a dark base on which the white building seemed to float (Cats. 226 and 235). Objects as diverse as Staffordshire pottery, jacquard coverlets (Cat. 242), fire screens, bandboxes (Cat. 239), embroidered pictures, and candelabra (Cat. 236) used these prints to create memorabilia. Even tobacco labels (Plate 22, Cat. 255) and sheet-music covers for patriotic marches reproduced views of the Capitol (Fig. 59; Cats. 243 and 244). Political and satirical prints in which the Capitol symbolized corruption (particularly pork-barrelling) began soon after the building was finished (Cat. 249). The Capitol has also been used as a backdrop in numerous twentieth-century advertisements to promote national sales because with the advent of railroads, manufactured goods need not be sold only locally (Cats. 261 and 262).

Success of the propaganda to represent the Capitol as America's "Temple of Freedom" can also be measured by its popularity as an anti-freedom symbol in abolitionist literature. As early as 1817, Dr. Jesse Torrey published an allegorical print of the Capitol as the frontispiece in *A Portraiture of Domestic Slavery in the United States* (Fig. 60; Cat. 246). A group of slaves and their master view the recently burned Capitol, which the text presents as a divine judgment against America because the country sanctioned slavery. The Capitol was portrayed in the background of many abolitionist tracts, as a backdrop for dehumanizing scenes and an ironic commentary on the dichotomy between the rhetoric and the reality of American liberty, freedom, and justice (Cats. 247 and 248).

Three architects with an intimate knowledge of the building at different stages in its development provided varied information about the Capitol and its artworks. George Hadfield wrote the only critical assessment, composed in 1820 but not published until after his death, in S. A. Elliot's *Washington Guide* (1826). Hadfield dissected Latrobe's interiors

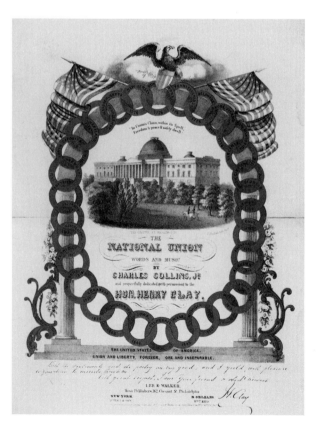

Fig. 59. Thomas S. Sinclair. "The Capitol March," 1850. Library of Congress.

Fig. 60. "A View of the Capitol of the United States After the Conflagration in 1814." Frontispiece in Jesse Torrey, *A Portraiture of Domestic Slavery in the United States, 1817.* Library of Congress.

at length, particularly the House chamber, noting that as an "admirer of chaste architecture" he "must be fully satisfied with [its] effect and scenic appearance," although everything in the south wing had been sacrificed to achieve its great volume. Hadfield found the variety of stones used in Latrobe's second House chamber inconsistent with the "economy and plainness suitable to our Republican Government," preferring the overall soft harmony of the brown Aquia sandstone of the first House Chamber.[52]

Hadfield's final judgment was damning with faint praise:

> However striking and agreeable the architecture of this room may appear to the common eye, it is nevertheless encumbered by many defects, which will strike the eye of architectural judgment with regret: the prostyle in front being of good proportion both in height and intercolumination, would certainly have been a chaste and good piece of architecture, had it not been destroyed by coupling the four center columns, and making the centre intercolumination wider than the rest. No reason appears to justify this unwarrantable deformity and weak construction.[53]

When Latrobe was pressed to finish the Capitol in 1811, he had hired Hadfield for three months to assist him with drawings; when Latrobe resigned in 1817, Hadfield was one of several architects recommended as his replacement. After Latrobe's death in 1820, Jefferson wrote to Hadfield's sister, his friend Maria Cosway, that her brother was "one of our first architects."[54]

In the early 1830s, the young New York architect Alexander Jackson Davis spent at least three summers in Washington testing the waters for government architectural work. One of the most accomplished architectural draftsmen in the United States, Davis did measured drawings of the completed Capitol preparatory to publishing a set of engravings (Figs. 61 and 62; Cats. 169, 172, 173; Plate 23, Cat. 171). Dozens of preliminary sketches and several finished watercolors have survived, including an east elevation, plans of every floor, and interior perspectives of the Rotunda and House chamber (Cats. 180.4 and 180.5). A few engravings and lithographs were done, the most spectacular being a reflected ceiling plan of the Capitol's

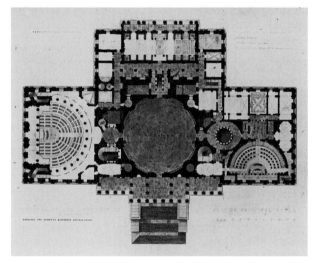

Fig. 61. Alexander Jackson Davis. "East Front of the Capitol,"
ca. 1832–1834. Library of Congress.

Fig. 62. Alexander Jackson Davis. "Capitol of the United States.
Plan of Principal Floor," ca. 1832–1834. Avery Architectural and Fine
Arts Library, Columbia University in the City of New York.

principal story, but apparently the project was never completed (Cat. 174). Of the many
sketches Davis did of the House chamber, the one he chose to finish and engrave is a
panorama of the room from behind the screen of columns that ran parallel to the south wall
(Fig. 63; Cat. 176). In his watercolor and subsequent engraving, Davis showed the tympanum
above the colonnade unfilled by the wall actually there, in order to open a view of Latrobe's
half-dome beyond (Plate 24, Cat. 178; Cat. 180). The impression from this vantage point is of
a circular, rather than semicircular, room. Davis may well have had Giambattista Piranesi's or
Giuseppe Vasi's similar views of the interior of the Roman Pantheon in mind when he
recorded the House chamber, which bore striking similarities to the ancient room (Cat. 179).

Davis's drawings are crucially important because they record the Capitol exactly as it was
completed by Bulfinch, giving more comprehensive information than any other visual documents. The most significant are a series of sketches and one grisaille watercolor of Bulfinch's

Library of Congress, a room destroyed by fire in 1851. Davis's views are the best existing graphic record of the library's appearance, as no important drawings by Bulfinch of it survive.

The influence of the Capitol on Davis's own work was profound. The five years he spent as a young man working at the *Alexandria Gazette* coincided with the surge under Bulfinch to complete the Capitol. His detailed drawings of the building prepared him to design several new state capitols done in partnership with Ithiel Town in the 1830s (Cats. 250 and 251). They adopted the national Capitol's classical form and details and its organization into legislative wings separated by a dome and portico. Davis seems to have been particularly impressed with Latrobe's semicircular hall for the House, with its perimeter colonnade, half-dome, and corner staircases, as he repeated this arrangement in many designs. Latrobe's corn order also impressed Davis, who used it as an exterior order on public and private buildings and even designed a 120-foot corn column to serve as the base of a statue of George Washington, which he submitted to the Virginia Washington Monument competition in 1849 (Cat. 252).

Robert Mills, a protégé of Jefferson's and student of Latrobe's who had apprenticed at the Capitol in the early years of the nineteenth century, published the most detailed descriptions of the Capitol and its artworks in several Washington guidebooks he wrote beginning in 1834. Mills settled in Washington in 1830, spending the remaining quarter-century of his life there and erecting the most important second-generation government buildings: the Treasury Building (1836–1840), the Patent Office (1836–1840), and the General Post Office (1839–1841). His Washington Monument design, chosen in 1845, took over an important commemorative function originally intended for the Capitol.

The Capitol also provided Mills with work, as he began to be consulted in 1829 about improvements to the hall of the House of Representatives and served as the building's care-

Fig. 63. Alexander Jackson Davis. "Perspective Sketch of the House of Representatives," ca. 1832. Avery Architectural and Fine Arts Library, Columbia University in the City of New York.

taker architect during the 1830s and 1840s. His knowledge of what he called "this splendid structure" was comprehensive, but his appreciation of its art and architecture was not wholly uncritical. He regretted Bulfinch's dome, "so disproportionate to the building, . . . a strange aberration from good taste." In many cases, Mills's interpretation of the Capitol's emblematic sculpture is a more complete statement of its contemporary evaluation than that provided by other documents. In 1826, Mills himself had submitted a design in the competition for the east pediment's sculpture, suggesting a chariot driven by Washington, who was "crowned by Liberty & Wisdom; the whole encircled by a glory, studded with thirteen stars, representing the Federal Union."[55]

~ EPILOGUE ~

"Freedom Triumphant in War and Peace"

The Capitol Extension

EXTENSION PLANS AND COMPETITION

Westward expansion and secure settlements during the 1810s and 1820s brought many new states into the union, with the result that the Capitol was simply too small to accommodate the new members almost as soon as it was finished. As early as the mid-1830s, Robert Mills and Alexander Jackson Davis suggested extending the Capitol with an east wing to balance the west one, creating a Greek cross-shaped building. On March 1, 1843, Congress itself requested the secretary of war to prepare a design "for the better accommodation of the sittings of the House of Representatives." During the next few years, several options were explored, including selecting one of Mills's proposals without holding another competition. The major problem was how to gain new and much enlarged Senate and House chambers without destroying the original Capitol's architectural integrity.[1]

In the fall of 1850, the Senate Committee on Public Buildings and Grounds announced an open competition. Designs, due by December 1, might be for extension by the construction of wings to the north and south or by the "erection of a separate and distinct building within the inclosure to the east" of the building. The members of the committee reserved the right to divide the $500 premium among several winners if they judged it desirable to select elements from many designs. The Senate committee's competition was not legally binding, nor did it represent the consensus of the joint Senate and House committees on public buildings.[2]

Although not so vociferous or active as the Senate committee, the House Committee on Public Buildings, composed of five members led by Richard H. Stanton of Kentucky, favored an extension to the east (Figs. 64 and 65; Cats. 182 and 183). In a letter to the editors of the *National Intelligencer,* Stanton enumerated the reasons against the north and south wings: extensive and expensive terracing of the grounds would be necessary; the Senate and House

95

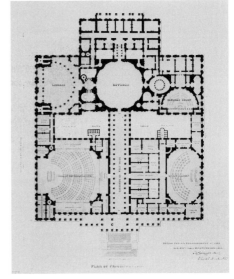

Fig. 64. Thomas U. Walter. "Perspective View of a Plan for Enlarging the U.S. Capitol," 1850. Architect of the Capitol.

Fig. 65. Thomas U. Walter. "Plan of Principal Story. Design for an Enlargement of the U.S. Capitol, Washington, D.C.," 1850. Architect of the Capitol.

chambers would be too distant from each other; circulation within the building would be circuitous at best; and the beauty of the original building would be impaired.[3]

In February 1851, designs from eight known competitors for both lateral and eastern extensions were sent to the White House for examination by President Millard Fillmore. After a four-hour meeting with six of the competing architects, Fillmore and his cabinet were still undecided. During the next three months, both Robert Mills and Philadelphia architect Thomas U. Walter met with Fillmore, lobbying for their respective designs (Cat. 181). Both submitted designs based on the two favored planning solutions (Plate 25, Cat. 184; Cat. 185). Fillmore made his decision on June 10, 1851: Walter was to be the architect of a modified version of the Senate plan, in which lateral wings would be attached to the original building by intervening corridors[4] (Plate 26, Cat. 186; Cat. 187).

THOMAS WALTER AND MONTGOMERY MEIG'S CAPITOL EXTENSION

On July 4, 1851, the cornerstone for the Capitol Extension was laid, the oration given by Daniel Webster. The inscription on the stone itself, composed by Webster, reflects the recent Compromise of 1850, a temporary solution to the slavery question, which was threatening the union of states:

> If, therefore, it shall hereafter be the will of God that this structure shall fall from its base, that its foundation be upturned and this stone be brought to light, BE IT KNOWN, that on this day the Union of the United States of America stands firm; that the Constitution still exists unimpaired, and with all its original usefulness and glory, growing every day stronger and stronger in the great body of the American people, and attracting more and more the admiration of the world. All here assembled, whether belonging to public life or to private life, with hearts devoutly thankful to Almighty God for the preservation of the liberty and happiness of the country, unite in sincere and fervent prayers that this deposit, all the walls and arches, the domes and towers, the columns and entablatures now to be executed over it may endure forever. God save the United States of America.[5]

Despite its long building history, the exterior of the Capitol as a whole is in harmony, but comparison of Thornton's facade with those adjoining by Bulfinch and Walter indicates differences among the three architects, as well as changes in interpretation of the classical tradition. Thornton's and Bulfinch's handling of the exterior walls was Neoclassical; Walter's was Victorian. In his additions, Walter was sympathetic to the original building, retaining the basic format of Thornton's Corinthian capitals and replicating Latrobe's east front portico as the east facade porticoes for both new wings (Fig. 66; Cats. 189 and 190). Yet Walter's extensions have their own distinct architectural character, a lively and sculptural synthesis of Italian Renaissance and French Baroque features that results in an American Victorian style predominantly Renaissance Revival in character. Although Walter had built his reputation during the 1830s and 1840s as a leading practitioner of the Greek Revival, he kept apace of the times and designed several houses and a church in Washington during the early 1850s in the Italianate style, another subcategory of Victorian architecture derived partially from Italian Renaissance architecture.

Walter continued all the horizontal regulating lines of the original building when designing his marble extensions, thus giving the impression from a distance that the Capitol was erected in a single building campaign. In their massing, the wing extensions are more three-dimensional than the original building, with colonnades on all their exposed facades. Walter's details also exhibit salient Victorian characteristics. Comparison between the windows and doors of the original building and those of the extensions shows that the frames, pediments, and brackets of the latter are more complex and sculpturally ornate (Cat. 191). In addition, the major architectural elements of the wing walls—windows and pilasters—are compressed more closely together, giving the extensions a more staccato and lively rhythm than the sedate, measured movement of the same elements on the original building.

Beginning in 1855, Walter consciously revived one of the Capitol's most venerable traditions. He designed two new American orders that are variants on the classical Corinthian order. For the Hall of Columns, which bisects the ground story of the House wing, he combined acanthus and tobacco leaves and added thistle flowers (Cat. 197). Walter's capitals for the columns in the new Senate vestibule (1858) combine tobacco and corn leaves and magnolia flowers with acanthus leaves and volutes of the canonical Corinthian order (Cat. 196).

Fig. 66. Thomas U. Walter and
Montgomery Meigs. "Eastern Elevation of
North Wing. Capitol Extension," 1853.
Architect of the Capitol.

This synthetic approach, in which American elements are fused with European, characterizes both the architecture and decoration of the Capitol Extension.

On March 4, 1853, authority for overseeing the construction of the extensions was transferred from the Department of the Interior to the Department of War. Secretary of War Jefferson Davis appointed Captain Montgomery C. Meigs of the Army Corps of Engineers as superintendent, with authority over Walter. Conflicts soon erupted into open enmity, with control not returned to Walter until 1862. Until he was relieved of his duties in 1859, Meigs contributed several important ideas to the Capitol's aesthetic and emblematic development. Originally, Walter had planned the new rectangular House and Senate chambers to be located on outside walls facing west, so they would be lit directly by natural light (Cat. 188). At Meigs's suggestion, the chambers were moved to the center of each wing and were encircled by broad corridors with offices and committee rooms located around the perimeters (Cats. 193 and 202). Meigs also suggested narrative themes for the Capitol's new sculpture and fresco paintings, and he supervised the artists who executed them.

Both the new House and new Senate chambers are double-story rectangles covered by flat ceilings, with public galleries around three sides. They were originally evenly illuminated from above, with light admitted through roof skylights and filtered through milk-glass panels inset into the ceiling's iron framework (Cat. 194). State seals painted on glass by Johannes A. Oertel about 1856 decorate the outer ring of panels in the House ceiling (Plate 27, Cat. 206). Walter designed the Senate chamber to have niches along the upper walls; one drawing shows standing mythological figures occupying them, but busts of vice presidents (the presidents of the Senate) actually occupy the niches (Plate 29, Cat. 195). Walter's House chamber was decorated in moss green and ocher; both rooms have extensive gilding of moldings and brackets. Meigs, apparently in reply to criticism of the House's decoration, defended it publicly in 1857:

> The rich and magnificent decoration of the new Hall—being the introduction in this country of a new style—when first seen, naturally excites surprise. The colors are so rich, so various, so intricate, so different from anything seen before, that the impression is that it must be, what "Gaudy!" But what is "gaudy?" Are the colors of our autumnal forests gaudy? Is there anything in this Hall more brilliant than the scarlet leafage of the gum or the maple, or the yellow of the oak and other trees? Has the great Artist who paints the forest made a gaudy picture?[6] (Plate 28, Cat. 204).

Meigs's need to link even the color of the Capitol's new interiors to something he considered quintessentially American reflects more than his own attitudes; the history of the Capitol's decoration, although overwhelmingly European in derivation, always had a consciously American rationale.

In 1858, Meigs commissioned sculptor William Henry Rinehart to model figures for the House of Representative clock (Cat. 205). The Great Seal eagle presides over a buckskinned-clad frontiersman who rests on his rifle, and a Plains Indian holds his bow. Both are in contemplative and peaceful poses, the entire composition both an elegy and an allegory: time marches on, leaving both figures and the groups they represent historical artifacts.

Jefferson Davis, now a senator from Mississippi serving on the Committee on Public Buildings and Grounds, vigorously promoted the Capitol's extensions. On June 1, 1858, he argued on the floor of the Senate that Latrobe's "old Hall is in a much higher style of architecture than the new. . . . The old Hall was made for beauty, the new Hall for use." In fact, the final decorative schemes of the chambers were more subdued than those of the corridors, office, and committee rooms surrounding the Senate and planned for the House wing. Walter's and Meigs's interiors of both the Senate and House chambers were replaced in 1949 and 1950 by sober and conservative neo-Georgian paneling and furnishings designed by Architect of the Capitol David Lynn.[7]

Fig. 67. Thomas U. Walter. "Elevation of Dome of U.S. Capitol," 1859. Architect of the Capitol.

CAPITOL DOME AND STATUE OF FREEDOM

The dome of the Capitol is one of America's greatest architectural spectacles (Fig. 67; Cat. 207). Its feat of engineering—placing nearly 4,500 tons of cast iron on a smaller stone drum—is often remarked on, but Walter's double-shell dome, which solved both exterior and interior design problems, is not fully appreciated. A dome was not part of the extensions authorized by Congress in 1850, but Walter and other architects competing for the design of the extension's design realized that a tall vertical element would eventually be needed to balance the new Capitol's great width.[8]

Walter's first dome design, completed by December 16, 1854, set the pattern of a lofty dome composed of five distinct layers: a peristyle of thirty-six free-standing columns at its base; a range of arched windows separated by pilasters; the dome itself; a tholos or cupola; and a monumental sculpted figure (Cat. 254). The technical success of Walter's new cast-iron room for the Library of Congress had convinced legislators that replacing the old dome with an iron one was feasible; Walter's spectacular watercolors of a dome atop the new building convinced them of its aesthetic value. The first dome appropriation was passed on March 3, 1855, and signed into law by President Franklin Pierce; responsibility for its erection was to be shared by Walter and Meigs.

The ultimate ancestor of Walter's dome is the great Renaissance dome of St. Peter's Basilica in Rome, distinguished by a high colonnaded drum supporting a soaring ribbed dome, the whole capped by a sculpturally complex cupola. But Walter's most imme-

Fig. 68. Thomas Crawford. "Second Design of *Freedom Triumphant in War and Peace*," 1855. Library of Congress.

Fig. 69. Thomas U. Walter. "Tholus on Dome of U.S. Capitol," 1859. Architect of the Capitol.

diate model was Auguste Ricard de Montferrand's cast-iron dome on St. Isaac's Cathedral (1824–1858) in St. Petersburg, itself one of several post-Renaissance domes influenced by that of St. Peter's (Cat. 208). The pyramidal composition of the Capitol dome—287 feet high, 135 feet in diameter at the base, and 88 feet at the cupola—resulted from structural necessity and aesthetic considerations. The distribution of its weight on the Rotunda and exterior foundation walls was of particular concern because of damage to the outside walls resulting from the 1814 fire (Plate 30, Cat. 209). A 14-foot-wide iron ring was cantilevered out from the existing masonry drum and supported by seventy-two iron brackets; the thirty-six columns of the peristyle rise from its outer edge. An iron wall, or skirt, below the columns hangs over the edge of the east wall behind the portico because the Rotunda is in the center of the Capitol's north-south axis, but not its east-west one. Between 1958 and 1962, the Capitol's east front was replicated in marble and moved forward 32 feet, offsetting the dome's looming appearance when viewed from the east.

The new dome's size was calculated on the basis of the great longitudinal length of the total building (751 feet), with its massiveness ameliorated by its openness. The skeletal cast-iron structure permits the insertion of vast expanses of glass on all four levels, flooding the interior with light, although only the peristyle windows are visible from the interior. The dome's sculptural three-dimensional quality in outline and in detail relates directly to the wings, drawing the whole into an integrated composition as much as possible given the disparate nature of the building's Neoclassical and Victorian architecture.

By the end of 1863, the outer dome was nearly complete, and on December 2 the final piece of Thomas Crawford's cast-bronze statue *Freedom Triumphant in War and Peace,* cast in five parts by Clark Mills at his nearby foundry, was hoisted into position. On May 11, 1855, Meigs had written to Crawford, who was in Rome: "We have too many Washingtons; we have America in the pediment, Victories and Liberties are rather pagan emblems, but a Liberty I fear is the best we can get." Crawford did three designs of Freedom, the first wearing a crown of stars and the second a liberty cap (Fig. 68; Cats. 210 and 211). Jefferson Davis, then secretary of war, objected to the liberty cap on the grounds that it was inappropriate to represent free-born Americans because the Roman liberty cap had been worn by freed slaves; he suggested that Crawford's Freedom wear a helmet. Crawford obliged with a helmet encircled with stars, its crest an eagle's head sprouting feathers "suggested by the costume of our Indian tribes" (Fig. 69; Cat. 212). Paws hanging beside Freedom's ears and the fur trim on her toga suggest that Crawford also included vestiges of a lion skin, one of the traditional attributes of Hercules. Once again, one single concept was not large enough to encompass the spirit of America, and Crawford combined features associated with Athena, Hercules, Liberty, and America to create a suitable symbol. Because the statue's final dimensions of 19 feet, 6 inches in height were larger than Walter had anticipated, the top of the dome had to be redesigned to accommodate the sculpture.[9]

CONSTANTINO BRUMIDI DECORATES THE CAPITOL

Meigs sought advice from critics and collectors to help identify talented American painters and sculptors to undertake the great cycle of historical and emblematic decoration he planned for the Capitol Extension. He wrote to Congressman Gouverneur Kemble on February 8, 1854: "I hope to see the day when the new portions of the Capitol will contain the germs of a collection worthy the most powerful and most wealthy nation of the earth. The only one that can point to a prosperous people and an overflowing treasury."[10] Public areas in the Capitol Extension that needed additional decoration, beyond the lavish architectural framework of variegated marbles that Walter and Meigs provided, were both numerous and imposing. Meigs planned for paintings on canvas to hang on staircase landings, as well as fresco paintings to be done directly on walls, although he was advised against the latter technique. This question was resolved when the Italian-born painter Constantino Brumidi applied for work at the Capitol in 1855. Meigs recounted the circumstances to John Durand, editor of *The Crayon,* who in October 1858 published an article critical of Brumidi's use of classical figures, dress, and situations to illustrate American personages and events:

> While debating in my own mind how I should meet this difficulty [decorating the walls of the Capitol Extension], in a fortunate moment an Italian artist applied to me for employment as a painter of fresco. He asked the use of a wall on which he might paint an example of his skill, saying that he could not carry fresco paintings with him, had executed none in the U. States to which he could refer me, but if I gave him the opportunity he would paint one at his own expense. *I hesitated but at length told him that the room in which I then sat,* which had only a rough coat of brown plaster, might be assigned to the Committee on Agriculture, and he might paint in the lunette of the wall a subject relating to agriculture, provided the sketch he should submit seemed to be worthy.
>
> He made some objection to our costume when asking for a subject and as he was a Roman (expatriated for his share in the last revolution) I suggested Cincinnatus called from the plough to defend his country—a favorite subject with all educated Americans, who associated with that name the Father of our Country.[11]

Thus Brumidi's twenty-five-year career as the Capitol's principal painter began by harking back to an allegorical analogy first made in the 1780s and suggested in 1793 as appropriate for the Capitol's decoration. He went on to execute or supervise the painting of extensive frescos of the so-called Brumidi Corridors, located on the first story of the Senate wing. Brumidi himself did the important lunette paintings above doors and within the arches formed by the vaulted ceilings, while assistants executed his decorative designs of a wide array of American flora and fauna. Portraits, landscapes, and patented American plows complement several historical scenes. All were painted in fresco (later varnished or overpainted in oils) directly on the walls and the curved ceilings in emulation of decorative paintings discovered when the Golden House of Nero (a.d. 64–68) was uncovered in 1516. These original Roman wall paintings formed the basis for a new Renaissance decorative style, which Brumidi in turn reinterpreted through an American Victorian Renaissance Revival lens.

During his career in Rome prior to emigrating to America, Brumidi had restored some of Raphael's Vatican ceilings painted before the discovery of the Golden House of Nero. Brumidi imported his first-hand knowledge of these Renaissance fresco paintings and their rich armature of carved and gilded plaster frames directly to the Capitol Extension. For instance, his ceiling design for the Vice-President's Room, but executed in the President's Room, is based directly on the plate "Coved Ceiling of the 'Stanza Della Segnatura' in the Vatican by

Raphalle D'Urbino," published by Lewis Gruner in *Specimens of Ornamental Art,* 1850 (Fig. 70; Cats. 200 and 201).[12]

Brumidi's intention was twofold: to impart to American political and technological accomplishments a timeless character, and to place them on a par with those of the Renaissance, the age hithertofore perceived to be the acme of human achievement. Meigs's boastful statement in 1854 that America was then the "most powerful and most wealthy nation of the earth" had a corollary: the belief that America's phenomenal success resulted from its national political structure, which fostered both individual and communal achievements.

In 1859, Brumidi made sketches for the Rotunda frieze, *America and History* (Cat. 216.1), responding to criticism of how he had portrayed actual historical events. Painted in monochromatic grisaille to imitate relief sculpture (originally intended by Meigs), Brumidi's frieze (1877-1889), which was finished by Flippo Costaggini, traces in sixteen narrative scenes American events from the landing of Columbus in the New World in 1492 to the discovery of gold in California in 1848. Pre-Revolutionary and Revolutionary-era events predominate, and all the figures are in the dress of their era. Brumidi depicted what he considered to be the most important American milestones: *The Landing of Columbus, 1492; The Entry of Cortez into the Halls of Montezuma, 1521* (Cat. 216.2); *Pizarro's Conquest of Peru, 1533; The Midnight Burial of De Soto in the Mississippi, 1542; Pocahontas Saving the Life of Captain John Smith, 1607; The Landing of the Pilgrims at Plymouth, Massachusetts, 1620; Penn's Treaty with the Indians, 1682; The Colonization of New England, Peace Between Governor Oglethorpe and the Indians, 1732* (Cat. 214); *The Battle of Lexington, 1775; The Reading of the Declaration of Independence, 1776* (Cat. 215); *The Surrender of Cornwallis at Yorktown, 1781; The Death of Tecumseh at the Battle of Thames, 1813* (Cat. 216.3); *The Entry of General Scott into the City of Mexico, 1847;* and *Discovery of Gold in California, 1848* (Cat. 216). Three additional scenes were added by Allyn Cox in 1953: *The Civil War, 1865; The Spanish-American War, 1898;* and *The Birth of Aviation in the United States, 1903.*

For *The Apotheosis of Washington,* his canopy painting suspended between the inner and outer domes, Brumidi chose to depict Washington's elevation to the status of a god in a suitably allegorical manner. His first sketches, done about 1859, focus on a group of Founding Fathers attended by a figure holding the Constitution and groups of figures representing commerce and husbandry (Cat. 217). A circle of female figures emanating from the central group represent the states; an eagle and the flag are in the center.

Brumidi's final version, executed in eleven months in 1864 and 1865, telescopes the circle to only thirteen figures (the original states), with Washington alone attended by Fame and Bellona (Fig. 71; Cat. 218). All wear billowing gowns, but Washington's Continental Army uniform is visible from the waist upward. Six allegorical groupings around the circle's perimeter dominate the composition. Directly beneath Washington, a composite figure of America-Freedom holding a raised sword and a shield of stars and stripes routs Tyranny and Kingly Power. Continuing clockwise, a helmeted figure of Minerva presides over and teaches a large group that includes Benjamin Franklin, Robert Fulton, and Samuel F. B. Morse—all notable American inventors. America's maritime prowess is represented by Neptune driving a chariot while his helpmates, including Venus, lay the transatlantic cable. Industrial smokestacks in the background separate this scene from the next, in which the god of commerce, Mercury, looms above a countinghouse where the chief actor is Robert Morris, financier of the Revolution. To the left, Vulcan, representing the mechanical arts, fashions cannon and cannonballs, perhaps a direct reference to the Civil War, which was still being fought when Brumidi began his work. In the final scene of agriculture, America, wearing a red liberty cap, hands

Ceres, carrying a full cornucopia, the reins of a team of horses that is pulling a reaping machine. Thus the two personifications flanking the central America-Freedom, representing commerce and agriculture, attest to the continuing validity of the Capitol's symbolic role as the magnet of the American population and the showplace of American enterprise.

THOMAS CRAWFORD'S SCULPTURE FOR THE SENATE WING PEDIMENT

Early in his tenure as superintendent of construction, Meigs suggested that the new east pediments contain sculpture, and he worked closely with Thomas Crawford in formulating the themes of his Senate wing pediment and bronze door and his statue of Freedom atop the dome. On August 18, 1853, Meigs wrote to the two most prominent American sculptors residing and working in Rome: Crawford and Hiram Powers. He asked Crawford for designs for the pediment and door of the Senate wing and Powers for those for the House, suggesting that they confer so that their "designs may be of such a character as to harmonize." He went on to expound a socio-politico-aesthetic theory that was commonly held at the time:

> The Pediments & doorways should be a part of the Original Construction of the building & I do not see why a Republic so much richer than the Athenian should not rival the Parthenon in the front of its first public edifice.
>
> Permit me to say that the sculpture sent here by our Artists is not altogether adapted to the taste of our people. We are not able to appreciate too refined & intricate allegorical representations and while the naked Washington of [Horatio] Greenough [commissioned by Congress in 1832 and placed in the Capitol rotunda a decade later] is the theme of admiration, to the few scholars, it is unsparingly denounced by the less refined multitude.
>
> Cannot sculpture be so designed as to please both? In this would be the triumph of the Artist whose works should appeal not to a class but to mankind.
>
> In our history of the struggle between civilized man and the savage, between the cultivated

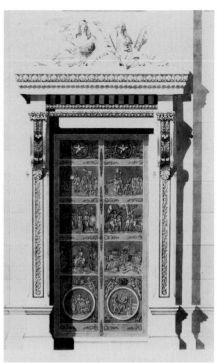

Fig. 72. Thomas Crawford. *The Progress of Civilization,* ca. 1853. Architect of the Capitol.

Fig. 73. Thomas U. Walter. "Front Door, U.S. Capitol," ca. 1854–1857. Architect of the Capitol.

and the wild nature, are certainly to be found themes worthy of the artist & capable of appealing to the feelings of all classes.[13]

Powers declined to submit a design. By October 31, Crawford responded with a pediment entitled *The Progress of Civilization,* and a bronze door with eight panels depicting scenes from George Washington's civic and military life, including his laying of the Capitol's cornerstone in 1793 (Figs. 72 and 73; Cats. 219, 192, and 70). The pediment's central classical figure, America, recalls Greek statues of Athena, as she wears a crown of stars and a liberty cap and stars decorate her mantle. The scene on the viewer's right illustrates the extermination of Native American culture—represented by a defeated and despairing Indian family—by the rapid advance of Euro-Americans, exemplified by a woodsman felling a tree. Four episodes to the viewer's left depict a Revolutionary War soldier, a merchant, a schoolmaster with three children, and a mechanic, or industrial worker. The only reference to agriculture is oblique: the woodsman clearing the forest for cultivation. Crawford sent Meigs a detailed description of the meaning of each individual element, accompanied with photographs of his design sketched in clay:

> The central figure of the composition represents America standing upon a rock against which the waves of the ocean are beating. She is attended by the Eagle of our country, while the sun rising at her feet indicates the light accompanying the march of liberty. In one hand she holds the rewards of civic and military merit—the laurel and oak wreath. The left hand is held out towards the pioneers for whom she asks the protection of the Almighty. . . .
>
> The Indian race and its extinction is explained by the group of the Indian chief and his family. Connecting this group with the backwoodsman are a few stumps of trees in which is seen retreating a rattlesnake. . . . In the statue of the Indian chief I have endeavoured to concentrate all the despair and profound grief resulting from the conviction of the white man's triumph.

The opposite half of the pediment is devote[d] to the effects of civilization and liberty. The first figure represents the soldier. I have given him this important position, as [our] freedom was obtained by the sword and must be preserved by it. I have clothed the statue with the military costume of our revolution as being suggestive of our country's struggle f[or] independence. . . .

Adjoining the soldier I have placed the merch[ant] sitting upon the emblems of commerce. His right ha[nd] rests upon the globe to indicate the extent of our trade. The anchor connects his figure with thos[e] of two boys, who are advancing cheerfully forward to devote themselves to the service of their country. The anchor at their feet is an easily understood emblem of hope for them in the future. Behind them si[ts] the teacher, emblematic of scholarship. He is instructing a child, whose career is shown by the advance of the boys his school mates. The mechanic completes this group. He rests upon the cogwheel, without which machinery is useless. In his hands are the implements of his profession, the hammer and compass; at his feet are seen [?] sheaves of wheat, expressive of fertility, activity, and abundance, in contradistinction to the emblem of Indian extinction—the grave—at the corresponding angle of the tympanum.[14]

The idealism that had pervaded the original Capitol's decoration was replaced in the extensions by a pragmatic ethnocentrism. Crawford's "march of liberty" was in reality an expansionist economic creed.

PAUL BARTLETT'S SCULPTURE FOR THE HOUSE WING PEDIMENT

Fig. 74. Paul Bartlett. Head of "Peace," from *Peace Protecting Genius,* cast 1927. James Monroe Museum and Memorial Library, Fredericksburg, Virginia.

Remarkably, the Capitol's final important iconographic decoration repeats, perhaps unknowingly, the basic themes first propounded as appropriate in the 1790s. Paul Bartlett's sculpture for the pediment of the House wing, *The Apotheosis of Democracy,* was not put in place until 1916 (Cat. 220). Beginning in 1908, Bartlett worked closely with a joint congressional committee to establish the pediment's meaning. Initially, the sculptor was told that there was a "vague feeling in the committee that the subject be taken from the history of the United States." During discussion, however, the sculptor and the legislators concluded that the pediment's "theme should be of the present rather than of the past. We thought because the House represents in its largest sense the people, that the people—the life and labors of the people—should be portrayed on this building, this temple of democracy."[15]

Bartlett's central allegory, "Peace Protecting Genius," is flanked by "two large figural groups representing, to the viewer's right, the labors of agriculture, and to the viewer's left, the labors of industry" (Fig. 74; Cats. 221 and 222). Waves at the corners of the pediment represent the Atlantic and Pacific oceans. In the twentieth century, agriculture is no longer cast allegorically as a classical figure of Ceres or as cornstalks, but as heroic American farmers—men, women, and children—accompanied by an ox, the animal that plowed nineteenth-century America. To signify industry, Bartlett chose to depict foundrymen smelting iron. This specificity of scenes of everyday labor, and Bartlett's naturalistic treatment of the farmers and ironworkers in their work clothes, were intended to engage the viewer in the pediment's democratic content. The classical figure of Mercury, suggested by several of the

Capitol's original competitors to represent commerce, and even Latrobe's tobacco order, do not have the immediacy and directness of Bartlett's sculpture.[16]

Bartlett reserved abstract personification for his central group. His towering "Peace," wrapped in a toga, has the austere remoteness of a classical deity. Her stance and some of her attributes—a breastplate and shield—link her to the warrior goddess Athena. The head of "Peace," particularly her peaked crown of laurel leaves, recalls Daniel Chester French's head of the Republic, created for the World's Columbian Exposition in Chicago in 1893. As Giuseppe Ceracchi, Benjamin Henry Latrobe, and Enrico Causici had conflated Minerva-Athena figures with those of Liberty and America, Bartlett continued to combine European and American models to generate a new American allegorical figure. The Capitol's earlier allegorical figures had been cast as guardians who fused multiple political virtues into one personification; Bartlett's "Peace," by protecting "Genius," the spirit of the people, glorifies the past settlement of the country and the development of its natural resources and looks to its future opportunities. Bartlett's *The Apotheosis of Democracy* is ultimately an allegory of good government: democracy makes these successes possible. Bartlett's figures literally represent the cultivators and forgers of the past and future of the United States and as such sum up the Capitol's meaning in American history.

The Capitol's original legislative chambers and the Rotunda are now museum rooms, frozen in time, while the surrounding offices and the wing extensions are living spaces that still respond to the needs of Congress and the American public. The Capitol was designed and redesigned to serve the Senate, the House of Representatives, the Supreme Court, the Library of Congress, and the American people. The Court's and the library's needs grew beyond the Capitol's ability to accommodate them, but Congress and the people have been continually served for two centuries.

Catalog of Objects in the Exhibition

Wherever possible, photograph negative numbers have been provided for items in the exhibition. Items in the Library of Congress collections are indicated by the prefix "LC." Numbers containing "USZ62" and "USA7" are for black-and-white images; those containing "USZC2" and "USZC4" represent color transparencies. "G & M" indicates negatives in the Geography and Map Division and "MSS" those in the Manuscript Division. The Library has photographs of and negative numbers for some exhibit items not in its collection. Some items in the exhibition do not yet have negative numbers, but may be assigned them in the future. Before ordering photographs, please check all information with the appropriate custodial division of the Library. Information on items not in the Library's collections may be obtained from the lending institutions.

1 Benjamin Franklin. "Join, or Die." *Pennsylvania Gazette.* (Philadelphia), May 9, 1754. Newspaper. 15 ⅝ x 10 in. Neg. no. LC-USZ62-9701. Serial and Government Publications Division, Library of Congress.

2 Paul Revere. "Join or Die." *Massachusetts Spy* (Boston), July 7, 1774. Newspaper. 17 ⅝ x 10 ½ in. Neg. no. LC-USZ62-7984. Serial and Government Publications Division, Library of Congress.

3 [Liberty Column Supported by Twelve Arms]. Title page of *Journal of the Proceedings of the [Continental] Congress, Held at Philadelphia, September 5, 1774* (Philadelphia: William and Thomas Bradford, 1774). 1 ½ in. diameter. Rare Book and Special Collections Division, Library of Congress.

4 Omitted.

4.1 Robert Wood. "Soffit of the door of the cell of the Temple." Table XVIII, H, in *The Ruins of Palmyra, Otherwise Tedmor in the Desart* [*sic*] (London, 1753). Copyprint. Rare Book and Special Collections Division, Library of Congress.

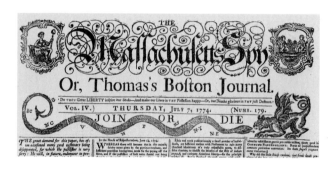

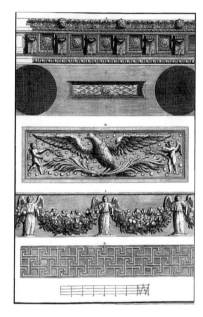

5 After John Faber. "Tomo Chachi Mico." Frontispiece in Samuel Urlsperger, *Ausfürliche nachricht von den saltzburgischen emigranten* (Halle: Wåysenhauses, 1744). Engraving in book. 8 ¾ x 6 ⅞ in. Neg. no. LC-USZ62-1921. Rare Book and Special Collections Division, Library of Congress.

6 Robert Scott. Indian Peace Medal, 1801. Bronze. 4 in. diameter. National Numismatic Collection, National Museum of American History, Smithsonian Institution.

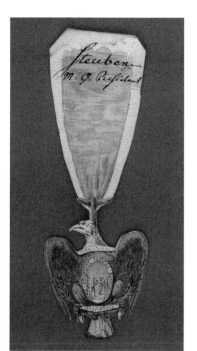

7 William Barton. Second Design for the Great Seal of the United States, 1782. Watercolor on paper. 14 ½ x 11 ⅞ in. National Archives and Records Administration.

8 Charles Thomson. Obverse, Great Seal of the United States, 1782. Ink and crayon on paper. 3 ⅞ in. diameter. Neg. no. LC-USZ62-45729. National Archives and Records Administration.

9 James Trenchard. "Arms of the United States." Page 33 in *The Columbian Magazine* (Philadelphia), September 1786. Engraving in book.

6 ⅞ x 4 ⅜ in. Rare Book and Special Collections Division, Library of Congress.

10 Pierre Charles L'Enfant. [Design for the Society of the Cincinnati Eagle], 1783. Watercolor on paper. 4 ½ x 1 ½ in. The Society of the Cincinnati Museum at Anderson House, Washington, D.C.

11 After Pierre Eugene du Simitière [Design for the Great Seal of the United States], 1776. Copyprint. 2 ½ x 7 ⅛ in. Neg. no. LC-USZ62-45728. Thomas Jefferson Papers, Manuscript Division, Library of Congress.

12 Photograph not available. See page 142.

13 "America Triumphant and Britannica in Distress," Boston, 1782. Engraving. 7 ¹⁄₁₆ x 8 ¼ in. Neg. no. LC-USZ62-45922. Prints and Photographs Division, Library of Congress.

14 Pierre Charles L'Enfant. [Society of the Cincinnati Certificate of John Yeamons], January 1784. Engraving on parchment. 14 ¼ x 20 ⅞ in. Manuscript Division, Library of Congress.

15 Benjamin Franklin, designer, and Claude-Michel Clodion, sculptor. *Allegory of the American Revolution*, 1783. Terra-cotta sculpture. 14 ⁹⁄₁₆ in. diameter. Musée National de la Coopération Franco-Améri-caine, Blérancourt, France.

16 François, Marquis de Barbé-Marbois, designer. "Allegory of the American Union," 1784. Watercolor on paper. 11 ½ x 8 ½ in. American Philosophical Society, Philadelphia.

17 Joseph Strutt, after Robert Edge Pine. "Allegory of America," London, 1781. Stipple engraving. 19 ⅛ x 24 in. Neg. no. LC-USZ62-15366. Prints and Photographs Division, Library of Congress.

18 W. D. Cooper. "America Trampling on Oppression." Frontispiece in *The History of North America* (London: E. Newberry, 1789). 4 ½ x 2 ⅝ in. Rare Book and Special Collections Division, Library of Congress.

19 Giuseppe Ceracchi. *Minerva as the Patroness of American Liberty*, 1792. 66 in. high. Copyprint of patinated terra-cotta bust. Library Company of Philadelphia.

110

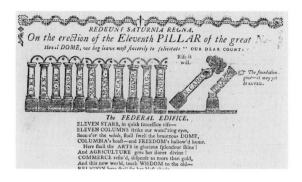

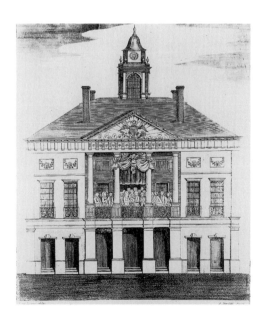

26 Jean-Antoine Houdon. Bust of George Washington, ca. 1786–1793. Plaster. 20 ⅞ in. high. © 1994 Board of Trustees, National Gallery of Art, Washington, D.C. Gift of Robert L. McNeil, Jr., in Honor of the Fiftieth Anniversary of the National Gallery of Art.

27 After Jean-Antoine Houdon. Bust of Thomas Jefferson, ca. 1784–1789, ca. 1948. Plaster. 27 in. high. Library of Congress. Franz Jantzen, photographer, 1994.

28 Thomas Jefferson. [Proposed Plan of the Federal City], 1791. Ink on paper. 15 ⁵⁄₁₆ x 9 ¾ in. G & M Neg. no. 1056. Thomas Jefferson Papers, Manuscript Division, Library of Congress.

29 Pierre Charles L'Enfant. "Plan of the City of Washington," March 1792. Engraving on paper. 13 ⅜ x 16 ½ in. Neg. no. 2438. Geography and Map Division, Library of Congress.

30 Thomas Jefferson. [Announcement of Capitol Design Competition]. *Dunlap's American Daily Advertiser* (Philadelphia), March 24, 1792. Newspaper. 21 ⅜ x 12 in. Serial and Government Publications Division, Library of Congress.

31 Attributed to Thomas Jefferson. [Possible Study for the Capitol, Plan and Elevation], ca. 1792. Ink sketch on paper. 7 ¾ x 4 ½ in. Nichols no. 387. Massachusetts Historical Society, Boston.

32 Thomas Jefferson. [Study for the Capitol, Plan], ca. 1792. Ink on paper. 7 ¼ x 7 in. Nichols no. 388. Massachusetts Historical Society, Boston.

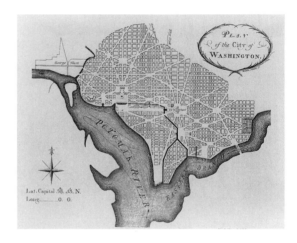

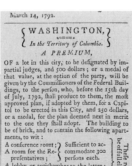
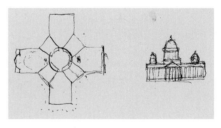

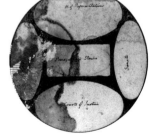

112

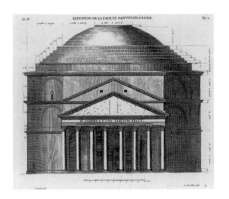

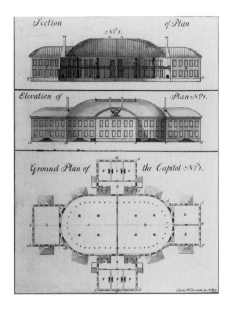

33 Antoine Desgodetz. "Elevation de la face du Pantheon, à Rome." Plate 3 in *Les Edifices antiques de Rome* (Paris: Claude-Antoine Jombert, 1779). Engraving in book. 12 x 13 ¾ in. Rare Book and Special Collections Division, Library of Congress.

34 Charles Wintersmith. [Section, Elevation, and Plan of Capitol Design No. 1], 1792. Ink and watercolor washes on paper. 21 ¼ x 16 ⅞ in. Acc. no. 76.88.42. Maryland Historical Society, Baltimore.

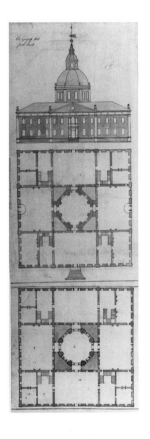

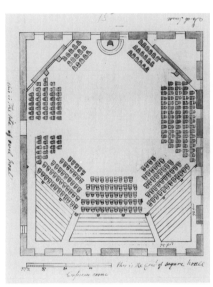

35 Jacob Small. "For Congress Hall," 1792. Ink and ink washes on paper. 20 ³⁄₁₆ x 10 ⁹⁄₁₆ in. Acc. no. 76.88.34. Maryland Historical Society, Baltimore.

36 Jacob Small. "Conference Roome [*sic*]," 1792. Ink, watercolor, and ink washes on paper. 11 ⅝ x 9 ⁹⁄₁₆ in. Acc. no. 76.88.31. Maryland Historical Society, Baltimore.

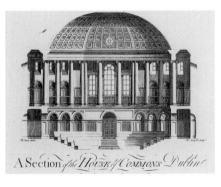

36.1 Rowland Omer. "A Section of the House of Commons, Dublin," 1767. Engraving on paper. 12 ½ x 15 ½ in. Courtesy of the National Library of Ireland, Dublin.

37 Philip Hart. "Elevation of a Capitol," 1792. Ink on paper. 18 ⅝ x 23 ¹⁵⁄₁₆ in. Acc. no. 76.88.12. Maryland Historical Society, Baltimore.

38 Robert Goin Lanphier. "Elevation for the Capitol," 1792. Ink and ink washes on paper. 25 15/16 x 29 3/8 in. Acc. no. 76.88.19. Maryland Historical Society, Baltimore.

39 James Diamond. "Section of the back Front on the Court Side," and "Back Front or Flank, to Plan No. 1 for a Capitol," 1792. Ink and ink washes on paper. 20 15/16 x 15 in. Acc. no. 76.88.50. Maryland Historical Society, Baltimore.

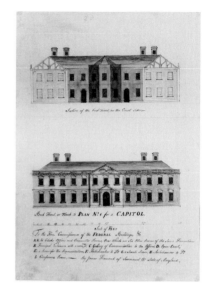

40 James Diamond. "An Elevation for a Capitol," 1792. Ink and ink washes on paper. 14 13/16 x 19 3/4 in. Acc. no. 76.88.51. Maryland Historical Society, Baltimore.

41 James Diamond. "An Elevation for a Capitol for Plan No. 2," 1792. Ink, watercolor, and ink washes on paper. 14 7/8 x 19 3/8 in. Acc. no. 76.88.52. Maryland Historical Society, Baltimore.

42 Giacomo Leoni, after Andrea Palladio. [Basilica, Vicenza]. Plate XX in *The Architecture of Palladio in Four Books*, 3rd ed., vol. 1 (London, 1742). Engraving in book. 12 3/4 x 8 7/8 in. Rare Book and Special Collections Division, Library of Congress.

43 Samuel Dobie. "No. 2 of Saml. Dobie invt & del. for a Capitol to be built in the City of Washington," 1792. Ink and ink washes on paper. 14 11/16 x 9 3/8 in. Acc. no. 76.88.40. Maryland Historical Society, Baltimore.

44 Omitted.

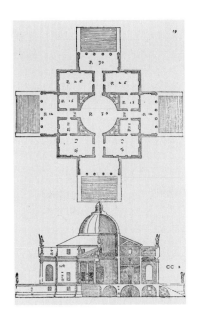

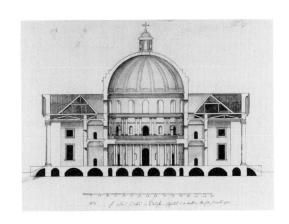

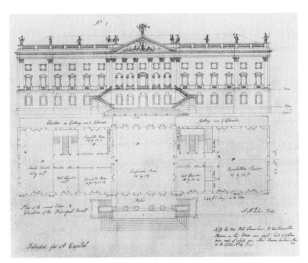

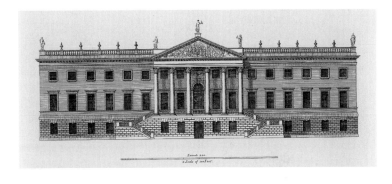

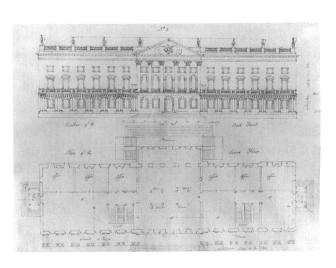

44.1 Andrea Palladio. [Villa Rotunda]. Page 19 of "Libro Secundo" in *I quattro libri dell'architettura* (Venice: Bartolomeo Carampello, 1601). 12 ½ x 8 ¼ in. Engraving in book. Prints and Photographs Division, Library of Congress.

45 Samuel Dobie. "No. 3 of Saml. Dobie inv. & del. for a Capital [*sic*] to be Built in the City of Washington," 1792. Ink and ink washes on paper. 13 ⁹⁄₁₆ x 19 in. Acc. no. 76.88.41. Maryland Historical Society, Baltimore.

46 Samuel McIntire. "Plan of the second Floor & Elevation of the Principal Front," 1792. Ink on paper. 14 ⅛ x 18 ⅜ in. Acc. no. 76.88.47. Maryland Historical Society, Baltimore.

47 Colen Campbell. "The First Design of the West Front of Wansted." Plate 22 in *Vitruvius Britannicus*, vol. 1 (London, 1715). Engraving in book. 9 ¾ x 15 in. Rare Book and Special Collections Division, Library of Congress.

48 Samuel McIntire. "No. 2. Elevation of the Back Front and Plan of the Lower Floor and Plan for Capitol Design," 1792. Ink and ink washes on paper. 13 ¼ x 17 ⅞ in. Acc. no. 76.88.45. Maryland Historical Society, Baltimore.

49a, 49b Samuel McIntire. [Sections for the Capitol Design], 1792. Ink and ink washes on paper. *(a)* 8 ⅞ x 18 ⁷⁄₁₆ in.; *(b)* 6 ¹¹⁄₁₆ x 18 ¼ in. *(a)* Acc. no. 76.88.44; *(b)* Acc. no. 76.88.48. Maryland Historical Society, Baltimore.

50 Andrew Mayfield Carshore. "Respective *[sic]* View of the Federal House," 1792. Ink and ink washes on paper. 10 ⅜ x 15 ⅞ in. Acc. no. 76.88.23. Maryland Historical Society, Baltimore.

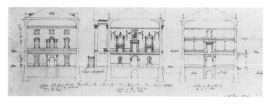

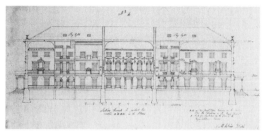

51 Stephen Hallet. [Elevation of First Design for the Capitol] "Plan B 2," ca. 1791. Ink and watercolor on paper. 14 ⅜ x 40 ⅛ in. Neg. nos. LC-USZ62-13187, LC-USZC4-224. Prints and Photographs Division, Library of Congress.

52 Israel Silvestre. "Veue et Perspective du Collège des 4 Nations." Adam Perelle, *Veues des Plus Belles Maisons de France* (Paris: I. Mariette, ca. 1700). Engraving in book. 11 ¾ x 30 in. Rare Book and Special Collections Division, Library of Congress.

53 Stephen Hallet. [Plan of Precompetition Design for the Capitol], ca. 1791. Ink on paper. 18 x 40 ⁹⁄₁₆ in. Neg. nos. LC-USZ62-37069, LC-USZC4-160. Prints and Photographs Division, Library of Congress.

54 Photograph not available. See page 142.

55 Stephen Hallet. [Plan of Capitol Competition Entry], 1792. Ink on paper. 16 ½ x 42 ¾ in. Neg. nos. LC-USZ62-37070, LC-USZC4-161. Prints and Photographs Division, Library of Congress.

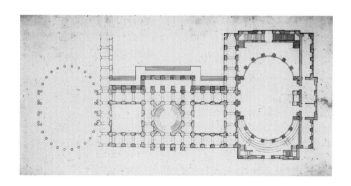

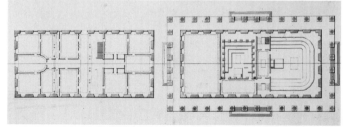

56 Benjamin Henry Latrobe. "View of the City of Richmond from the Bank of the James River," 1798. Watercolor on paper. 7 x 10 ¼ in. Maryland Historical Society, Baltimore.

57 See Plate 3.

58 Stephen Hallet. [Elevation of Fourth Design for the Capitol], 1793. Ink and watercolor on paper. 19 ⅛ x 42 ½ in. Neg. no. LC-USZ62-37080. Prints and Photographs Division, Library of Congress.

59 Stephen Hallet. [Section of Fourth Design for the Capitol], 1793. Ink and watercolor on paper. 19 ¾ x 44 ⅛ in. Neg. no. LC-USZ62-63154. Prints and Photographs Division, Library of Congress.

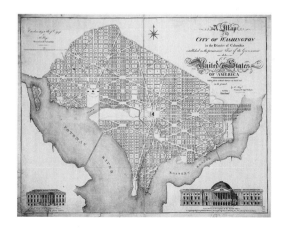

60 William Thornton. [West Elevation, "Tortola" Plan for a Capitol], 1792. Watercolor on paper. 9 x 27 ⅞ in. The Prints and Drawings Collection, The Octagon, The Museum of the American Architectural Foundation, Washington, D.C.

61 William Thornton. [East Elevation, "Tortola" Plan for a Capitol], 1792. Ink and watercolor on paper. 9 ¼ x 18 ¾ in. The Prints and Drawings Col-

lection, The Octagon, The Museum of the American Architectural Foundation, Washington, D.C.

62 Robert King. "A Map of the City of Washington in the District of Columbia," 1818. Engraving. 24 x 31 in. Neg. no. 1080.1. Geography and Map Division, Library of Congress.

63 Don Alexander Hawkins. Reconstruction of William Thornton's West Front of 1793, 1994. Copyprint from silver-gelatin print. Courtesy of Don Alexander Hawkins.

64 Don Alexander Hawkins. Reconstruction of William Thornton's Principal Floor Plan of 1793, 1994. Copyprint from silver-gelatin print. Courtesy of Don Alexander Hawkins.

65 Stephen Hallet. [Elevation of Fifth Design for the Capitol], 1793. Watercolor on paper. 19 ¼ x 39 ¼ in. Neg. nos. LC-USZ62-94657, LC-USZC4-164. Prints and Photographs Division, Library of Congress.

66 See Plate 4.

67 Stephen Hallet. [Principal Floor, Plan of Fifth Design for the Capitol], 1793. Ink and watercolor on paper. 21 ½ x 44 ½ in. Neg. nos. LC-USZ62-37079, LC-USZC4-170. Prints and Photographs Division, Library of Congress.

68 Stephen Hallet. [Conference Plan for the Capitol], 1793. Ink on paper. 14 ⅞ x 21 ⅝ in. Neg. nos. LC-USZ62-37064, LC-USZC4-125. Prints and Photographs Division, Library of Congress.

69 Stephen Hallet. [Post-Conference Plan for the Capitol], 1793–1794. Ink on paper. 17 ½ x 22 ⅜ in. Neg. no. LC-USZ62-13239. Prints and Photographs Division, Library of Congress.

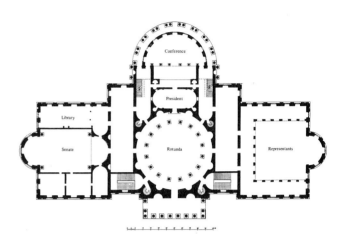

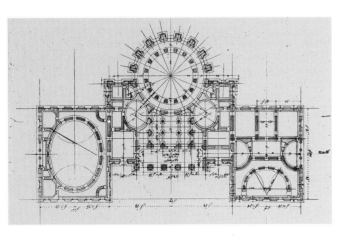

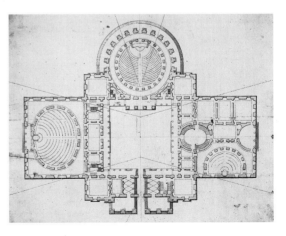

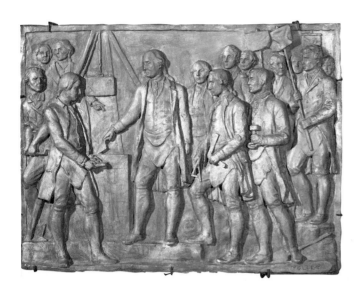

70 After Thomas Crawford, [?] Nolley, maker. [Laying the Cornerstone of the United States Capitol], n. d. Plaster relief sculpture. 22 x 27 ⅞ x 3 ⅛ in. Architect of the Capitol. Donated by the U.S. Capitol Historical Society.

71 Charles-Balthazar-Julien Févret de Saint-Mémin. Portrait of William Thornton, ca. 1799–1804. Chalk on paper. 26 x 20 in. The Octagon, The Museum of the American Architectural Foundation, Washington, D.C.

72 See Plate 5. **73** See Plate 6.

74 Architectural Model of William Thornton's Revised Design for the Capitol, 1994. Plastic. 54 x 48 x 21 in. Architect of the Capitol.

75 William Thornton. [Sketch of Section of Monument and Conference Room], ca. 1797. Ink on paper. 18 x 14 in. Neg. no. LC-USZ62-56088. Prints and Photographs Division, Library of Congress.

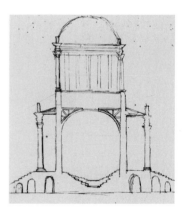

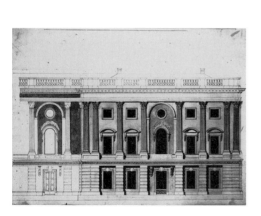

76 William Thornton. [East Elevation for the North Wing], 1795–1797. Watercolor on paper. 17 ⅝ x 23 ⅞ in. Neg. nos. LC-USZ62-37194, LC-USZC4-274. Prints and Photographs Division, Library of Congress.

77 William Thornton and Charles Bulfinch. Corinthian Capital from the East Front Portico of the Capitol, 1825. Copyprint of Aquia sandstone sculpture. 67 ½ in. high. Architect of the Capitol.

119

78 "The Corinthian Order." Plate 12F in Sir William Chambers, *A Treatise on Civil Architecture* (London: John Haberkorn, 1759). Engraving in book. 16 ⅛ x 11 ¾ in. Prints and Photographs Division, Library of Congress.

79 Attributed to Alexander Jackson Davis, after George Hadfield. "Plan for the Capitol, Washington, by George Hadfield, first Arc. 1795," ca. 1831–1834. Watercolor on paper. 14 ⅜ x 10 ¼ in. Machen Collection, The Historical Society of Washington, D.C.

80 After George Hadfield. [Perspective of the West Front of the Capitol]. *Washington Gazette*, February 2, 1819. Copyprint from newspaper. Serial and Government Publications Division, Library of Congress.

81a, 81b Attributed to George Hadfield. [East and West Elevations of the Capitol], ca. 1795. Ink on paper. *(a)* 9 ⅝ x 18 1/16 in.; *(b)* 9 ⅝ x 19 in. *(a)* Acc. no. 76.88.01; *(b)* Acc. no. 76.88.02. Maryland Historical Society, Baltimore.

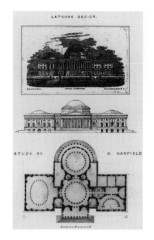

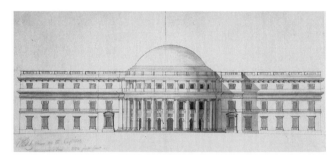

82 Office of the Architect of the Capitol. [Conjectural Reconstruction of the House of Representatives in 1804], 1989. Photograph. Architect of the Capitol.

83 See Plate 14.

84 Charles Willson Peale. Benjamin Henry Latrobe, ca. 1804. Oil painting. 22 ½ x 19 ½ in. The White House, Washington, D.C.

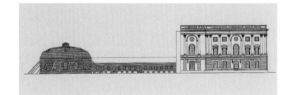

120

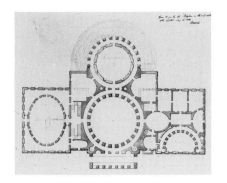

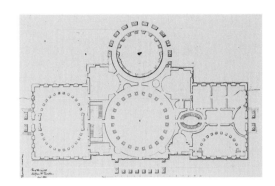

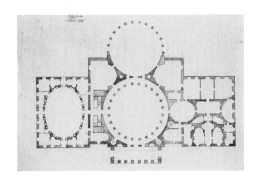

85 William Thornton. [Plan of the Ground Story of the Capitol], ca. 1795–1797. Ink and watercolor on paper. Neg. no. LC-USZ62-13238. Prints and Photographs Division, Library of Congress.

86 William Thornton. [Plan of the Principal Floor of the Capitol], ca. 1795–1797. Ink and watercolor on paper. 17 ⅜ x 24 ½ in. Neg. no. LC-USZ62-13237. Prints and Photographs Division, Library of Congress.

87 William Thornton. [Plan of the Ground Story of the Capitol], ca. 1804. Ink and watercolor on paper. 18 ⅛ x 21 ½ in. Neg. no. LC-USZ62-13236. Prints and Photographs Division, Library of Congress.

88 See Plate 7.

88.1 Robert Wood. "Temple." Table XIV in *The Ruins of Palmyra, Otherwise Tedmor in the Desart* [*sic*] (London, 1753). 9 ¾ x 15 ¼ in. Engraving in book. Rare Book and Special Collections Division, Library of Congress.

89 Benjamin Henry Latrobe. [Study for a West Front], ca. 1808–1809. Watercolor on paper. 21 ⅞ x 30 ⅝ in. Neg. nos. LC-USZ62-13250, LC-USZC4-217. Prints and Photographs Division, Library of Congress.

90 Benjamin Henry Latrobe. [Perspective View of the Capitol from the Northeast], 1810. Watercolor on paper. 17 x 25 ⅜ in. Acc. no. 1897.1.1. Maryland Historical Society, Baltimore.

91 [Panathenaic Procession]. Plate XVIII in James Stuart and Nicholas Revett, *Antiquities of Athens*, vol. 2 (London: John Haberkorn, 1762). Engraving in book. 30 x 22 in. Prints and Photographs Division, Library of Congress.

92 Benjamin Henry Latrobe. [Plan of the Mall and the Capitol Grounds], 1815. Watercolor on paper. 23 x 18 ½ in. Neg. no. 1147. Geography and Map Division, Library of Congress.

93 Architectural Model of Benjamin Henry Latrobe's Design for the Capitol of ca. 1811, 1994. Plastic. 54 x 48 x 21 in. Architect of the Capitol.

94 See Plate 9. **95** See Plate 8. **96** See Plate 10.

97 Charles Turner, after John James Hall. "Admiral Sir John Cockburn," 1819. Engraving. 24 ¼ x 14 ¹³⁄₁₆ in. Neg. no. LC-USZ62-12334. Prints and Photographs Division, Library of Congress.

98 George Heriot. [View of the Burned Capitol], 1815. Watercolor on paper. 4 ⅛ x 8 in. Neg. no. 23679. Collection of The New-York Historical Society, New York.

99 Mather Brown. *Portrait of Charles Bulfinch*, 1786. Copyprint of oil painting. 30 x 25 ⅛ in. Courtesy of the Harvard University Portrait Collection, Harvard University Art Museums, Cambridge, Mass. Gift of Francis V. Bulfinch.

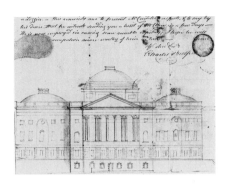

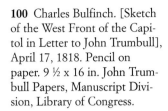

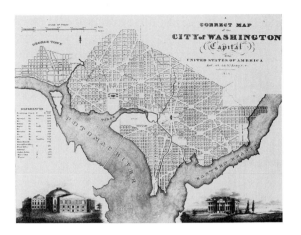

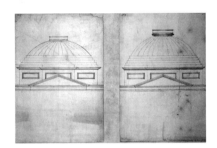

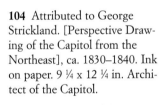

100 Charles Bulfinch. [Sketch of the West Front of the Capitol in Letter to John Trumbull], April 17, 1818. Pencil on paper. 9 ½ x 16 in. John Trumbull Papers, Manuscript Division, Library of Congress.

101 W. I. Stone. "Correct Map of the City of Washington," 1820. Engraving. 16 ½ x 20 ⅞ in. G & M neg. no. 1081. Geography and Map Division, Library of Congress.

102 Charles A. Busby. "The Capitol at Washington. Elevation of the Principal Front," 1823. Etching on paper. 18 ¾ x 25 ⅜ in. Neg. no. USA7-35663. Prints and Photographs Division, Library of Congress.

103 Charles Bulfinch. [Alternative Designs for the Capitol Dome], ca. 1824. Ink on paper. 21 ⅜ x 15 ⅛ in. each. Neg. no. LC-USZ62-33562. Prints and Photographs Division, Library of Congress.

104 Attributed to George Strickland. [Perspective Drawing of the Capitol from the Northeast], ca. 1830–1840. Ink on paper. 9 ¼ x 12 ¼ in. Architect of the Capitol.

105 [West Front of the Capitol], ca. 1848. Copyprint. Architect of the Capitol.

106 Architectural Model of
Charles Bulfinch's Capitol of
1829, 1994. Plastic. 96 x 72 x
21 in. Architect of the Capitol.

107 Charles Bulfinch.
[Site Plan of the Capitol], ca.
1826–1829. Watercolor on
paper. 23 ⅞ x 33 ½ in. Neg.
nos. LC-USZ62-37103, LC-
USZC4-238. Prints and Photographs Division, Library of
Congress.

108 See Plate 2.

109 Charles Burton. [View
of the Capitol], 1824. Watercolor on paper. 16 x 20 ¼ in.
Acc. no. 42.138; Neg. no. MM
129651 B. Lent by The Metropolitan Museum of Art, New
York. Purchase, Joseph
Pulitzer Bequest, 1942.

110 John Rubens Smith. [West
Front of the Capitol], ca. 1828.
Pencil on paper. 19 ½ x 23 in.
John Rubens Smith Collection,
Prints and Photographs Divi-
sion, Library of Congress. Gift
of the Madison Council and
Mrs. Joseph Carson.

111 See Plate 11. **112** See
Plate 13. **113** See Plate 12.

114 John Plumbe. [East Front
of the Capitol], 1846. Copyprint from glass negative. Neg.
no. LC-USZ62-46801. Prints
and Photographs Division,
Library of Congress.

115 After Luigi Persico.
Genius of America of
1825–1828, 1959–1960. Marble. 9 ft. high. Photograph of
sculpture. Architect of the
Capitol.

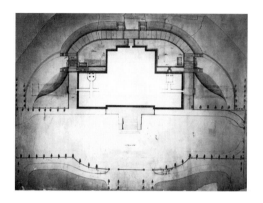

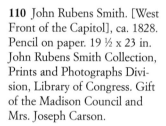

116 After Luigi Persico. *War* of 1834, 1958. Marble. 8 ¾ ft. high. Photograph of sculpture. Architect of the Capitol.

117 After Luigi Persico. *Peace* of 1834, 1958. Photograph of sculpture. Architect of the Capitol.

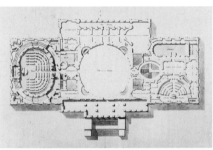

118 Benjamin Henry Latrobe. "Plan of the Principal Story of the Capitol, U.S.," 1806. Watercolor on paper. 19 ⁵⁄₁₆ x 29 ⅞ in. Neg. no. LC-USZ62-5464. Prints and Photographs Division, Library of Congress.

119 Benjamin Henry Latrobe. "Plan of the Principal Floor at the Capitol, U.S.," 1817. Watercolor on paper. 21 ⅛ x 31 ¾ in. Neg. nos. LC-USZ62-11125, LC-USZC4-199. Prints and Photographs Division, Library of Congress.

120 Benjamin Henry Latrobe. General View of the Supreme Court of 1808–1810, ca. 1976. Photograph. Architect of the Capitol.

121 Photograph not available. See page 142.

122 Benjamin Henry Latrobe. "Sections of the Court Room, N. Wing, Capitol," ca. 1808. Watercolor on paper. 14 ⁷⁄₁₆ x 19 ⁷⁄₁₆ in. Neg. nos. LC-USZ62-13235, LC-USZC4-124. Prints and Photographs Division, Library of Congress.

123 See Plate 16.

124 Omitted.

124.1 Thomas Major. "Members and Measures of the Hexastyle Ipetral Temple." Table XII in *Ruins of Paestum, Otherwise Posidonia, in Magna Graecia* (London: T. Major, 1768). Engraving in book. 10 ¾ x 14 ¾ in. Rare Book and Special Collections Division, Library of Congress.

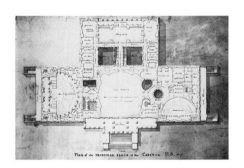

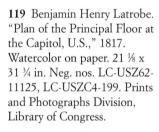
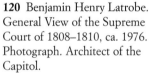

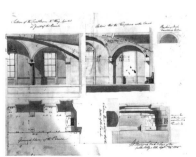
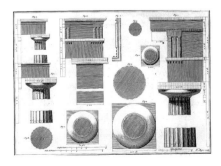

125

125 Giuseppe or Carlo Franzoni. *Justice*, ca. 1809–1815. Pencil on paper. 5 x 8 in. Neg. no. LC-USA7-35656. The Historical Society of Washington, D.C.

126 Giuseppe or Carlo Franzoni. *Justice,* ca. 1809–1815. Pencil on paper. 4 x 6 ½ in. Neg. no. LC-USA7-35655. The Historical Society of Washington, D.C.

127 Photograph not available. See page 142.

128 Benjamin Henry Latrobe. "Plan of the Principal Story of the North Wing of the Capitol U.S. as authorised to be built," 1817. Ink and watercolor on paper. 20 x 31 ⅜ in. Neg. no. LC-USZ62-11127. Prints and Photographs Division, Library of Congress.

129 Benjamin Henry Latrobe. Corn Capital Vestibule to the Supreme Court of 1808, ca. 1976. Copyprint. Architect of Capitol.

130 Alexander Jackson Davis. ["Corn Order" from the Capitol, Washington], ca. 1831–1834. Copyprint of ink and wash drawing. Acc. no. 24.66.1407, Vol. VIII, leaf 5 (9); neg. no. MM84920B. Courtesy of The Metropolitan Museum of Art, New York. Harris Brisbane Dick Fund, 1924.

131 See Plate 15.

132 Photograph not available. See page 142.

133 Benjamin Henry Latrobe. [Sketch of the Tobacco-Leaf Capital in Letter to Thomas Jefferson], November 5, 1816. Ink on paper. 9 ⅞ x 7 ¾ in. Neg. no. LC-MSS-027748-43. Thomas Jefferson Papers, Manuscript Division, Library of Congress.

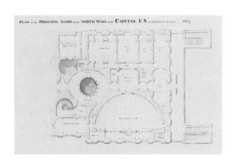

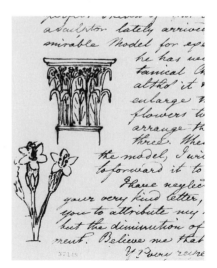

134 Benjamin Henry Latrobe, designer, and Francesco Iardella, sculptor. Tobacco-Leaf Capital, 1817. Sandstone. 18 x 21 x 21 in. Monticello/Thomas Jefferson Foundation, Inc., Charlottesville, Va.

135 Benjamin Henry Latrobe. Old Senate Chamber, 1815–1817, ca. 1976. Copyprint. Architect of the Capitol.

136 Julien David LeRoy. [Ionic Order]. Plate XX in *Les Ruines plus beaux des monuments de la Grèce* (Paris: H. L. Guerin and L. F. Delatour, 1758). Engraving in book. 18 ½ x 12 ½ in. Prints and Photographs Division, Library of Congress.

137 See Plate 18.

138 Omitted.

139 Benjamin Henry Latrobe. "Details of the Upper Columns in the Gallery of the Entrance of the Chamber of the Senate, U[nited] States," 1809. Watercolor on paper. 28 ¼ x 20 in. Neg. no. USZ62-13253. Prints and Photographs Division, Library of Congress.

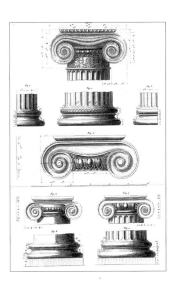

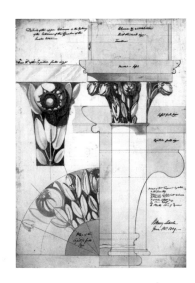

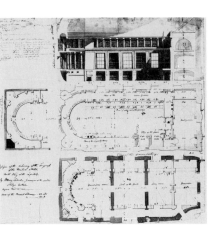

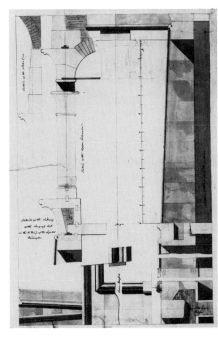

140 Benjamin Henry Latrobe. "Design of the Library of Congress of the United States, North Wing of the Capitol," 1808. Ink and watercolor on paper. 21 ⅜ x 24 ⅜ in. Neg. no. LC-USZ62-10823. Prints and Photographs Division, Library of Congress.

141 Benjamin Henry Latrobe. "Details of the Library of the Congress U.S. in the N. Wing of the Capitol Washington," ca. 1808–1816. Watercolor on paper. 26 ⅜ x 18 ⅞ in. Neg. no. LC-USZ62-10822. Prints and Photographs Division, Library of Congress.

142 See Plate 19.

127

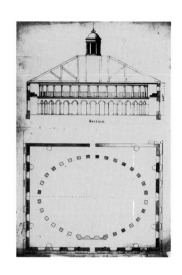

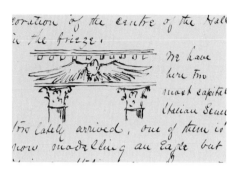

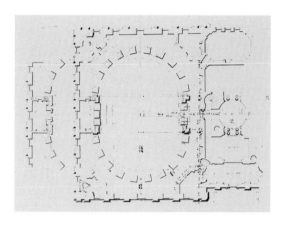

143 Attributed to James Hoban. [Projected Design of Hall for the House of Representatives], ca. 1801. Ink and ink washes on paper. 14 ¾ x 20 ¼ in. Nichols no. 390, Thomas Jefferson Papers, Alderman Library, University of Virginia, Charlottesville.

144 See Plate 21.

145 Benjamin Henry Latrobe. [Eagle in Entablature in Letter to Charles Willson Peale], April 18, 1806. Ink on paper. 14 ⅝ x 20 in. Benjamin Henry Latrobe Papers, Manuscript Division, Library of Congress.

146 Benjamin Henry Latrobe. [Plan of the House of Representatives], ca. 1808–1813. Ink and watercolor on paper. 18 ¹⁵⁄₁₆ x 24 ⅜ in. Neg. no. LC-USZ62-13244. Prints and Photographs Division, Library of Congress.

147 Omitted.

148 Benjamin Henry Latrobe. "Sketch of a Section of the Capitol of the United States at Washington, of the Doric Order, Roman," 1804. Watercolor on paper. 13 ⅝ x 22 in. Neg. no. LC-USZ62-13247. Prints and Photographs Division, Library of Congress.

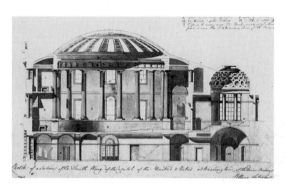

149 Benjamin Henry Latrobe. "Plan of the Framing of the Roof of the Hall of Rep.[resentatives], Wash.[ington]" and "Ceiling of the Hall of Representatives, Capitol, Washington," 1805. Ink and watercolor on paper. 22 ½ x 27 ³⁄₁₆ in. Neg. no. LC-USZ62-5650. Prints and Photographs Division, Library of Congress.

150 See Plate 20.

151 Attributed to Giovanni Andrei. [The House of Representatives After the Burning of the Capitol by the British, 1814], ca. 1815. Pencil, ink, and ink washes on paper. 7 ⅝ x 16 in. Architect of the Capitol.

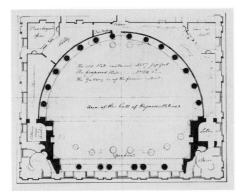

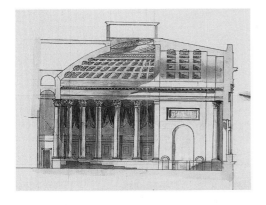

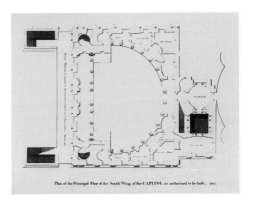

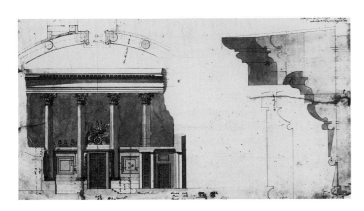

152 See Plate 17.

153 Benjamin Henry Latrobe. "Sketch of a Design for altering the plan of the House of Representatives in the Capitol U.S. Washington," 1815. Ink and watercolor on paper. 11 ⅝ x 7 in. Architect of the Capitol. Donated by the U.S. Capitol Historical Society.

154 Benjamin Henry Latrobe. "Design Proposed for the Hall of Representatives, U.S., Section from North to South," 1815. Ink and watercolor on paper. 12 ⅛ x 6 ⅞ in. Architect of the Capitol. Donated by the U.S. Capitol Historical Society.

155 Benjamin Henry Latrobe. "Plan of the Principal Floor of the South Wing of the Capitol as authorized to be built, 1817." Ink and watercolor on paper. 21 x 32 in. Neg. no. LC-USZ62-11126. Prints and Photographs Division, Library of Congress.

156 Samuel F. B. Morse. Study for the House of Representatives. ca. 1822. Oil sketch. 9 x 15 in. National Museum of American Art, Smithsonian Institution. Museum Purchase through a Grant from the Morris and Gwendolyn Cafritz Foundation.

157 Photograph not available. See page 142.

158 Benjamin Henry Latrobe. [Details of the Hall of Representatives], 1815. Ink and watercolor on paper. 19 1/16 x 27 ¾ in. Neg. nos. LC-USZC4-1250, LC-USZ62-11128. Prints and Photographs Division, Library of Congress.

159 Charles Bulfinch. [Composite Capital], ca. 1817–1829. Ink and wash on paper. 15 x 13 ¼ in. Neg. no. LC-USZ62-63161. Prints and Photographs Division, Library of Congress.

160 [Choragic Monument of Lysicrates]. Plate VI in James Stuart and Nicholas Revett, *Antiquities of Athens*, vol 1 (London: John Haberkorn, 1762). Engraving in book. 13 ¾ x 9 ¼ in. Rare Book and Special Collections Division, Library of Congress.

161 Benjamin Henry Latrobe. "Ground Story of the Capitol, U.S.," 1806. Watercolor on paper. 19 ⅞ x 30 ⅛ in. Neg nos. LC-USZC4-1441, LC-USZ62-38081. Prints and Photographs Division, Library of Congress.

162 Charles Bulfinch. "Ground Plan of the Capitol of the United States showing the Projection and Division of the Center," ca. 1818–1821. Ink and watercolor on paper. 21 ⅞ x 24 ⅛ in. Neg. nos. LC-USZC4-239, LC-USZ62-37104. Prints and Photographs Division, Library of Congress.

163 Charles A. Busby. "The Capitol at Washington. Plan of the Principal Floor," 1823. Copyprint from glass negative. Neg. no. LC-J71-10021. Prints and Photographs Division, Library of Congress.

164 John Trumbull. Section Through the Rotunda and Crypt with Stairs, 1818. Pencil on paper. 7 ⅛ x 5 ½ in. Neg. no. 52533. John Trumbull Album, Collection of The New-York Historical Society, New York.

165 Charles Bulfinch. [Plan of Center Building with Crypt], ca. 1818–1822. Ink on paper. 32 ¾ x 22 ⅝ in. Neg. nos. LC-USZ62-37105, LC-USZC4-240. Prints and Photographs Division, Library of Congress.

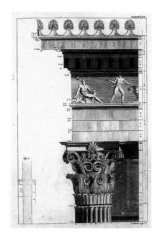

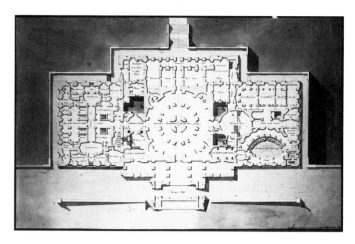

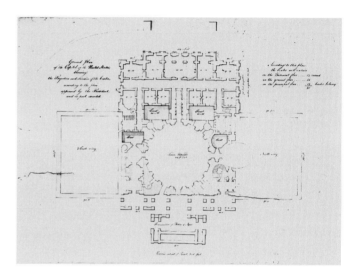

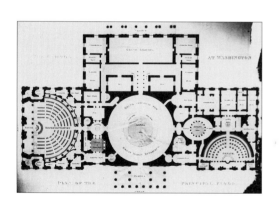

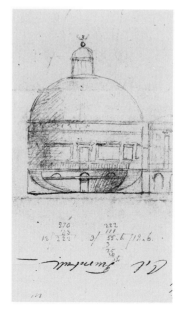

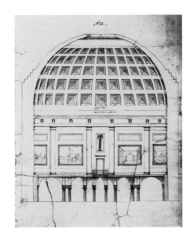

166 [Crypt of the Capitol], ca. 1900. Copyprint. Neg. no. LC-USZ62-2630. Prints and Photographs Division, Library of Congress.

167 Charles Bulfinch. "No. 2" [Section of Rotunda], ca. 1824. Ink on paper. 21 ¼ x 14 ¹³⁄₁₆ in. Neg. nos. LC-USZ62-33563, LC-USZC4-352. Prints and Photographs Division, Library of Congress.

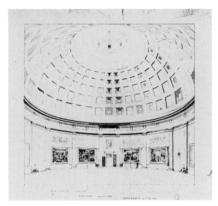

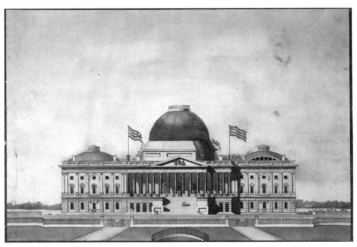

168 Alexander Jackson Davis. "Perspective View of Capitol Rotunda," ca. 1832–1834. Pencil on paper. 11 ⅜ x 14 ¾ in. Acc. no. 940.001.00059; Davis no. J1.11. From the A. J. Davis Collection, Division of Drawings and Archives, Avery Architectural and Fine Arts Library, Columbia University in the City of New York.

169 Alexander Jackson Davis. "East Front of the Capitol," ca. 1832–1834. Ink and watercolor on paper. 13 ½ x 20 in. Neg. no. LC-USZ62-10170. Prints and Photographs Division, Library of Congress.

170 Omitted.

171 See Plate 23.

172 Alexander Jackson Davis. "Capitol of the United States. Plan of Principal Floor," ca. 1832–1834. Ink and ink wash on paper. 14 ⅛ x 19 ⅞ in. Acc. no. 1940.001.00178; Davis no. J1-29a. From the A. J. Davis Collection, Division of Drawings and Archives, Avery Architectural and Fine Arts Library, Columbia University in the City of New York.

173 Alexander Jackson Davis. "Capitol of the United States. Plan of the Principal Floor," ca. 1832–1834. Ink and watercolor on paper. 14 ⅞ x 22 ⅜ in. Neg. no. LC-USZ62-63158. Prints and Photographs Division, Library of Congress.

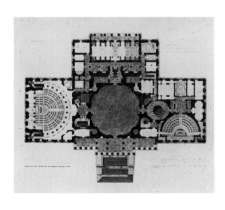

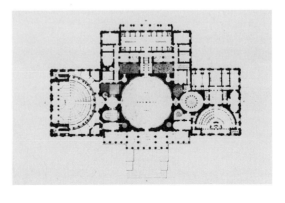

174 Alexander Jackson Davis. "Plan of the Ceilings of the Capitol of the United States, Washington," ca. 1832–1834. Engraving on paper. 16 ⅝ x 21 ¾ in. Neg. no. LC-USA7-36537. Prints and Photographs Division, Library of Congress.

175 Photograph not available. See page 142.

176 Alexander Jackson Davis. [Perspective Sketch of the House of Representatives], ca. 1832. Pencil on paper. 6 ¾ x 8 ¼ in. Acc. no. 1940.001.00070R; Davis no. J1-23. From the A. J. Davis Collection, Division of Drawings and Archives, Avery Architectural and Fine Arts Library, Columbia University in the City of New York.

177 Omitted.

178 See Plate 24.

179 "Veduta interna del Panteon d' Agrippa. . . ." Giuseppi Vasi, *Raccolta delle piu Belle vedute antiche, e Moderne di Roma* (Rome, 1786). Engraving in book. 6 ¼ x 16 in. The John Work Garrett Library, Special Collections Department, The Johns Hopkins University, Baltimore.

180 Alexander Jackson Davis. "Interior of the Hall of Representatives," ca. 1832–1834. Engraving on paper. 11 x 13 ⅛ in. Acc. no. 1940.001.00055; Davis no. J1-3. From the A. J. Davis Collection, Division of Drawings and Archives, Avery Architectural and Fine Arts Library, Columbia University in the City of New York.

180.1, 180.2, 180.3 Photographs not available. See page 142.

180.4 Alexander Jackson Davis. [Perspective View of the Rotunda, Capitol], ca. 1832–1834. Pencil on paper. 11 ¼ x 14 ¼ in. Acc. no. 1940.001.00060; Davis no. J1-12. From the A. J. Davis Collection, Division of Drawings and Archives, Avery Architectural and Fine Arts Library, Columbia University in the City of New York.

180.5 Alexander Jackson Davis. [Corinthian Capitals from the House of Representatives] ca. 1832. Pencil on paper. 7 ⅛ x 6 ½ in. Acc. no. 1940.001.00079R; Davis no. J1-32. From the A. J. Davis Collection, Division of Drawings and Archives, Avery Architectural and Fine Arts Library, Columbia University in the City of New York.

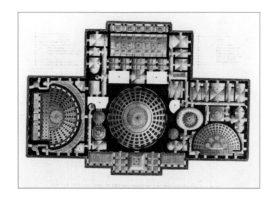

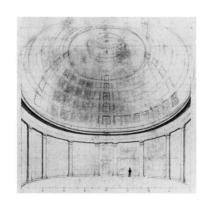

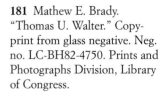

181 Mathew E. Brady. "Thomas U. Walter." Copy-print from glass negative. Neg. no. LC-BH82-4750. Prints and Photographs Division, Library of Congress.

182 Thomas U. Walter. "Perspective View of a Plan for Enlarging the U.S. Capitol," 1850. Watercolor on paper. 18 ½ x 27 ³⁄₁₆ in. Architect of the Capitol.

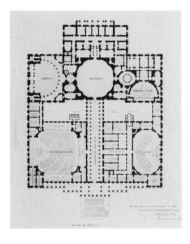

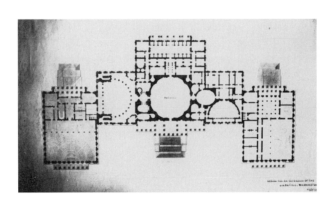

183 Thomas U. Walter. "Plan of Principal Story. Design for an Enlargement of the U.S. Capitol, Washington, D.C.," 1850. Watercolor on paper. 27 ³⁄₁₆ x 18 ⅛ in. Architect of the Capitol.

184 See Plate 25.

185 Thomas U. Walter. "Design for an Extension of the U.S. Capitol. Washington, D.C.," 1851. Watercolor on paper. 22 ¹⁄₁₆ x 42 ⅛ in. Architect of the Capitol.

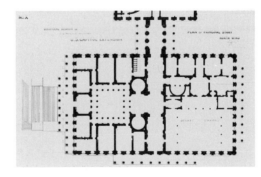

186 See Plate 26.

187 Frederick Law Olmsted. "General Plan for the Improvement of the U.S. Capitol Grounds," 1874. Ink and watercolor on paper. 44 ⅞ x 32 ¼ in. Architect of the Capitol.

188 Thomas U. Walter. "Plan of Principal Story, North Wing," 1851. Ink and watercolor on paper. 22 ¾ x 34 ¾ in. Architect of the Capitol.

133

189 Thomas U. Walter and Montgomery Meigs. "Eastern Elevation of North Wing. Capitol Extension," 1853. Ink and watercolor on paper. 25 ¼ x 39 ⅝ in. Architect of the Capitol.

190 Thomas U. Walter. "Exterior Order. Extension of U.S. Capitol," 1854. Ink and watercolor on paper. 26 ⅜ x 21 ⅛ in. Architect of the Capitol.

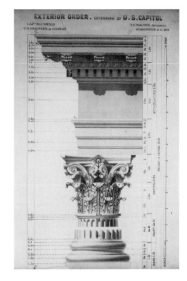

191 Thomas U. Walter. "Design for Eastern Doors. Extension of U.S. Capitol," ca. 1854. Ink and watercolor on paper. 28 ⅛ x 23 ⅛ in. Architect of the Capitol.

192 Thomas U. Walter. "Front Door, U.S. Capitol," ca. 1854–1857. Ink and watercolor on paper. 25 ¾ x 21 ½ in. Architect of the Capitol.

193 Thomas U. Walter. "Plan of Principal Story, North Wing," ca. 1856. Ink and ink washes on paper. 21 ¼ x 26 ½ in. Architect of the Capitol.

194 Thomas U. Walter. "Plan of Attic Story, North Wing, U.S. Capitol Extension," ca. 1853. Ink and watercolor on paper. 22 x 26 ½ in. Architect of the Capitol.

195 See Plate 29.

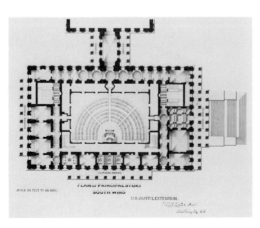
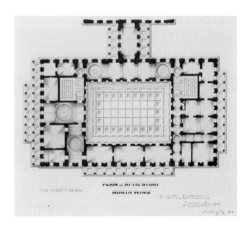

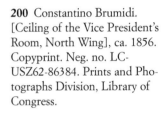

196 Thomas U. Walter. [American Order in the Senate Vestibule], 1858. Photograph. Architect of the Capitol.

197 Thomas U. Walter. [American Order in the Hall of Columns, South Wing], 1855. Photograph. Architect of the Capitol.

198, 199 Omitted.

200 Constantino Brumidi. [Ceiling of the Vice President's Room, North Wing], ca. 1856. Copyprint. Neg. no. LC-USZ62-86384. Prints and Photographs Division, Library of Congress.

201 "Coved Ceiling of the 'Stanza Della Segnatura' in the Vatican by Raphalle D'Urbino." Page 80 in Lewis Gruner, *Specimens of Ornamental Art* (London: Thomas McLean, 1850). Color engraving in book. 16 ¼ x 14 ½ in. General Collections, Library of Congress.

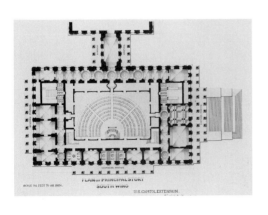

202 Thomas U. Walter. "Plan of Principal Story, South Wing," 1856. Ink and watercolor on paper. 21 x 26 ¾ in. Architect of the Capitol.

203 Photograph not available. See page 142.

204 See Plate 28.

205 Montgomery C. Meigs, Thomas U. Walter, with figures by William Henry Rinehart. "Design for Clock for Hall of Representatives," 1858. Photograph, ink, and watercolor on paper. 26 x 21 ⅛ in. Architect of the Capitol.

206 See Plate 27.

207 Thomas U. Walter. "Elevation of Dome of U.S. Capitol," 1859. Ink and watercolor on paper. 42 ½ x 24 ⅝ in. Architect of the Capitol.

208 Auguste Ricard de Montferrand. [Dome of St. Isaac's Cathedral, St. Petersburg, 1818–1858]. Copyprint of architectural drawing. Architect of the Capitol.

209 See Plate 30.

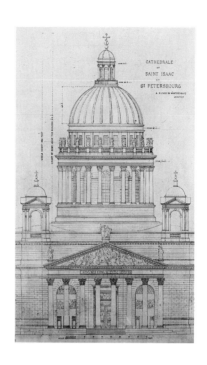

210 Thomas Crawford. [Second Design of *Freedom Triumphant in War and Peace*], 1855. Copyprint. Library of Congress.

211 After Thomas Crawford. [Figure of *Freedom Triumphant in War and Peace*], ca. 1855. Sculpture, zinc with nickel-plated stars. 20 in. high; 10 ¼ in. figure. Courtesy of Mr. and Mrs. Set Charles Momjian.

212 Thomas U. Walter. "Tholus on Dome of U.S. Capitol," 1859. Ink and watercolor on paper. 41 ½ x 25 ⅜ in. Architect of the Capitol.

213 Omitted.

214 Constantino Brumidi. "Peace Between General Oglethorpe and the Muscogee Chief, 1732," 1859. Oil wash on kraft paper. 12 ⅞ x 15 ¾ in. Architect of the Capitol.

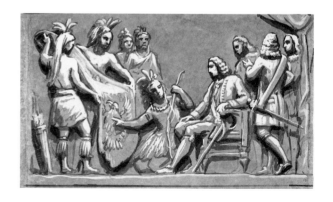

215 Constantino Brumidi. "Lexington Insurrection, 1775," and "Declaration of the Independence, 1776," 1859. Oil wash on kraft paper. 12 ¾ x 32 in. Architect of the Capitol.

216 Constantino Brumidi. "A Laborer in the Employ of Cap. Sutter," ca. 1859. Oil wash on kraft paper. 12 ⅞ x 23 ¾ in. Architect of the Capitol.

216.1, 216.2, 216.3 Photographs not available. See page 142.

217 Constantino Brumidi. *The Apotheosis of George Washington,* ca. 1859–1862. Oil on canvas. 24 ⅞ in. diameter. The Athenaeum of Philadelphia.

218 Constantino Brumidi. "Brumidi's Allegorical Painting," ca. 1865. Color lithograph. 16 ½ x 16 ½ in. Prints and Photographs Division, Library of Congress.

219 Thomas Crawford. *The Progress of Civilization,* ca. 1853. [Preliminary Sketch for Model of the East Pediment of the North Wing, U.S. Capitol]. Ink and ink washes on paper. 19 x 38 ½ in. Architect of the Capitol.

220 Paul Bartlett. *The Apotheosis of Democracy,* 1908–1909. [Preliminary Sketch Model of the South Wing Pediment]. Bronze. 5 ⅝ x 29 in. James Monroe Museum and Memorial Library, Fredericksburg, Va.

221 Paul Bartlett. Head of "Peace," from "Peace Protecting Genius" [Central Group, South Wing Pediment], cast 1927. Bronze. 10 ¾ in. high. James Monroe Museum and Memorial Library, Fredericksburg, Va.

222 Photograph not available. See page 142.

223 Peder Anderson. "View of the City of Washington," 1838. Color lithograph. 16 ⁷⁄₁₆ x 36 ³⁄₁₆ in. Neg. no. LC-USZ62-15281. Prints and Photographs Division, Library of Congress.

224 Robert P. Smith. "View of Washington," 1850. Color lithograph. 19 x 29 ¼ in. Prints and Photographs Division, Library of Congress.

224.2 Photograph not available. See page 142.

225 See Plate 1.

226 August Kollner. "West Front of the United States Capitol" (New York: Goupil, Vibert, 1839). Lithograph. 9 ½ x 11 ⅝ in. Neg. no. LC-USZ62-2908. Prints and Photographs Division, Library of Congress.

227, 228 Omitted.

229 "Commercial Directory." J.C. Kayser, 1823. Engraving. 9 ½ x 7 ⅜ in. Prints and Photographs Division, Library of Congress.

230 Photograph not available. See page 142.

231 H. and J. Stokes, after Charles Bulfinch. "United States Capitol." Page 87 in *The Jackson Wreath* (Philadelphia: Jacob Maas, 1829). Engraving in book. 4 ⅞ x 8 ¼ in. Rare

Book and Special Collections Division, Library of Congress.

232 William Pratt. "Elevation of the Eastern Front of the Capitol of the United States" (Washington, D.C.: William Fischer, 1839). Lithograph. 16 ¾ x 22 ¹⁄₁₆ in. Neg. no. LC-USZ62-58543. Prints and Photographs Division, Library of Congress.

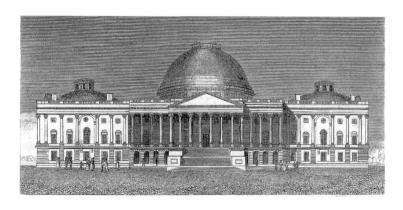

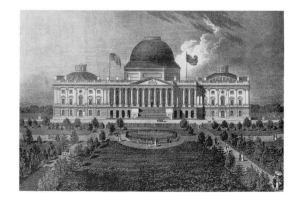

138

ASCENT TO THE CAPITOL, WASHINGTON.

ENTRÉE DU CAPITOLE, À WASHINGTON.   DER WEG ZAR CAPITOL HINAUF, ZU WASHINGTON.

233, 234 Omitted.

235 W. H. Bartlett. "Ascent to the Capitol." Opposite page 37 in Nathaniel P. Willis, *American Scenery*, vol. 1 (London: Virtue, 1840). Engraving in book. 5 ¼ x 8 in. Neg. no. LC-USA7-32900. Rare Book and Special Collections Division, Library of Congress.

236 Attributed to Henry Hooper and Company, Boston. Pair of Reverse-glass-painted Candelabra Depicting the West Front of the Capitol, ca. 1850. Ormolu. 16 ¼ x 18 x 9 in. Courtesy of Murray B. Woldman and Joel M. Woldman, Woldman & Woldman Antiques, Alexandria, Va.

237 W. H. Bartlett. "View of the Capitol at Washington." Frontispiece in Nathaniel P. Willis, *American Scenery*, vol. 1 (London: Virtue, 1840). Engraving in book. 10 ½ x 7 ¾ in. Neg. no. LC-USZ62-3741. Rare Book and Special Collections Division, Library of Congress.

238 Photograph not available. See page 142.

239 Bandbox with Wallpaper View of the Capitol, ca. 1840. Cardboard and paper. 12 x 18 in. oval. Courtesy of J. and D. Louv, Mizzentop Farm Antiques.

240, 241 Photographs not available. See page 142.

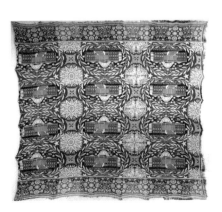

242 Double-Weave Jacquard Coverlet with Medallion of the Capitol in a Laurel Wreath, 1846. Woven wool fabric. 78 x 86 in. Neg. no. 26875. Collection of The New-York Historical Society, New York.

243 Thomas S. Sinclair. "The Capitol March," 1850. Sheet-music cover. 12 ½ x 8 ¾ in. Prints and Photographs Division, Library of Congress.

139

244 Thomas S. Sinclair. "The National Union," 1851. Sheet-music cover. 10 ¾ x 7 ⅞ in. Neg. no. LC-USZ62-57570. Music Division, Library of Congress.

245 Photograph not available. See page 142.

246 "A View of the Capitol of the United States After the Conflagration in 1814." Frontispiece in Jesse Torrey, *A Portraiture of Domestic Slavery in the United States* (Philadelphia: Jesse Torrey, 1817). Engraving in book. 5 x 4 ¼ in. Rare Book and Special Collections Division, Library of Congress.

UNITED STATES SLAVE TRADE. 1830.

247 "United States Slave Trade, 1830." Engraving on woven paper. 4 x 6 ¾ in. Neg. no. LC-USZ62-89701. Prints and Photographs Division, Library of Congress.

248 Photograph not available. See page 142.

249 Adam Weingaertner. "The Happy Family" (New York: Nagel and Weingaertner, 1851). Lithograph. 10 ⅝ x 16 ⅛ in. Neg. no. 58549. Collection of The New-York Historical Society, New York.

designers. "Longitudinal Section Through the Senate Chamber, the Rotondo, and Representatives Hall," 1837. [Indiana State Capitol Design]. Ink and watercolor on paper. 10 ½ x 15 in. Acc. no. 24.66.1406 (26); neg. no. MM 62346 B. Lent by The Metropolitan Museum of Art, New York. Harris Brisbane Dick Fund, 1924.

250 Alexander Jackson Davis. [Plan of the Principal Floor and the Basement Floor of the State Capitol, Raleigh, North Carolina], 1853. Watercolor on paper. Acc. no. 24.66.1403 (10); neg. no. MM 72362. Lent by The Metropolitan Museum of Art, New York. Harris Brisbane Dick Fund, 1924.

251 Alexander Jackson Davis and Ithiel Town,

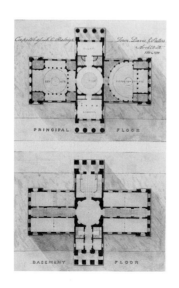

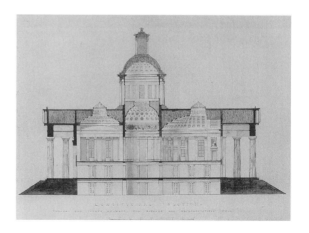

THE GREAT NATIONAL DRINK

Coca-Cola

DELICIOUS! HEALTHFUL! REFRESHING!

The greatest building on this Continent — the Capitol at Washington — is fitted with the most perfect plumbing ever devised —

THE DURHAM SYSTEM.

Owners of smaller buildings will be interested in page 25 of our pamphlet (sent free).

Durham House Drainage Co.

158–160 West 27th Street, New-York City.

252 Alexander Jackson Davis. [Design for the Washington Monument in Richmond], 1849. Copyprint of ink and watercolor drawing. Acc. no. 24.66.1553.5; neg. no. MM 75480. Courtesy of The Metropolitan Museum of Art, New York. Harris Brisbane Dick Fund, 1924.

253 Photograph not available. See page 142.

254 "Panoramic View of Washington City from the Dome of the Capitol, Looking East" (Washington, D.C.: Casimir Bohn, 1857). Lithograph. 20 1/16 x 32 5/16 in. Neg.

no. LC-USZ62-64266. Prints and Photographs Division, Library of Congress.

255 See Plate 22.

256 [National Motor Vehicle Company Advertisement]. *Cosmopolitan* (New York), February 1909. Copyprint from magazine. General Collections, Library of Congress.

257 [Coca-Cola Advertisement]. *Everybody's Magazine*, December 1906. Copyprint from magazine. 9 3/8 x 12 3/8 in. General Collections, Library of Congress.

258, 259, 260 Photographs not available. See page 142.

261 [Durham System Advertisement], ca. 1925. Copyprint. United States Senate Collection, Washington, D.C.

262 [Baker Motor Vehicle Company Advertisement]. *Life* (New York), March 31, 1910. Copyprint from magazine. United States Senate Collection, Washington, D.C.

263, 264, 265 Omitted.

266 Photograph not available. See page 142.

Objects in the Exhibition Not Shown in Catalog

12 After Benjamin West. "The Hon. James Otis, jun., Esq." Frontispiece in *Isaac Bickerstaff's Almanack* (Boston, 1770). Engraving in book. 4 ½ x 3 ½ in. Rare Book and Special Collections Division, Library of Congress.

54 Isidore-Stanislas Helman, after Charles Monnet. "Assemblée nationale, Abandon de tous les privilèges dans la séance de la nuit du 4 au 5 août 1789," 1789. Engraving. 15 x 39 ½ in. Bibliothèque Nationale de France, Paris, Cabinet des Estampes.

121 Benjamin Henry Latrobe. "Ground Plan of the North Wing of the Capitol of the United States," 1806. Watercolor on paper. 15 x 20 ¾ in. Neg. no. LC-USA7-13766. Architect of the Capitol.

127 Benjamin Henry Latrobe. "Plan, shewing the alterations proposed in the principal Story of the North Wing of the Capitol," 1806. Ink and watercolor on paper. 15 x 20 ¾ in. Architect of the Capitol. Donated by the U.S. Capitol Historical Society.

132 Alexander Jackson Davis. [Partial Ceiling Plans of Library of Congress and Tobacco-Order Rotunda], ca. 1831–1834. Pencil on paper. 14 x 8 ⅜ in. Acc. no. 1940.001.00068; Davis no. J1.15. From the A. J. Davis Collection, Division of Drawings and Archives, Avery Architectural and Fine Arts Library, Columbia University in the City of New York.

157 Jean-François-Thérèse Chalgrin. [Senate Chamber, Luxembourg Palace, Paris], ca. 1840. Engraving. 15 x 38 ½ in. Bibliothèque Nationale de France, Paris, Cabinet des Estampes.

175 Alexander Jackson Davis. [Sketch of the House of Representatives], ca. 1832–1834. Pencil on paper. 6 ⅞ x 9 ½ in. Acc. no. 1940.001.00066; Davis no. J1-19. From the A. J. Davis Collection, Division of Drawings and Archives, Avery Architectural and Fine Arts Library, Columbia University in the City of New York.

180.1 Alexander Jackson Davis. [Details of the West Wing Exterior], ca. 1831–1834. Pencil on paper. 11 ⅛ x 17 in. Acc. no. 1940.001.00065V; Davis no. J1-17. From the A. J. Davis Collection, Division of Drawings and Archives, Avery Architectural and Fine Arts Library, Columbia University in the City of New York.

180.2 Alexander Jackson Davis. [Details of the Rotunda Frieze], ca. 1832–1834. Pencil on paper. 8 x 9 ⅞ in. Acc. no. 1940.001.00061V; Davis no. J1-13. From the A. J. Davis Collection, Division of Drawings and Archives, Avery Architectural and Fine Arts Library, Columbia University in the City of New York.

180.3 Alexander Jackson Davis. [Details of the Library of Congress], ca. 1832–1834. Pencil on paper. 11 ¼ x 8 ⅞ in. Acc. no. 1940.001.00177V; Davis no. J1-18. From the A. J. Davis Collection, Division of Drawings and Archives, Avery Architectural and Fine Arts Library, Columbia University in the City of New York.

203 Edward Sachse. "The House of Representatives, U.S. Capitol, Washington, D.C.," 1866. Color lithograph. 18 x 23 ½ in. Neg. no. LC-USZC2-1319. Prints and Photographs Division, Library of Congress.

216.1 Constantino Brumidi. "America and History," 1859. Oil wash on kraft paper. 12 ⅞ x 27 ¾ in. Architect of the Capitol.

216.2 Constantino Brumidi. "Cortez and Montezuma at Mexican Temple," 1859. Oil wash on kraft paper. 12 ⅞ x 35 ⅜ in. Architect of the Capitol.

216.3 Constantino Brumidi. "Col. Johnson & Tecumseh," 1859. Oil wash on kraft paper. 12 ⅞ x 41 ¾ in. Architect of the Capitol.

222 Paul Bartlett. Head of "Genius," from "Peace Protecting Genius" [Central Group, South Wing Pediment], ca. 1911–1913. Plaster. 14 x 10 in. Tudor Place Foundation, Inc., Washington, D.C.

224.2 Benjamin Franklin Smith, Jr. *Washington, D.C.* (New York: F. Michelin, 1852). Lithograph. 24 ⅝ x 42 ⁵⁄₁₆ in. Neg. nos. LC-USZ62-58856, LC-USZC4-579. Prints and Photographs Division, Library of Congress.

230 Staffordshire Teapot and Sugar Bowl with View of the Capitol, after 1823. Stoneware Teapot, 6 x 11 in.; Sugar Bowl, 6 x 6 ½ in. National Museum of American History, Smithsonian Institution.

238 Staffordshire Platter with View of the West Front of the Capitol, after 1840. Stoneware. 14 x 19 ¼ in. National Museum of American History, Smithsonian Institution.

240 "Capitol of the United States, Washington." Page 458 in John Howard Hinton, *The History of the United States from the Earliest Period . . .* (London: J. and F. Tallis, ca. 1843). Steel engraving in book. 3 ¾ x 6 ⅛ in. Neg. no. LC-USZ62-1631. Rare Book and Special Collections Division, Library of Congress.

241 Staffordshire Platter with View of the Capitol. Stoneware. 15 ½ x 20 ⅝ in. National Museum of American History, Smithsonian Institution.

245 Needlepoint Picture of the West Front of the Capitol, ca. 1840. Wool yarn on fabric. 16 x 18 ¾ in. Courtesy of Clarence and Joyce Brown.

248 "A Sketch from God's Description of the Consequences of Emancipation." *The American Anti-Slavery Almanac for 1837* (Boston: N. Southard and D. K. Hitchcock, 1837). Pamphlet. 2 ¾ x 3 ⅛ in. Rare Book and Special Collections Division, Library of Congress.

253 "View of Washington City" (Baltimore: Edward Sachse & Co., 1852). Lithograph. 20 x 27 ⅜ in. Neg. nos. LC-USZ62-4509, LC-USZC4-771. Prints and Photographs Division, Library of Congress.

258 [Uneeda Biscuit Advertisement], ca. 1900. Copyprint. 9 ½ x 4 ½ in.

259 Capitol Tobacco Label, ca. 1880. Tobacco label. 7 x 4 ½ in. Neg. no. LC-USZC2-1880. Prints and Photographs Division, Library of Congress.

260 [Quaker Wheat Berries Advertisement], ca. 1900. Copyprint. 7 x 5 in. Warshaw Collection, National Museum of American History, Smithsonian Institution.

266 Architectural Model of the Present Capitol, ca. 1960. Plastic. 54 x 86 x 24 in. Architect of the Capitol.

Notes

PROLOGUE

1. James Wilson, "Address before the Pennsylvania Legislature," September 11, 1787, in *The Debate of the Several State Conventions on the Adoption of the Federal Constitution,* compl. Jonathan Elliot (Philadelphia: Lippincott, 1866), 2:529; Marquis de Lafayette, "Address to the Continental Congress, December 11, 1784," in *Lafayette in the Age of the American Revolution,* ed. Stanley J. Idzerda et al. (Ithaca, N.Y.: Cornell University Press, 1983), 5:281; Kenneth R. Bowling, *The Creation of Washington, D.C.: The Idea and Location of the American Capital* (Fairfax, Va.: George Mason University Press, 1991).

2. George Washington to commissioners, November 9, 1975, in "The Writings of George Washington Relating to the National Capital," *Records of the Columbia Historical Society* 17 (1914): 148.

3. Benjamin Henry Latrobe to Thomas Law, November 10, 1816, in *The Correspondence and Miscellaneous Papers of Benjamin Henry Latrobe,* ed. John C. Van Horne et al. (New Haven, Conn.: Yale University Press, 1984–1988), 3:828.

4. Anne Royall, *Sketches of History, Life and Manners in the United States* (New Haven, Conn.: Printed for the Author, 1826), 130.

5. Henry James, *The American Scene* (New York: Harper & Brothers, 1907), 346.

CHAPTER I

1. Quoted in Bruce Granger, *Satire in the American Revolution* (Ithaca, N.Y.: Cornell University Press, 1960), 203.

2. Sinclair Hamilton, "'The Earliest Device of the Colonies' and Some Other Early Devices," *Princeton University Library Chronicle* 10 (1949): 117–23; J. A. Leo Lemay, "The American Aesthetic of Franklin's Visual Creations," *Pennsylvania Magazine of History and Biography* 111 (1987): 465–99.

3. Richard S. Patterson and Richardson Dougall, *The Eagle and the Shield: A History of the Great Seal of the United States* (Washington, D.C.: Department of State, 1978), 6–110.

4. Quoted in Charles C. Jones, Jr., *Historical Sketches of Tomo-chi-chi* (Albany, N.Y.: Munsell, 1968), 64–65.

5. Francis Bacon, "A Brief Discourse Touching the Happy Union of the Kingdoms of England and Scotland," in *The Works of Francis Bacon,* ed. James Spedding, Robert Leslie Ellis, and Douglas Denon Heath (1860–1864; reprint, St. Clair Shores, Mich.: Scholarly Press, 1969), 3:91.

6. Thomas Jefferson, Account book entry, 1774, in *The Papers of Thomas Jefferson,* ed. Julian Bond et al. (Princeton, N.J.: Princeton University Press, 1950–   ), 1:495.

7. Bernard F. Reilly, *American Political Prints: A Catalog of the Collection in the Library of Congress* (New York: Hall, 1991), cat. 1782–1.

8. Hugh Honour, *The European Vision of America* (Cleveland: Cleveland Museum of Art, 1976), items 215, 216; Anne L. Poulet and Guilhem Scherf, *Clodion, 1738–1814* (Paris: Louvre, 1992), 204–7.

9. E. McClung Fleming, "The American Image as Indian Princess, 1765–1783," *Winterthur Portfolio* 2 (1965): 65–81, and "From Indian Princess to Greek Goddess: The American Image, 1783–1815," *Winterthur Portfolio* 3 (1967): 37–66.

10. [Hedy Backlin], *The Four Continents from the Collection of James Hazen Hyde* (New York: Cooper Union Museum, n.d.), cat. 73; Winfried Schleiner, "The Infant Hercules: Franklin's Design for a Medal Commemorating American Liberty," *Eighteenth Century Studies* 10 (1976–1977): 235–44; Poulet and Scherf, *Clodion,* 204–7; *The French in America* (Detroit: Detroit Institute of Arts, 1951), cat. 213.

11. Quoted in Robert G. Stewart, *Robert Edge Pine: A British Portrait Painter in America, 1784–1788* (Washington, D.C.: National Portrait Gallery, 1979), 16–19. The author gratefully thanks Sam Daniel of the Prints and Photographs Division of the Library of Congress for bringing this reference to her attention.

12. John Adams to Abigail Adams, August 14, 1776, in *Adams Family Correspondence,* ed. Lyman Butterfield (Cambridge, Mass.: Harvard University Press, 1963), 2:96–97.

13. Georgia was not represented in the first Continental Congress, and the North Carolina delegates did not arrive until a week after the opening session. The full complement of delegates numbered fifty -five.

14. David L. Ammerman, "The First Continental Congress and the Coming of the American Revolution" (Ph.D. diss., Cornell University, 1966); Richard Tyler, *"The Common Cause of America": A Study of the First Continental Congress* (Philadelphia: National Park Service, 1974), 123–28.

15. Kenneth R. Bowling, *The Creation of Washington, D.C.: The Idea and Location of the American Capital* (Fairfax, Va.: George Mason University Press, 1991).

16. James Trenchard, "Behold! a Fabric now to Freedom rear'd," *Columbian Magazine, or Monthly Miscellany* 2 (1788): frontispiece.

17. Louis Torres, "Federal Hall Revisited," *Journal of the Society of Architectural Historians* 29 (1970): 327–38.

18. Ibid., 330.

19. [James Madison,] *Notes of Debates in the Federal Convention of 1787 Reported by James Madison* (New York: Norton, 1969), 659.

20. Ibid.

CHAPTER II

1. Benjamin Henry Latrobe, "A Private Letter to the Individ-

ual Members of Congress, on the Subject of the Public Buildings of the United States at Washington," November 28, 1806, in *The Correspondence and Miscellaneous Papers of Benjamin Henry Latrobe,* ed. John C. Van Horne et al. (New Haven, Conn.: Yale University Press, 1984–1988), 2:305–6.

2. The Capitol competition drawings are at the Maryland Historical Society and form part of Latrobe's papers. S. A. Elliot, *The Washington Guide* (Washington, D.C.: Elliot, 1826), 22.

3. "I. Jefferson's Draft of Agenda for the Seat of Government," in *The Papers of Thomas Jefferson,* ed. Julian P. Boyd et al. (Princeton, N.J.: Princeton University Press, 1950–   ) 17:460, 464.

4. "An Advertisement for the Capitol," in *Jefferson Papers,* 23:226–27.

5. Thomas Jefferson to Pierre Charles L'Enfant, April 10, 1791, in *Jefferson Papers,* 20:1982, 1986; Richard W. Stephenson, *"A Plan Whol[l]y New": Pierre Charles L'Enfant's Plan of the City of Washington* (Washington, D.C.: Library of Congress, 1993), 39.

6. Samuel Blodget, Jr., to Thomas Jefferson, June 25, 1792, in *Jefferson Papers*, 24:120.

7. Jeanne F. Butler, "Competition 1792: Designing a Nation's Capitol," *Capitol Studies* 4 (1976): 10–96.

8. Quoted in Pamela Scott, "L'Enfant's Washington Described: The City in the Public Press, 1791–1795," *Washington History* 3 (1991): 97–111.

9. Helen Park, *A List of Architectural Books Available in America Before the Revolution* (Los Angeles: Hennessey & Ingalls, 1973); Janice G. Schimmelman, *Architectural Treatises and Building Handbooks Available in American Libraries and Bookstores Through 1800* (Worcester, Mass.: American Antiquarian Society, 1986).

10. Butler, "Competition 1792," 70–72; Charles Wintersmith to Thomas Jefferson, July 17, 1792, in *Jefferson Papers,* 24:238–39.

11. Butler, "Competition 1792," 54–62.

12. Ibid., 35–42.

13. Ibid., 43–46.

14. Ibid., 78–79; Kim Snyder Rice, "Joseph Clark, Maryland Architect," *Antiques* 115 (1979): 552–55.

15. Butler, "Competition 1792," 18–23.

16. Ibid., 24–29.

17. Ibid., 47–53; George Cabot to commissioners, June 14, 1792, Records of the Commissioners of Public Buildings and Grounds, Record Group 42, National Archives.

18. Butler, "Competition 1792," 75–78, 85–86; George Washington to commissioners, July 23, 1792, RG 42, National Archives.

19. Butler, "Competition 1792," 15–18.

20. Alexandra Cushing Howard, "Stephen Hallet and William Thornton at the U.S. Capitol, 1791–1797" (M.A. thesis, University of Virginia, 1974); Fiske Kimball and Wells Bennett, "William Thornton and the Design of the United States Capitol," *Art Studies* 1 (1923): 76–92.

21. Pamela Scott, "Stephen Hallet's Designs for the United States Capitol," *Winterthur Portfolio* 27 (1992): 145–70.

22. Commissioners to The Municipality of Bordeaux, January 4, 1793, RG 42, National Archives.

23. Stephen Hallet, "Observations upon the Prospect East of the Capitol," November 1794, manuscript, Architect of the Capitol, Curator's Office.

24. Arthur M. Schlesinger, "Liberty Tree: A Genealogy," *New England Quarterly* 25 (1952): 435–58.

25. Commissioners to George Washington, March 1793, RG 42, National Archives.

26. Commissioners to Thomas Jefferson, October 14, 1792, in *Jefferson Papers,* 24:481; Stephen Hallet to Thomas Jefferson, March 15, 1793, in *Jefferson Papers,* 25:385.

27. Minor Myers, Jr., *Liberty without Anarchy: A History of the Society of the Cincinnati* (Charlottesville: University Press of Virginia, 1983); Gary Wills, *Cincinnatus: George Washington and the Enlightenment* (New York: Doubleday, 1984).

28. Quoted in Michael Kammen, *A Machine That Would Go of Itself: The Constitution in American Culture* (New York: Knopf, 1987), 41.

29. Thomas Jefferson to Daniel Carroll, February 1, 1793, in *Jefferson Papers,* 25:110.

30. Hallet to Jefferson, March 15, 1793, in *Jefferson Papers,* 25:384–86.

31. Thomas Jefferson to George Washington, July 17, 1793, in *Thomas Jefferson and the National Capitol,* ed. Saul K. Padover (Washington, D.C.: Government Printing Office, 1946), 184–86; [George Washington,] Journal entry, Monday 15 July 1793, in *The Journal of the Proceedings of the President, 1793–1797,* ed. Dorothy Twohig (Charlottesville: University Press of Virginia, 1981), 198–99.

CHAPTER III

1. Mark Boatner, *Encyclopedia of the American Revolution* (New York: McKay, 1966), 1230–50.

2. James Wilson, "Address before the Pennsylvania Legislature," September 11, 1787, in *The Debates of the Several State Conventions on the Adoption of the Federal Constitution,* comp. Jonathan Elliot (Philadelphia: Lippincott, 1866), 2:529; George Washington, First inaugural address, April 30, 1789, in *The Papers of George Washington,* Presidential Series, ed. W. W. Abbott et al. (Charlottesville: University Press of Virginia, 1987–   ), 2:152–77.

3. Francis Hopkinson, "The New Roof," *Pennsylvania Packet,* December 29, 1787.

4. Robert L. Alexander, "The Grand Federal Edifice," *Documentary Editing* 9 (1987): 13–17.

5. Francis Hopkinson, "Account of the Grand Federal Procession in Philadelphia, July 4, 1788," *American Museum* 4 (1788): 57–75.

6. Whitfield J. Bell, Jr., "The Federal Processions of 1788," *New-York Historical Society Quarterly* 46 (1962): 4–39.

7. Thomas Lee Shippen to William Shippen, 15 September 1790, Thomas Lee Shippen Papers, Manuscript Division, Library of Congress.

8. Pamela Scott, "'This Vast Empire': Development of the

Mall from 1791 to 1848," in *The Mall in Washington, 1791–1991,* ed. Richard Longstreth (Washington, D.C.: National Gallery of Art, 1991), 37–58.

9. Pierre Charles L'Enfant to Alexander Hamilton, April 8, 1791, in *The Papers of Alexander Hamilton,* ed. Harold C. Syrett (New York: Columbia University Press, 1961–1987), 8:254; Elizabeth S. Kite, *L'Enfant and Washington* (Baltimore: Johns Hopkins Press, 1929), 45, 55.

10. Thomas Johnson to Thomas Jefferson, February 29, 1792, in *The Papers of Thomas Jefferson,* ed. Julian Boyd et al. (Princeton, N.J.: Princeton University Press, 1950–), 23:165–66; Scott, "This Vast Empire," 42.

11. Thomas Jefferson to Thomas Johnson, March 8, 1792, in *Jefferson Papers,* 23:237; Commissioners Proceedings, January 7, 1792, RG 42, National Archives.

12. "Essay on the City of Washington," *Gazette of the United States,* February 11, 12, 13, 1795.

13. Thomas Jefferson to Pierre Charles L'Enfant, April 10, 1791, in *Jefferson Papers,* 20:86.

14. Thomas Jefferson to William Short, March 16, 1791, in *Jefferson Papers,* 19:578–79.

15. Charles Brownell, "United States Capitol," in Brownell et al., *The Making of Virginia Architecture* (Richmond: Virginia Museum of Fine Arts, 1992), 218.

16. Charles Dickens, *American Notes* (1842; reprint, New York: St. Martin's Press, 1985), 106.

17. Benjamin Henry Latrobe to Thomas Jefferson, August 15, 1807, in *The Correspondence and Miscellaneous Papers of Benjamin Henry Latrobe,* ed. John C. Van Horne et al. (New Haven, Conn.: Yale University Press, 1984–1988), 2:464.

18. Robert Mills, *Guide to the Capitol and National Executive Offices of the United States* (Washington, D.C.: Greer, 1847–1848), 35.

19. William Thornton, Description of Capitol design, April 1793, in the J. Henly Smith Collection of the Papers of William Thornton, Letterbook 18, 51–57, Manuscript Division, Library of Congress; transcribed in Alexandra Cushing Howard, "Stephen Hallet and William Thornton at the U.S. Capitol, 1791–1797" (M.A. thesis, University of Virginia, 1974), 179–89.

20. Quoted in Howard, "Hallet and Thornton at the U.S. Capitol," 182–83.

21. Charles Warren, "How Politics Intruded into the Washington Centenary of 1832," *Proceedings of the Massachusetts Historical Society* 65 (1932): 37.

22. Frederick L. Harvey, *History of the Washington National Monument and Washington National Monument Society,* 57th Cong., 2nd sess., 1902–1903, S. Doc. 224, 13–14.

23. Quoted in Howard, "Hallett and Thornton at the U.S. Capitol," 188.

24. Quoted in "Washington Centenary of 1832," 37.

25. William Thornton to John Marshall, January 2, 1800, Thornton Papers.

26. [William Thornton,] "The Comparative Merits of a Mausoleum and Monument," *National Intelligencer,* December 8, 1800.

27. Benjamin Henry Latrobe, Journal entry, March 18, 1819, in *The Journals of Benjamin Henry Latrobe, 1799–1820,* ed. Edward C. Carter II et al. (New Haven, Conn.: Yale University Press, 1977–1980): 3:264–66.

28. *Annals of Congress,* 6th Cong., 1st sess., 178–79, 181, 203–9, 708, 711–12.

29. "Essay on the City of Washington," February 11, 1795.

30. Alexander White, Broadside, January 21, 1796, RG 42, National Archives.

31. William Thornton to Samuel Lane, April 13, 1820, Thornton Papers, 7:6.

32. Commissioners to George Washington, November 18, 1795, in *Documentary History of the Construction and Development of the United States Capitol Building and Grounds* (Washington, D.C.: Government Printing Office, 1904), 37–38.

33. George Hadfield, in *Washington Gazette,* February 6, 1819.

34. Benjamin Henry Latrobe to Thomas Jefferson, December 7, 1806, in *Latrobe Correspondence,* 2:321, 323n.

35. Thomas Sunderland published an aquatint of Latrobe's 1810–1811 perspective in London in 1825. It is illustrated in Bates Lowry, ed., *The Architecture of Washington, D.C.* (Washington, D.C.: Dunlap Society, 1979), 2:213, C6.

36. Thornton to Lane, April 13, 1820, Thornton Papers, 7:6.

37. Thomas Jefferson to Benjamin Henry Latrobe, July 12, 1812, in *Thomas Jefferson and the National Capitol,* ed. Saul K. Padover (Washington, D.C.: Government Printing Office, 1946), 471.

38. Charles Bulfinch to Samuel Lane, February 5, 1818, in *Documentary History of the Capitol,* 201; Neil Bingham, *C. A. Busby: The Regency Architect of Brighton and Hove* (London: Heinz Gallery, 1991), 52–55.

39. Charles Bulfinch to Joseph Elgar, December 9, 1822, Records of the House of Representatives, RG 233, National Archives.

40. A Citizen of the World [James Boardman], *America, and the Americans* (London: Longman, Rees, Ormie, Brown, Green & Longman, 1833), 224–25.

41. Godfrey T. Vigne, *Six Months in America* (Philadelphia: Ash, 1833), 53.

42. Egon Verheyen, "John Trumbull and the U.S. Capitol: Reconsidering the Evidence,"in *John Trumbull: The Hand and Spirit of a Painter,* ed. Helen A. Cooper (New Haven, Conn.: Yale University Press, 1982), 260–71.

43. Charles Bulfinch to Enrico Causici, July 8, 1822, RG 42, National Archives.

44. Architect of the Capitol, *Art in the United States Capitol* (Washington, D.C.: Government Printing Office, 1978), 130–45, 292–96.

45. John Quincy Adams, Diary entry, May 31, 1825, in *Memoirs of John Quincy Adams,* ed. Charles Francis Adams (Philadelphia: Lippincott, 1875), 7:20; Vivien Green Fryd, *Art and Empire: The Politics of Ethnicity in the U.S. Capitol, 1815–1860* (New Haven, Conn.: Yale University Press, 1992), 181–83.

46. Quoted in Fryd, *Art and Empire,* 11–12.

47. Ibid., 92–105.

48. [Timothy Flint,] "A Tour," *Western Monthly Review* 2 (1828): 206.

49. Petition of John Foy, Records of the House of Representatives, RG 233, National Archives. The story of James Maher's career has not yet been compiled; documents relating to his work as the public gardener are in RG 42, National Archives, and the Toner Collection, Manuscript Division, Library of Congress.

CHAPTER IV

1. Thomas Jefferson to Benjamin Henry Latrobe, April 14, 1811, in *The Correspondence and Miscellaneous Papers of Benjamin Henry Latrobe,* ed. John C. Van Horne et al. (New Haven, Conn.: Yale University Press, 1984–1988), 3:57–58.

2. William Seale, *The President's House* (Washington, D.C.: White House Historical Association, 1986), 1:31.

3. Abbé Brothier, "Premier mémoire sur les jeux du cirque, considérés dans les vues politiques des Romains: Lû janvier 1781," *Histoire de l'Académie d'architecture et belles-lettres, 1780–1784* 45 (1793): 478–94; "Second mémoire . . . ," 495–508; "Troisième mémoire . . . ," 509–24.

4. William Thornton to George Washington, November 2, 1795, in the J. Henly Smith Collection of the Papers of William Thornton, Manuscript Division, Library of Congress.

5. John Trumbull to Jonathan Trumbull, September 23, 1794, Letters Received, RG 42, National Archives.

6. Benjamin Henry Latrobe, Journal entry, August 12, 1806, in *The Journals of Benjamin Henry Latrobe, 1799–1820,* ed. Edward C. Carter II et al. (New Haven, Conn.: Yale University Press, 1977–1980), 3:72.

7. Alexander White, Broadside, January 21, 1796, RG 42, National Archives.

8. James Hoban, Annual Report, November 18, 1799, in *Documentary History of the Construction and Development of the United States Capitol Building and Grounds* (Washington, D.C.: Government Printing Office, 1904), 88.

9. Benjamin Henry Latrobe to Thomas Jefferson, May 23, 1808, in *Latrobe Correspondence,* 2:622.

10. Benjamin Henry Latrobe to Thomas Jefferson, enclosing a "Report on the U.S. Capitol," April 4, 1803, in *Latrobe Correspondence,* 1:268–84.

11. Benjamin Henry Latrobe to John Lenthall, May 5, 1803, in *Latrobe Correspondence,* 1:288–90; Latrobe to Lenthall, May 6, 1803, in *Latrobe Correspondence,* 1:290–92.

12. Benjamin Henry Latrobe to Thomas Jefferson, August 31, 1805, in *Latrobe Correspondence,* 2:131; Latrobe to Jefferson, August 13, 1807, in *Latrobe Correspondence,* 2:463; Latrobe to Jefferson, August 15, 1807, in *Latrobe Correspondence,* 2:466; Jefferson to Latrobe, September 8, 1807, in *Latrobe Correspondence,* 2:485n.1.

13. Thomas Jefferson to Benjamin Henry Latrobe, April 26, 1818, in *Latrobe Correspondence,* 2:612–13.

14. Benjamin Henry Latrobe to Thomas Jefferson, September 11, 1808, in *Latrobe Correspondence,* 2:658.

15. Benjamin Henry Latrobe, "A Private Letter to the Individual Members of Congress, on the Subject of the Public Buildings of the United States at Washington," November 28, 1806, in *Latrobe Correspondence,* 2:306.

16. Thomas Jefferson to Benjamin Henry Latrobe, October 10, 1809, in *Latrobe Correspondence,* 2:777. C. Ford Peatross, Curator of Architectural Collections at the Library of Congress, has correctly identified Latrobe's magnolia-flower order, previously supposed to be based on cotton flowers. *Thomas Jefferson: Notes on the State of Virginia,* ed. Thomas Perkins Abernethy (New York: Harper Torchbooks, 1964), 41.

17. Benjamin Henry Latrobe to Thomas Jefferson, August 28, 1809, in *Latrobe Correspondence,* 2:749–53; Jefferson to Latrobe, August 27, 1816, in *Latrobe Correspondence,* 3:809–9; John H. B. Latrobe, *The Capitol and Washington at the Beginning of the Present Century* (Washington, D.C.: Privately printed, 1881), 19.

18. Francis Hopkinson, "Account of the Grand Federal Procession in Philadelphia, July 4, 1788," *American Museum* 4 (1788): 57–75; Benjamin Henry Latrobe to Thomas Jefferson, November 5, 1816, in *Latrobe Correspondence,* 3:822–23.

19. Robert Mills, *Guide to the Capitol and National Executive Offices of the United States* (Washington, D.C.: Greer, 1847–1848), 10.

20. Benjamin Henry Latrobe to Samuel Lane, April 29, 1817, quoted in *Latrobe Correspondence,* 2:335n2.

21. Benjamin Henry Latrobe to James Madison, September 8, 1809, in *Latrobe Correspondence,* 2:764.

22. Benjamin Henry Latrobe to Thomas Jefferson, July 12, 1815, in *Latrobe Correspondence,* 3:671.

23. Giuseppe Franzoni, Proposal for Sculpture for Senate Chambers, July 21, 1812, RG 42, National Archives; Benjamin Henry Latrobe to Thomas Law, November 10, 1816, in *Latrobe Correspondence,* 3:826.

24. Latrobe to Law, November 10, 1816, in *Latrobe Correspondence,* 3:828.

25. George Watterston, *A New Guide to Washington* (Washington, D.C.: Eliot, 1826).

26. Latrobe, *Capitol and Washington,* 27–28.

27. James Hoban, Report to commissioners, December 14, 1801, in *Documentary History of the United States Capitol,* 99.

28. *American and Baltimore Daily Advertiser,* December 10, 1801.

29. George Hadfield, Leonard Harbaugh, and George Blagden to Thomas Jefferson, October 24, 1802, RG 42, National Archives.

30. *Virginia Gazette and General Advertiser,* December 25, 1802.

31. Latrobe to Jefferson, April 4, 1803, in *Latrobe Correspondence,* 1:278.

32. Benjamin Henry Latrobe to Thomas Jefferson, February 27, 1804, in *Latrobe Correspondence,* 1:437.

33. Benjamin Henry Latrobe to Philip R. Thompson, February 28, 1804, in *Latrobe Correspondence,* 1:445.

34. Benjamin Henry Latrobe to Thomas Jefferson, October 29, 1806, in *Latrobe Correspondence,* 2:277–82.

35. Thomas Jefferson to Benjamin Henry Latrobe, September 8, 1805, in *Latrobe Correspondence,* 2:140.

36. Thomas Jefferson to Benjamin Henry Latrobe, April 22, 1807, in *Latrobe Correspondence,* 2:411.

37. Benjamin Henry Latrobe to Thomas Jefferson, May 21, 1807, in *Latrobe Correspondence,* 2:428.

38. Benjamin Henry Latrobe to Samuel Harrison Smith, editor of the *National Intelligencer,* November 22, 1807, in *Latrobe Correspondence,* 2:504.

39. Benjamin Henry Latrobe to Thomas Jefferson, March 29, 1804, in *Latrobe Correspondence,* 1:466–73; Jefferson to Latrobe, April 29, 1804, *Latrobe Correspondence,* 1:485.

40. Benjamin Henry Latrobe to John Lenthall, August 5, 1804, in *Latrobe Correspondence,* 1:528.

41. Benjamin Henry Latrobe to Philip Mazzei, March 6, 1805, in *Latrobe Correspondence,* 2:21–24.

42. U.S. Congress, "Committee of the Whole House," *Reports of Select Committees,* 12th Cong., 1st sess., February 4, 1814, 291; Philip Mazzei to Benjamin Henry Latrobe, September 12, 1805, in *Latrobe Correspondence,* 2:141–45; Charles Willson Peale to Benjamin Henry Latrobe, April 21, 1806, in *Latrobe Correspondence,* 2:218; Benjamin Henry Latrobe to Philip Maz-zei, May 29, 1806, in *Latrobe Correspondence,* 2:225–31; Latrobe to Mazzei, December 19, 1806, in *Latrobe Correspondence,* 2:328.

43. Latrobe to Smith, editor of the *National Intelligencer,* November 22, 1807, in *Latrobe Correspondence,* 2:504.

44. Benjamin Henry Latrobe to Thomas Jefferson, September 11, 1808, in *Latrobe Correspondence,* 2:658; Benjamin Henry Latrobe to Charles Willson Peale, December 10, 1808, in *Latrobe Correspondence,* 2:684:85.

45. Thomas Jefferson to Nathaniel Macon, January 12, 1816, Papers of Thomas Jefferson, Manuscript Division, Library of Congress.

46. Benjamin Henry Latrobe to James Todd, October 26, 1804, *Latrobe Correspondence,* 1:551–52.

47. John H. B. Latrobe, *Capitol and Washington,* 21.

48. Latrobe to Jefferson, July 12, 1815, in *Latrobe Correspondence,* 3:670–71.

49. Benjamin Henry Latrobe to Robert Goodloe Harper, August 13, 1815, in *The Papers of Benjamin Henry Latrobe,* ed. Edward C. Carter II (Clifton, N.J.: James T. White for the Maryland Historical Society, 1976), fiche 127/C6.

50. Vivien Green Fryd, *Art and Empire: The Politics of Ethnicity in the U.S. Capitol, 1815–1860* (New Haven, Conn.: Yale University Press, 1992), 187–88.

51. Jefferson to Latrobe, October 10, 1809, in *Latrobe Correspondence,* 2:777.

52. S. A. Elliot, *The Washington Guide* (Washington, D.C.: Elliot, 1826), 16–17.

53. Ibid, 18.

54. [T.] Fairfax to Samuel Lane, November 21, 1817, Letters Received of Application for Employment and of Recommendation, 1792–1870, RG 42, National Archives; Thomas Jefferson to Maria Cosway, October 24, 1822, Papers of Thomas Jefferson, Manuscript Division, Library of Congress.

55. Robert Mills, *Guide to the Capitol of the United States* (Washington, D.C.: Privately printed, 1834), 12.

EPILOGUE

1. *Alteration of the Capitol: Letter from the Secretary of War,* 28th Cong., 1st. sess., H. Doc. 51, Serial 441.

2. Glenn Brown, *History of the United States Capitol* (1900–1903; reprint, New York: Da Capo Press, 1970), 116.

3. R. H. Stanton, "To the Editors," *National Intelligencer,* March 5, 1851.

4. *National Intelligencer,* March 3, 1851.

5. Brown, *History of the Capitol,* 121.

6. Montgomery C. Meigs, "The New Representatives' Hall," *National Intelligencer,* December 7, 1857.

7. *The Papers of Jefferson Davis,* ed. Lynda Lasswell Crist and Mary Seaton Dix (Baton Rouge: Louisiana State University Press, 1989), 6:181.

8. William C. Allen, *The Dome of the United States Capitol: An Architectural History* (Washington, D.C.: Government Printing Office, 1992).

9. Ibid., 42–43.

10. Charles E. Fairman, *Art and Artists of the Capitol of the United States of America* (Washington, D.C.: Government Printing Office, 1927), 150.

11. Montgomery C. Meigs to John Durand, October 11, 1858, John Durand Papers, Manuscript Division, New York Public Library.

12. Lewis Gruner, *Specimens of Ornamental Art* (London: Thomas McLean, 1850). This comparison has been made by Brumidi scholar Barbara Wolanin in *Constantino Brumidi: Artist of the Capitol* (Washington, D.C.: Government Printing Office, forthcoming).

13. Montgomery C. Meigs to Thomas Crawford and Hiram Powers, August 18, 1853, Montgomery C. Meigs Letterbooks, Office of the Architect of the Capitol.

14. Robert L. Gale, *Thomas Crawford, American Sculptor* (Pittsburgh: University of Pittsburgh Press, 1964), 111–12.

15. Thomas P. Somma, *The Apotheosis of Democracy, 1908–1916: The Pediment for the House Wing of the United States Capitol* (Newark: University of Delaware Press, 1994), 56–57.

16. Ibid., 56.

Bibliography

Adams, John Quincy. *Memoirs of John Quincy Adams.* Ed. Charles Francis Adams. 7 vols. Philadelphia: Lippincott, 1875.

Adams, William Howard, ed. *Jefferson and the Arts: An Extended View.* Washington, D.C.: National Gallery of Art, 1976.

Alexander, Robert L. "The Grand Federal Edifice." *Documentary Editing* 9 (1987): 13–17.

Allen, William C. *The Dome of the United States Capitol: An Architectural History.* Washington, D.C.: Government Printing Office, 1992.

American and Baltimore Daily Advertiser, December 10, 1801.

Ammerman, David L. "The First Continental Congress and the Coming of the American Revolution." Ph.D. diss., Cornell University, 1966.

Architect of the Capitol, *Art in the United States Capitol.* Washington, D.C.: Government Printing Office, 1978.

[Backlin, Hedy.] *The Four Continents from the Collection of James Hazen Hyde.* New York: Cooper Union Museum, n.d.

Bacon, Francis. *The Works of Francis Bacon.* Ed. James Spedding, Robert Leslie Ellis, and Douglas Denon Heath. 15 vols. 1860–1864. Reprint. St. Clair Shores, Mich.: Scholarly Press, 1969.

Bell, Whitfield J., Jr. "The Federal Processions of 1788." *New-York Historical Society Quarterly* 46 (1962): 4–39.

Bennett, Wells. "Stephen Hallet and His Designs for the National Capitol, 1791–94." *Journal of the American Institute of Architects* 4, nos. 7–10 (1916): 290–95, 324–30, 376–83, 411–18.

Bingham, Neil. *C. A. Busby: The Regency Architect of Brighton and Hove.* London: Heinz Gallery, 1991.

Boatner, Mark. *Encyclopedia of the American Revolution.* New York: McKay, 1966.

Bowling, Kenneth R. *The Creation of Washington, D.C.: The Idea and Location of the American Capital.* Fairfax, Va.: George Mason University Press, 1991.

Brown, Glenn. *History of the United States Capitol.* 1900–1903. Reprint. New York: Da Capo Press, 1970.

Brownell, Charles E., Calder Loth, William M. S. Rasmussen, and Richard Guy Wilson. *The Making of Virginia Architecture.* Richmond: Virginia Museum of Fine Arts, 1992.

Brothier, Abbé. "Premier mémoire sur les jeux du cirque, considérés dans les vues politiques des Romains: Lû janvier 1781." *Histoire de l'Académie d'architecture et belles-lettres, 1780–1784* 45 (1793): 478–94.

———. "Second mémoire sur les jeux du cirque, considérés dans les vues politiques des Romains: Lû janvier 1781." *Histoire de l'Académie d'architecture et belles-lettres, 1780–1784* 45 (1793): 495–508.

———. "Troisième mémoire sur les jeux du cirque, considérés dans les vues politiques des Romains: Lû janvier 1781." *Histoire de l'Académie d'architecture et belles-lettres, 1780–1784* 45 (1793): 509–24.

Butler, Jeanne F. "Competition 1792: Designing a Nation's Capitol." *Capitol Studies* 4 (1976): 10–96.

Butterfield, Lyman, ed. *Adams Family Correspondence.* 4 vols. Cambridge, Mass.: Harvard University Press, 1963.

A Citizen of the World [James Boardman]. *America, and the Americans.* London: Longman, Rees, Ormie, Brown, Green & Longman, 1833.

Cooper, W. D. *The History of North America.* London: Newberry, 1789.

Davis, Jefferson. *The Papers of Jefferson Davis.* Ed. Lynda Lasswell Christ and Mary Seaton Dix. 7 vols to date. Baton Rouge: Louisiana State University Press, 1989.

Deák, Gloria-Gilda. *Picturing America, 1497–1899.* Princeton, N.J.: Princeton University Press, 1988.

Detroit Institute of Arts. *The French in America.* Detroit: Detroit Institute of Arts, 1951.

Dickens, Charles. *American Notes.* 1842. Reprint. New York: St. Martin's Press, 1985.

Documentary History of the Construction and Development of the United States Capitol Building and Grounds. Washington, D.C.: Government Printing Office, 1904.

Dowd, Mary-Jane M., comp. *Records of the Office of Public Buildings and Public Parks of the National Capital.* Washington, D.C.: National Archives and Records Administration, 1992.

Elliot, Jonathan., comp. *The Debates of the Several State Conventions on the Adoption of the Federal Constitution.* 5 vols. Philadelphia: Lippincott, 1866.

Elliot, S. A. *The Washington Guide.* Washington, D.C.: Elliot, 1826. "Essay on the City of Washington." *Gazette of the United States,* February 11, 12, 13, 1795.

Fairman, Charles E. *Art and Artists of the Capitol of the United States of America.* Washington, D.C.: Government Printing Office, 1927.

Fleming, E. McClung. "The American Image as Indian Princess, 1765–1783." *Winterthur Portfolio* 2 (1965): 65–81.

———. "From Indian Princess to Greek Goddess: The American Image, 1783–1815." *Winterthur Portfolio* 3 (1967): 37–66.

[Flint, Timothy.] "A Tour." *Western Monthly Review* 2 (1828): 206.

Foreman, Carolyn T. *Indians Abroad, 1493–1938.* Norman: University of Oklahoma Press, 1942.

Frary, I. T. *They Built the Capitol.* Richmond, Va.: Garrett and Massie, 1940.

Fryd, Vivien Green. *Art and Empire: The Politics of Ethnicity in the U.S. Capitol, 1815–1860.* New Haven, Conn.: Yale University Press, 1992.

Gale, Robert L. *Thomas Crawford, American Sculptor.* Pittsburgh: University of Pittsburgh Press, 1964.

Gamboni, Dario, and Georg Germann. *Emblèmes de la liberté:*

L'image de la république dans l'art due XVIe au XXe siècle. Berne: Editions Staempfi, 1991.

Granger, Bruce. *Satire in the American Revolution.* Ithaca, N.Y.: Cornell University Press, 1960.

Gruner, Lewis. *Specimens of Ornamental Art.* London: Thomas McLean, 1850.

Gunmere, Richard M. *The American Colonial Mind and the Classical Tradition.* Cambridge, Mass.: Harvard University Press, 1963.

Hamilton, Alexander. *The Papers of Alexander Hamilton.* Ed. Harold C. Syrett. 27 vols. New York: Columbia University Press, 1961–1987.

Hamilton, Sinclair. "'The Earliest Device of the Colonies' and Some Other Early Devices." *Princeton University Library Chronicle* 10 (1949): 117–23.

Hamlin, Talbot. *Benjamin Henry Latrobe.* New York: Oxford University Press, 1955.

Harvey, Frederick L. *History of the Washington National Monument and Washington National Monument Society.* 57th Cong., 2nd sess., 1902–1903.

Hawkins, Don Alexander. "William Thornton's Lost Design of the United States Capitol." Unpublished paper, n.d.

Hazelton, George C., Jr. *The National Capitol: Its Architecture, Art, and History.* New York, 1897.

Honour, Hugh. *The European Vision of America.* Cleveland: Cleveland Museum of Art, 1976.

Hopkinson, Francis. "Account of the Grand Federal Procession in Philadelphia, July 4, 1788." *American Museum* 4 (1788): 57–75.

———. "The New Roof." *Pennsylvania Packet,* December 29, 1787.

Howard, Alexandra Cushing. "Stephen Hallet and William Thornton at the U.S. Capitol, 1791–1797." M.A. thesis, University of Virginia, 1974.

Idzerda, Stanley J., et al., eds. *Lafayette in the Age of the American Revolution.* 5 vols. Ithaca, N.Y.: Cornell University Press, 1977–1983.

Isaacson, Philip M. *The American Eagle.* New York: New York Graphic Society, 1975.

James, Henry. *The American Scene.* New York: Harper & Brothers, 1907.

Jefferson, Thomas. *The Papers of Thomas Jefferson.* Ed. Julian P. Boyd et al. 25 vols. to date. Princeton, N.J.: Princeton University Press, 1950– .

———. *Thomas Jefferson: Notes on the State of Virginia.* Ed. Thomas Perkins Abernethy. New York: Harper Torchbooks, 1964.

Jones, Charles C. *Historical Sketches of Tomo-chi-chi.* Albany, N.Y.: Munsell, 1868.

Kamman, Michael. *A Machine That Would Go of Itself: The Constitution in American Culture.* New York: Knopf, 1987.

Kerwood, John R., comp. *The United States Capitol: An Annotated Bibliography.* Norman: University of Oklahoma Press, 1973.

Kimball, Fiske, and Wells Bennett. "William Thornton and the Design of the United States Capitol." *Art Studies* 1 (1923): 76–92.

Kite, Elizabeth S. *L'Enfant and Washington.* Baltimore: Johns Hopkins Press, 1929.

Lane, Mills. *Architecture of the Old South: Virginia.* New York: Abbeville Press, 1984.

Latrobe, Benjamin Henry. *The Correspondence and Miscellaneous Papers of Benjamin Henry Latrobe.* Ed. John C. Van Horne et al. 3 vols. New Haven, Conn.: Yale University Press, 1984–1988.

———. *The Journals of Benjamin Henry Latrobe, 1799–1820.* Ed. Edward C. Carter II et al. 3 vols. New Haven, Conn.: Yale University Press, 1977–1980.

———. *The Papers of Benjamin Henry Latrobe.* Ed. Edward C. Carter II. Clifton, N.J.: James T. White for the Maryland Historical Society, 1976.

Latrobe, John H. B. *The Capitol and Washington at the Beginning of the Present Century.* Washington, D.C.: Privately printed, 1881.

Lemay, J. A. Leo. "The American Aesthetic of Franklin's Visual Creations." *Pennsylvania Magazine of History and Biography* 111 (1987): 465–99.

Lowry, Bates, ed. *The Architecture of Washington, D.C.* 2 vols. Washington, D.C.: Dunlap Society, 1976–1979.

[Madison, James.] *Notes of Debates in the Federal Convention of 1787 Reported by James Madison.* New York: Norton, 1969.

Matthews, Albert. "Centennial Celebrations." *Colonial Society of Massachusetts Publications* 26 (1926): 402–26.

———. "The Snake Devices, 1754–1776, and the Constitutional Courant, 1765." *Colonial Society of Massachusetts Publications* 11 (1906): 409–53.

Meigs, Montgomery C. "The New Representatives' Hall." *National Intelligencer,* December 7, 1857.

Miller, Lillian. *Patrons and Patriotism.* Chicago: University of Chicago Press, 1966.

Mills, Robert. *Guide to the Capitol and National Executive Offices of the United States.* Washington, D.C.: Greer, 1847–1848.

———. *Guide to the Capitol of the United States.* Washington, D.C.: Privately printed, 1834.

Myers, Minor, Jr. *Liberty without Anarchy: A History of the Society of the Cincinnati.* Charlottesville: University Press of Virginia, 1983.

Norton, Paul F. *Latrobe, Jefferson and the National Capitol.* New York: Garland, 1977.

Olson, Lester C. *Emblems of American Community in the Revolutionary Era.* Washington, D.C.: Smithsonian Institution Press, 1991.

Padover, Saul K., ed. *Thomas Jefferson and the National Capitol.* Washington, D.C.: Government Printing Office, 1946.

Park, Helen. *A List of Architectural Books Available in America Before the Revolution.* Los Angeles: Hennessey & Ingalls, 1973.

Patterson, Richard S., and Richardson Dougall. *The Eagle and the Shield: A History of the Great Seal of the United States.* Washington, D.C.: Department of State, 1978.

Peterson, Charles E. "Iron in Early American Roofs." *Smithsonian Journal of History* 3 (1968): 41–76.

Poulet, Anne L., and Guilhem Scherf. *Clodion, 1738–1814*. Paris: Louvre, 1992.

Reilly, Bernard F. *American Political Prints: A Catalog of the Collection in the Library of Congress*. New York: Hall, 1991.

Reinhold, Meyer. *Classica Americana: The Greek and Roman Heritage in the United States*. Detroit: Wayne State University Press, 1984.

Rice, Kim Snyder. "Joseph Clark, Maryland Architect." *Antiques* 115 (1979): 552–55.

Riley, Edward M. "The Independence Hall Group." *Transactions of the American Philosophical Society* 43 (1980): 7–42.

Ripa, Cesare. *Della piu che novissima Iconologia de Cesare Ripa Perugino*. Padua: Donato Pasquardi, 1630.

Rosenberger, Homer T. "Thomas Ustick Walter and the Completion of the United States Capitol." *Records of the Columbia Historical Society* 50 (1952): 273–322.

Royall, Anne. *Sketches of History, Life and Manners in the United States*. New Haven, Conn.: Printed for the Author, 1826.

Schimmelman, Janice G. *Architectural Treatises and Building Handbooks Available in American Libraries and Bookstores Through 1800*. Worcester, Mass.: American Antiquarian Society, 1986.

Schleiner, Winfried. "The Infant Hercules: Franklin's Design for a Medal Commemorating American Liberty." *Eighteenth Century Studies* 10 (1976–1977): 235–44.

Schlesinger, Arthur M. "Liberty Tree: A Genealogy." *New England Quarterly* 25 (1952): 435–58.

Scott, Pamela. "L'Enfant's Washington Described: The City in the Public Press, 1791–1795." *Washington History* 3 (1991): 97–111.

———. "Stephen Hallet's Designs for the United States Capitol." *Winterthur Portfolio* 27 (1992): 145–70.

———. "'This Vast Empire': Development of the Mall from 1791 to 1848." In *The Mall in Washington, 1791–1991*, ed. Richard Longstreth, 37–58. Washington, D.C.: National Gallery of Art, 1991.

Seale, William. *The President's House*. 2 vols. Washington, D.C.: White House Historical Association, 1986.

Sifton, Paul G. "Pierre Eugene du Simitière (1737–1748): Collector of Revolutionary America." Ph.D. diss., University of Pennsylvania, 1960.

Somma, Thomas P. *The Apotheosis of Democracy, 1908–1916: The Pediment for the House Wing of the United States Capitol*. Newark: University of Delaware Press, 1994.

Sommer, Frank H. "Benjamin Franklin: Stoves, 'Scripture Histories,' and 'Moral Prints.'" In *Delaware Antiques Show 1979*, 27–49. Wilmington: Wilmington Antiques Show, 1979.

———. "Emblem and Device: The Origin of the Great Seal of the United States." *Art Quarterly* 24 (1961): 57–76.

———. "The Metamorphoses of Britannia." In *American Art, 1750–1800: Towards Independence*, ed. Charles F. Montgomery and Patricia Kane, 40–49 Boston: New York Graphic Society, 1976.

Stephenson, Richard W. *"A Plan Whol[l]y New": Pierre Charles L'Enfant's Plan of the City of Washington*. Washington, D.C.: Library of Congress, 1993.

Stewart, Robert G. *Robert Edge Pine: A British Portrait Painter in America, 1784–1788*. Washington, D.C.: National Portrait Gallery, 1979.

[Thornton, William.] "The Comparative Merits of a Mausoleum and Monument." *National Intelligencer*, December 8, 1800.

Torres, Louis. "Federal Hall Revisited." *Journal of the Society of Architectural Historians* 29 (1970): 327–38.

Trenchard, James. "Behold! a Fabric now to Freedom rear'd." *Columbian Magazine, or Monthly Miscellany* 2 (1788): frontispiece.

Tyler, Richard. *"The Common Cause of America": A Study of the First Continental Congress*. Philadelphia: National Park Service, 1974.

U.S. Congress. "Committee of the Whole House." *Reports of Select Committees*. 12th Cong., 1st sess., February 4, 1814.

Verheyen, Egon. "John Trumbull and the U.S. Capitol: Reconsidering the Evidence." In *John Trumbull: The Hand and Spirit of a Painter*, ed. Helen A. Cooper, 260–71. New Haven, Conn.: Yale University Press, 1982.

Vigne, Godfrey T. *Six Months in America*. Philadelphia: Ash, 1833.

Virginia Gazette and General Advertiser, December 25, 1802.

Warren, Charles. "How Politics Intruded into the Washington Centenary of 1832." *Proceedings of the Massachusetts Historical Society* 65 (1932): 37–62.

Washington, George. *The Journal of the Proceedings of the President, 1793–1797*. Ed. Dorothy Twohig. Charlottesville: University Press of Virginia, 1981.

———. *The Papers of George Washington*. Presidential Series. Ed. W. W. Abbot et al. 4 vols to date. Charlottesville: University Press of Virginia, 1987– .

———. "The Writings of George Washington Relating to the National Capital." *Records of the Columbia Historical Society* 17 (1914): 3–258.

Washington Gazette, February 6, 1819.

Watterston, George. *A New Guide to Washington*. Washington, D.C.: Eliot, 1826.

Weigley, Russell F. "Captain Meigs and the Artists of the Capitol: Federal Patronage of Art in the 1850's." *Records of the Columbia Historical Society* 47 (1969–1970): 285–305.

Wills, Garry. *Cincinnatus: George Washington & the Enlightenment*. New York: Doubleday, 1984.

Wolanin, Barbara. *Constantino Brumidi: Artist of the Capitol*. Washington, D.C.: Government Printing Office, forthcoming.

Wood, Gordon S. *The Creation of the American Republic, 1776–1787*. Chapel Hill: University of North Carolina Press, 1969.

Wood, Robert. *The Ruins of Palmyra Otherwise Tedmor in the Desart [sic]*. London, 1753.

Index